access to history

Cambridge International AS Level

International History 1870–1945

David Williamson

Exam-style questions and sample answers have been written by the authors. References to assessment and/or assessment preparation are the publisher's interpretation of the syllabus requirements and may not fully reflect the approach of Cambridge Assessment International Education. Cambridge International recommends that teachers consider using a range of teaching and learning resources in preparing learners for assessment, based on their own professional judgement of their students' needs.

Dedication: To Luca, Marco, Saul and Jonah

Orders: please contact Bookpoint Ltd, 130 Park Drive, Milton Park, Abingdon, Oxon OX14 4SE. Telephone: +44 (0)1235 827827. Fax: +44 (0)1235 400401. Email education@bookpoint.co.uk Lines are open from 9 a.m. to 5 p.m., Monday to Saturday, with a 24-hour message answering service. You can also order through our website: www.hoddereducation.com

ISBN: 978 1 5104 4867 4

First published in 2019 by
Hodder Education,
An Hachette UK Company
Carmelite House
50 Victoria Embankment
London EC4Y 0DZ

www.hoddereducation.com

Impression number 10 9 8 7 6 5 4 3 2 1

Year 2023 2022 2021 2020 2019

Illustrations by Integra Software Services

Typeset in Palatino LT Std Light 10/13 by Integra Software Services Pvt. Ltd, Pondicherry, India

Printed by Bell & Bain Ltd, Glasgow

A catalogue record for this title is available from the British Library.

Contents

Introduction

This book has been written to support your study of the International Option: International History, 1870–1945 for Cambridge International AS Level History (syllabus code 9489).

This introduction gives you an overview of:

- the content you will study for the International Option: International History, 1870–1945 – structure of the syllabus
- the different features of this book and how these will aid your learning.

 What you will study

This book is a study of international relations and international history from 1870 to 1945, which is dominated by the emergence of the 'New Imperialism', the two world wars, turmoil in China and the emergence of two new imperial powers, Japan and the USA. Yet these were also years when there were attempts to create a new international system of peace and security through the League of Nations.

Between 1870 and 1914 the European imperial powers partitioned and colonized Africa, leaving only Liberia and Ethiopia independent. Only great power rivalry saved China from a similar fate. The years 1870–1914 saw the development of both Japan and the USA as imperial powers, which began to play important roles in the power politics of the time. The year 1870 was also the date when Prussia defeated France and created the German Reich (Empire) which was to become, for most of the period studied by this book, the dominant power in continental Europe. The tensions created by the emergence of this new great power led to the formation of rival alliance systems and ultimately to the outbreak of war in 1914. The First World War and the Russian Revolution of 1917 were seismic events that influenced the history of not just Europe but of the world for the rest of the century. Although the focus of the war was the European continent, by November 1918 Japan, the USA and China had been sucked into the conflict and the peoples and economies of the British and French empires mobilized for the struggle. The post-war peace treaties proved deeply flawed and were perceived by the defeated powers as acts of revenge. Between 1919 and 1939, Soviet Russia gave support to communist groups in central and western Europe and encouraged nationalist and communist movements in the French and British colonial empires and particularly in China.

In 1924 the USA's new willingness to play a leading financial role in the reconstruction of Germany's economy and the atmosphere of *détente* opened the way up for the gradual peaceful revision of the Treaty of Versailles and the more effective functioning of the League of Nations. Yet this period was short-lived. The Wall Street Crash and the Great Depression were significant causes of the rise of extremism and nationalism in Germany and Japan, leading to the failure of both disarmament and the League of Nations.

As a consequence of the impact of the Great Depression on the Japanese economy, the influence of the army in Japanese politics became dominant. From 1931, with the seizure of Manchuria, until defeat in 1945, Japan was engaged in steadily escalating conflict first with China and then with Britain and the USA after the attack on Pearl Harbor in 1941. In Germany the Great Depression was instrumental in bringing Hitler and the Nazis to power, whose aggression caused the outbreak of the Second World War despite the appeasement policies of Britain and France.

This book covers the following topics:

- Chapter 1 explores the impact of European imperialism on the rest of the world, particularly Africa and China before 1914, as well as the impact of this imperialism on relations between the European powers. It looks, too, at the emergence of two new world powers, the USA and Japan.
- Chapter 2 analyzes the peace settlements of 1919–20 and their impact on Europe, as well as attempts to solve the reparation problem and to reconcile France and Germany. It also looks at the aims, membership and development of the League of Nations and efforts to secure global disarmament during the 1920s.
- Chapter 3 looks at the impact of the Wall Street Crash and the Great Depression, which brought Adolf Hitler to power in Germany. The consequences of this for both disarmament and the League of Nations and the causes of the Second World War are the main themes of this chapter.
- Chapter 4 explores developments in China and Japan in the period 1912–45. The 'warlord era', Chiang Kai-shek's response to the Communists and the role of Mao Zedong up to 1945 are all discussed, as well as the establishment of a military dictatorship in Japan and its consequences.

2 Structure of the syllabus

The Cambridge International AS Level History course will be assessed through two papers, a Document Paper and an Outline Study.

- Paper 1: For Paper 1 you need to answer one two-part document question on one of the options given. You will need to answer both parts of the option you choose. This counts for 40 per cent of the AS Level.
- Paper 2: For Paper 2 you need to answer two two-part questions from three on one of the options given. You must answer both parts of the question you choose. This counts for 60 per cent of the AS Level.

AS Level topics rotate between Papers 1 and 2 year-on-year – the prescribed topic for Paper 1 in the June and November series of any given year is not used for Paper 2.

Examination questions

For Paper 1 there will be two parts to each question. For part (a) you will be expected to consider two sources on one aspect of the material. For part (b) you will be expected to use all the sources and your knowledge of the period to address how far the sources support a given statement.

For Paper 2 you will select two questions from the option on International History 1870–1945. There will be two parts to each question. Part (a) requires a causal explanation and Part (b) requires you to consider and weigh up the relative importance of a range of factors. You will need to answer both parts of the question you choose.

Command words

When choosing the two essay questions, keep in mind that it is vital to answer the actual question that has been asked, not the one that you might have hoped for. A key to doing well is understanding the demands of the question. Cambridge International AS Level History uses key terms and phrases known as command words. The command words are listed in the table below, with a brief explanation of each.

Command word	What it means
Assess	Make an informed judgement
Compare	Identify/comment on similarities and/or differences
Contrast	Identify/comment on differences
Discuss	Write about issue(s) or topic(s) in depth in a structured way
Evaluate	Judge or calculate the quality, importance, amount or value of something
Explain	Set out purposes or reasons/make the relationships between things evident/provide why and/or how and support with relevant evidence

Questions may also use phrases such as:

- How far do/does X support…?
- To what extent…?
- Account for…

Key concepts

The syllabus also focuses on developing your understanding of a number of key concepts and these are also reflected in the nature of the questions set in the examination. The key concepts for AS History are:

Cause and consequence

The events, circumstances, actions and beliefs that have a direct causal connection to consequential events and developments, circumstances, actions or beliefs. Causes can be both human and non-human.

Change and continuity

The patterns, processes and interplay of change and continuity within a given time frame.

Similarity and difference

The patterns of similarity and difference that exists between people, lived experiences, events and situations in the past.

Significance

The importance attached to an event, individual or entity in the past, whether at the time or subsequent to it. Historical significance is a constructed label that is dependent upon the perspective (context, values, interests and concerns) of the person ascribing significance and is therefore changeable.

The icons above appear next to questions to show where key concepts are being tested and what they are.

Answering the questions

With Paper 1, the Document Paper, you have 1 hour 15 minutes to answer the two parts to the question. On Paper 2, the Outline Study, you have 1 hour and 45 minutes to answer two two-part questions. It is important that you organize your time well. In other words do not spend 70 minutes on one question on Paper 2 and leave yourself just 35 minutes to do the second question. Before you begin each question, take a few minutes to draw up a brief plan of the major points you want to make and your argument. You can then tick them off as you make them. This will help you produce a coherent and well-argued answer. A good essay will be well organized with well-supported arguments and a conclusion while a bad essay will lack coherence and jump from point to point.

The answers that you write for both papers will be read by trained examiners. The examiners will read your answers and check what you write against the mark scheme. The mark scheme offers guidance to the examiner but is not comprehensive. You may write an answer that includes analysis and evidence that is not included in the mark scheme and that is fine. It is also worth remembering that the examiner who marks your answers is looking to reward arguments that are well supported, not to deduct for errors or mistakes.

Answering source questions

For the Comparison Question (a) you should be able to:

- make a developed comparison of the two sources
- explain why points of similarity and difference exist
- use contextual knowledge or source evaluation to explain the similarities and differences
- evaluate the source to reach a supported judgement as to how far the sources support the statement.

Answering essay questions

Both the short and long answer questions should:

- be well focused
- be well supported by precise and accurate evidence
- reach a relevant and supported conclusion or judgement
- demonstrate knowledge and understanding of historical processes
- demonstrate a clear understanding of connections between causes.

Your essay should include an introduction which sets out your main points. Do not waste time copying out the question but do define any key terms that are in the question. The strongest essays show awareness of different possible approaches to the question. You will need to write an in-depth analysis of your main points in several paragraphs, providing detailed and accurate information to support them. Each paragraph will focus on one of your main points and be directly related to the question. Finally, you should write a concluding paragraph. All of these skills are developed throughout the book in the Study skills section at the end of each chapter.

What will the examination paper look like?

Cover

The cover of the examination paper states the date of the examination and the length of time you have to complete it. Instructions state that you should answer questions from only **one** section, Section A, the International option. The cover will also tell you the total number of marks for the paper – 40 for Paper 1 and 60 for Paper 2 – and will also tell you the number of marks for each question or part question.

Questions

Read through Section A, the International option. With Paper 1 you will have no choice but to answer the document question from that section, but for Paper 2 choose which two out of three questions you can answer most fully.

With Paper 1 you might find it helpful to:

- spend ten minutes reading the sources carefully
- identify the key terms and phrases in the question so that you remain focused on the actual question
- underline any quotations you will use to support your arguments.

If you spend about 10 minutes carefully reading the sources you will have about 1 hour left to answer the two questions. It is advisable to spend somewhere around 20–25 minutes answering (a) and 35–40 minutes answering (b).

With Paper 2 you might find it helpful to:

- circle the two questions you intend to answer
- identify the command terms and key words and phrases so that you remain focused on them.

Then spend time drawing up plans. If, for Paper 2, you allow 5 minutes to decide which questions to answer you will have 50 minutes for each question, 5 minutes to plan and 45 minutes to write answers to part (a) and (b). It is advisable to spend somewhere around 15–20 minutes answering (a) and 30–35 minutes on (b).

About this book

Coverage of the course content

This book addresses the key areas listed in the Cambridge International syllabus. The content follows closely the layout and sequence of the Cambridge syllabus with each chapter representing each topic.

Chapters start with an introduction outlining key questions they address. Each key question is accompanied by content that you are expected to understand and deploy when addressing the key question.

Throughout the chapters you will find the following features to aid your study of the course content.

Key terms

Key terms are the important terms you need to know to gain an understanding of the period. These are emboldened in the text the first time they appear in the book and are defined in the margin. They also appear in the glossary at the end of the book.

Key figures and profiles

Key figures highlight important individuals and can be found in the margin. Some chapters contain profiles that offer a more information about the importance and impact of the individual. This information can be very useful in understanding certain events and providing supporting evidence to your arguments.

Sources

Throughout the book you will encounter both written and visual sources. Historical sources are important components in understanding more fully why specific decisions were taken or on what contemporary writers and politicians based their actions. The sources are accompanied by questions to help you dig deeper into International History, 1870–1945. To help with analyzing the sources think about the message of the source, its purpose, and its usefulness for a particular line of inquiry. The questions that accompany the source will help you with this.

Extension boxes

Sometimes it is useful to go beyond the syllabus to help further your understanding of the topic. The extension boxes will include a variety of additional information such as useful debates and historians' views.

Activities

Activities and tasks throughout the book will help you develop conceptual understanding and consolidate knowledge.

Summary diagrams

At the end of each section is a summary diagram which gives a visual summary of the content of the section. It is intended as an aid for revision.

Chapter summaries

At the end of each chapter is a short summary of the content of that chapter. This is intended to help you consolidate your knowledge and understanding of the content.

Refresher questions

Questions at the end of each chapter will serve as a useful tool to test your knowledge of what you have read. These are not exam-style questions, but will serve as prompts and show where you have gaps in your knowledge and understanding.

Study skills

At the end of each chapter you will find guidance on how to approach both writing a successful essay and how to evaluate sources. We also analyze and comment on some sample answers. These are not answers by past candidates. We have written them to help you to see what part of a good essay and piece of source analysis might look like.

End of the book

The book concludes with the following sections:

Glossary

All key terms in the book are defined in the glossary.

Further reading

This contains a list of books and websites which may help you with further independent research. At this level of study, it is important to read around the subject and not just solely rely on the content of this textbook. The further reading section will help you with this. You may wish to share the contents of this area with your school or local librarian.

Online teacher support

In addition to this book there is an online teacher resource* for sale that will provide support for all three AS Level Paper 1 and Paper 2 options:

- The History of the USA, 1820–1941
- Modern Europe, 1750–1921
- International History, 1870–1945

The online material can be found here: **www.hoddereducation.com**

It includes:

- simple factual knowledge recall tests
- quizzes to test understanding of definitions and key terms to help improve historical understanding and language
- schemes of work
- worksheets to be used in the classroom or study at home
- sample exam-style questions and answers
- links to websites and additional online resources.

*The online teacher support component is not endorsed by Cambridge International.

CHAPTER 1

Empire and the emergence of world powers, c.1870–1919

This chapter considers the expansion of established colonial powers – Britain and France – and the emergence of Germany, Japan and the USA as imperial powers between 1870 and 1919. It analyzes their ambitions, particularly in Africa and China, and their acquisition of colonies and protectorates throughout the world under the following headings:

★ Why was imperialism a significant force for late nineteenth-century Europe?

★ What was the impact of imperial expansion on international relations?

★ Why did Japan emerge as a world power and what was the impact on international relations?

★ Why did the USA emerge as a world power and what was the impact on international relations?

KEY DATES

1870–71	Defeat of France and German unification
1882	Egyptian nationalists defeated by the British at Tel el Kebir
1884–85	Foundations of German colonial empire laid
1884–85	Berlin West Africa Conference
1894–85	Sino-Japanese war
1898	Fashoda crisis USA occupies Cuba, Puerto Rico and the Philippines
1902	Anglo-Japanese alliance
1904	Anglo-French colonial agreement (*Entente cordiale*)
1904–05	Russo-Japanese war
1905–06	First Moroccan crisis
1914 July	Sarajevo incident, which leads to the First World War
1917 April	USA declares war on Germany
1918 November	German armistice

Why was imperialism a significant force for late nineteenth-century Europe?

Economic and political motives for imperial expansion

There was a 'Scramble for Africa' as European powers took control of areas of not formally controlled before; there was also expansion in southeast Asia by France (Indochina) and Britain (Burma). The US became a colonial power in the Pacific (Hawaii, Philippines) and Japan acquired overseas possessions in the Pacific. The powers hastened to acquire ports in China while Russia expanded her control over areas of Central Asia and the Far East. **Imperialism** became a major element in the world with a new belief in the destiny of great powers to dominate other peoples.

Economic motives

European states were expanding their trade and industry and looking for markets for the goods they manufactured, and businessmen and investors thought that it would be profitable to invest in the new trading companies that were being formed to trade in Africa and China. Also, since more and more countries were introducing **tariffs**, the possession of colonies was seen as the only way to guarantee access to vital raw materials needed by modern industrial economies. Businessmen in Marseilles, Liverpool and Hamburg were, for example, constantly pushing their governments into annexing areas where they had important trading interests. There was often an exaggerated and wildly inaccurate belief in the potential wealth of new colonies.

KEY TERMS

Imperialism The policy of acquiring and controlling dependent territories carried out by a state.

Tariffs Taxes placed on imported goods to protect the home economy.

New Imperialism The period of intensive colonization by the European powers, Japan and the USA roughly in the period 1890–1914.

Free trade Trade between nations unimpeded by tariffs.

Political motives

However, economic factors are really only half the explanation for the **New Imperialism**. It can just as well be argued that politics and international diplomacy played as great or even greater part. Britain's occupation of Egypt in 1882 (see page 6), which was carried out to safeguard the Suez Canal as the main route to India, and the draft Anglo-Portuguese Treaty of 1884 concerning the Congo, set off a chain reaction among the other European powers that, even if it didn't directly lead to the partition of Africa, certainly sped the process up.

The emergence of the 'New Imperialism'

In the middle of the nineteenth century, interest in colonies had declined in Europe. In an era of **free trade** it seemed that political control of overseas markets was unnecessary. In 1865 a Parliamentary Committee even recommended that Britain should withdraw from its bases on the west coast of Africa. However, within just 20 years the political climate had dramatically changed, and the European governments, egged on by their populations, were fiercely competing for colonies in Africa and by 1900 seemed poised to carve up China. Between 1870 and 1900 the empires of the European nations underwent a spectacular expansion. The British Empire, which was by far the largest, increased in size by nearly 5 million square miles (13 million km^2) and in 1900 comprised of one-fifth of the world, while the French Empire expanded from 700,000 square miles (1.8 million km^2) to 6 million (15.5 million km^2) and its population grew from 5 million to 52 million.

At the same time Germany, Italy, Japan and the USA all acquired colonial possessions, the size of which, however, were dwarfed by the long-established, substantial British and French empires. It was this dramatic expansion overseas that historians have called the 'New Imperialism'. It was made possible by the technological lead the European powers had over

Figure 1.1 The partition of Africa up to 1895.

Africa, China and much of the rest of Asia. The **maxim gun**, the steamboat, **quinine** and financial power made the Europeans ultimately invincible.

KEY TERMS 

Maxim gun The first machine gun invented in 1883.

Quinine An anti-malaria drug.

Nature and purpose of the 'scramble for Africa'

The early stages

In 1870 only ten per cent of the African continent was under European control. By 1900, only Liberia and Ethiopia were independent. At the start of this period little was known about the interior of Africa, and any attempts by Europeans to explore it proved suicidal because of disease and the lack of suitable transport. However, interest was growing in Africa for a number of reasons:

- The development of steamboats enabled merchants to sell manufactured goods and textiles in exchange for tropical products such as groundnuts, peanuts and palm oil.
- Missionary societies and churches were also keen to open up Africa to Christianity and convert the Africans. This was made all the more urgent by their determination to stamp out the slave trade, which still existed in Africa despite attempts to prohibit it by Britain after 1807.
- The press and the newly founded geographical societies increasingly interested Europeans in the dramatic journeys across the African continent undertaken by explorers.
- Governments welcomed the discoveries of the explorers, hoping that they would open up Africa to their countries' exports.

KEY FIGURES

Dr David Livingstone (1813–1873) A Scottish missionary and explorer of Africa.

Henry Morton Stanley (1841–1904) A Welsh-American explorer famous for his explorations of central Africa.

It was **David Livingstone** whose explorations in Africa made such an impression on both Americans and Europeans. In 1854–56 he was the first European to cross the African continent. He discovered Lake Nyasa and the Zambezi, which he hoped would become highways for the new steamboats. In an adroit PR gesture he named the great Mosiotunya Falls ('the smoke that thunders') the Victoria Falls. Livingstone's book *Missionary Travels and Researches in South Africa* was aimed at persuading public opinion and the government to support his plans for establishing a British colony of settlers in the Zambian Highlands. He was convinced that once this was established it would, in the words of the historian Niall Ferguson, 'radiate civilising waves, until the whole continent had been cleansed of superstition and slavery'.

Livingstone was arguably the most famous of the explorers, but there were others, such as Richard Burton, John Speke, Verney Cameron, **Henry Morton Stanley**, the German Gustav Nachtigal and the Frenchman Jules Devreux, whose discoveries revealed the potential of Africa to the European states and played a key part in the first stages of 'the scramble for Africa'.

KEY FIGURES 

King Leopold (1835–1909) King of Belgium, 1865–1909, and founder of the Congo Free State.

Pierre Brazza (1852–1905) A French explorer of Italian extraction.

King Leopold of Belgium and the scramble for the Congo

In September 1876 **King Leopold** set up the International African Association (IAA). Its declared aim was to suppress the slave trade and open up central Africa to international commerce, but in reality he was secretly scheming, as he wrote to the Belgian ambassador in London, 'of getting us a slice of this magnificent African cake'. In 1879, with his encouragement, **Pierre Brazza** and Stanley organized two separate expeditions in the name of the IAA to open up the lower Congo. Unknown to Leopold, Brazza had secret instructions to annex the territory of the lower Congo for France. Despite initial successes he failed, but on his return to France, unsuccessful and bankrupt, he found himself a hero, and gained widespread public support for French ambitions in the Congo.

The Anglo-French quarrel over Egypt and its consequences

KEY TERM 

Khedive The title used by the governor and ruler of Egypt and the Sudan.

Egypt was a self-governing territory within the Turkish Empire which was ruled by the **Khedive**. The Suez Canal, which was opened in 1869, was built by a French company and rapidly became a key link in Britain's communications with India, which was Britain's wealthiest and most important possession. In April 1876, Egypt went bankrupt and could no longer pay the interest on the money lent by Europeans investors. Britain and France (the majority shareholder in the Suez Canal Company) took over joint control of Egypt's finances. In 1881 both powers were challenged by a nationalist uprising led by officers in the Egyptian army. As the French parliament vetoed the dispatch of French troops, it was left to the British to defeat the uprising. The British now became the masters of Egypt and, despite repeated assurances that they would leave as soon as order had been restored, did not do so.

The impact of the quarrel on Anglo-French relations in West Africa

Inevitably this infuriated the French, who set out to thwart British ambitions both in Egypt and in West Africa. Alarmed by the prospect of a French advance into the Congo, in May 1884 Britain signed the draft Congo Treaty with Portugal, which acknowledged Portugal's claims to the lower Congo, while allowing Britain to trade freely there and to have a monopoly of navigation rights on the Congo River. This, the British government hoped, would provide an effective barrier to any French expansion. In protest France appealed to Otto von Bismarck, the German chancellor, to force Portugal to renounce the Congo Treaty. In November, despite British objections, Bismarck summoned a conference in Berlin attended by fifteen other countries, which decided that the Congo was to be administered by Leopold's International African Association and to allow the other colonial powers to trade freely there (see page 29).

Otto von Bismarck

1815	Born
1848	Supported the Prussian Crown during the revolts of 1848–49
1851–8	Prussian ambassador at the German Confederation at Frankfurt
1862	Appointed Chief Minister of Prussia
1866	Established North German Confederation after the defeat of Austria
1871–90	Chancellor of the German **Reich**
1890	Dismissed by Kaiser Wilhelm II
1898	Died

Bismarck was born into an old, established, landed family in Prussia. He entered politics in 1847 and made a reputation for himself as an extreme **counter-revolutionary** when he supported the Prussian King during the revolutionary turmoil of the years 1848–49. As a reward he was appointed Prussian ambassador to the German Confederation in 1851. He rapidly became critical of Austria's attempt to dominate the Confederation and at every opportunity urged Prussia to seize the leadership of Germany. He became the Prime Minister of Prussia in 1862 and, after defeating both Austria and France, created the German Reich in 1871. Up to 1871 he was intent on challenging the existing order, but once Germany was unified he was anxious to avoid any further changes which might destroy what he had created.

KEY TERMS 

Reich Empire.

Counter-revolutionary Person who opposes a revolution and wants to reverse its results.

El Dorado Spanish for a fabulously wealthy city or state.

German participation: the creation of the German colonial empire, 1884–85

In 1884–85 Bismarck had surprised both his own ministers and the other imperial powers by annexing territory in South West Africa, the Cameroon and east Africa (see map, page 4). What persuaded Bismarck so suddenly to create a German empire in Africa?

- His main motive was probably to place himself in a position where he could co-operate with France against the British in order to distract the French from their intention of revenging their defeat of 1870 by Germany when France lost the provinces of Alsace-Lorraine (see page 17).
- He was also influenced by the cries for help from the north German colonial traders, such as F.L. Lüderitz, the Bremen tobacco merchant, to recognize his acquisition of a small trading post on the south-west African coast at Angra Pequena. The mercantile cities of Hamburg and Bremen also feared that their merchants might be shut out of the African markets.
- German public opinion, influenced by the newly founded German Colonial Union and newspapers, was convinced that Africa was an '**El Dorado**' of enormous wealth.

KEY TERM 

Social imperialism A policy aimed at uniting all social classes behind plans for creating and expanding an empire.

- Bismarck, like **Disraeli**, the British Prime Minister, also grasped how imperialism could unite the German people and discourage criticism of the government. One eminent German historian, H-U. Wehler, has called this '**social imperialism**'.

Rewrite Source A in your own words so that its meaning is clear. How far does Source A explain Bismarck's colonial policy?

SOURCE A

Bismarck rejects the German acquisition of colonies. Extract from the Memoirs of the former German ambassador in Paris, Prince Hohenlohe, from Medlicott, W. and Coveney, D., *Bismarck and Europe*, London, Arnold, 1971, pp. 137–8

In the evening [of 22 February 1880] I had dinner with Bismarck … At table we drank much port and Hungarian wine. Afterwards I sat with the Chancellor and spoke of many things. The Chancellor refuses all talk of colonies. He says that we haven't an adequate fleet to protect them and our bureaucracy [civil service] is not skilful enough to direct the government of such territories. The Chancellor also alluded to my report on the French plans for Morocco, and thought we could only rejoice if France annexed it. She would then be very occupied, and we could let her expand into Africa as compensation for Alsace-Lorraine…

KEY FIGURES 

Benjamin Disraeli (1804–81) Conservative Prime Minister, 1868 and 1874–80. He was an ardent imperialist who believed that patriotism and nationalism could overcome class divisions.

Cecil Rhodes (1853–1902) British businessman and Prime Minister of Cape Colony, 1890–96, and founder of Rhodesia (now Zimbabwe and Zambia).

The scramble completed, 1885–98

The Berlin Conference (see page 29) speeded up the scramble for Africa as rules were now drawn up for defining how the imperial powers could legitimately claim African territory 'on the coasts' of the continent and exclude their rivals. This could only happen if the powers already 'effectively' controlled the area they wished legally to annex (see Sources B and I). Yet this did not lead to an amicable partition of the rest of Africa. On the contrary, over the next 13 years there was intense rivalry between the colonising powers. As one French minister put it, the 'scramble' became a 'steeplechase'. Competition for territory, influence and trading rights focused on the Sudan, East Africa, the west African hinterland and the ambitious plans of **Cecil Rhodes** to create a vast area of British territory between the Transvaal in southern Africa and what later became Rhodesia (see page 27):

- Britain and Germany partitioned east Africa, 1886–90.
- West Africa was partitioned between Germany, France and Britain, 1884–99.
- The Anglo-Egyptian **Condominium** was established in the Sudan.
- The British expanded in South Africa and annexed the Boer Republics of Transvaal and Natal and the territory which later became Rhodesia, 1890–1902.

KEY TERM

Condominium Joint control of a territory by two states.

The reasons for the accelerated partition of Africa after 1885 were diverse and complex:

1. Economic factors continued to be important. In east Africa where British and German interests clashed, Britain had major trading interests in Zanzibar, which imported British cloth and manufactured goods and exported ivory, rubber and hides from the interior of Africa. Beyond the

coastal region lay the temperate areas lying between Lakes Victoria and Tanganyika, which was suitable for European settlement and farming. To control this profitable area intense competition developed between the German East African Company and the Imperial British East Africa Company. Similarly, in both west and south Africa economic factors had a role to play. In west Africa between 1886 and 1889 **Sir George Goldie's** Royal Niger Company aggressively advanced British interests on the Lower Niger and Benue Rivers, as well as defending British economic interests from French competition beyond the borders of what later became Nigeria. In South Africa, Cecil Rhodes' annexation of what was later to be called Rhodesia was financed by the **British South African Company** and the diamond trade (see map, page 4).

2 Political factors, particularly nationalism, were important in European colonial expansion in the Sudan and in both west and south Africa. To compensate for its defeat by Germany in Europe in 1870 (see page 17) and its humiliation in Egypt by Britain (see page 6), France aimed to carve out for herself a massive sphere of influence stretching from Algeria and Tunis to the Gulf of Guinea – nearly a quarter of the African continent. In August 1890 Britain accepted French claims in west Africa, but the boundaries of the three British colonies of Nigeria, the Gold Coast and Gambia were left undefined. Consequently, on-the-spot rivalry between Goldie's Royal Niger Company and French traders backed up by locally based French military units continued until 1899. It was nationalism, too, that motivated French attempts to block British attempts to re-establish Anglo-Egyptian control over the Sudan by dispatching the Marchand expedition to occupy the Upper Nile (see page 10).

In South Africa, German support and sympathy for the Boers enflamed public opinion in Britain, while the **Boer War**, in its early stages anyway, had massive public support in Britain. Conversely, the war antagonized public opinion in Germany and France.

Strategic aims of the imperial powers also influenced the scramble for Africa. In South Africa, for instance, the discovery of gold in the Transvaal, and the growth of German economic and political influence there, convinced the British that the Boer republics of the Orange Free State and Transvaal needed to be absorbed into British South Africa before they drew too close to Germany (see page 27). Again it was strategic reasons (see page 10) that ensured that control of Egypt and ultimately of Sudan was firmly in British hands. Sometimes strategic reasons could also dictate concessions by the imperial powers. In 1890 the German government conceded Zanzibar to Britain in exchange for the return of the important North Sea naval base of Heligoland. Once France recognized British control of Egypt and the Sudan, Britain was ready to recognize French claims in west Africa.

KEY FIGURE

Sir George Goldie (1846–1925) Founder of the Royal Niger Company.

KEY TERMS 

British South African Company Formed by Cecil Rhodes from the amalgamation of two companies: the Central Search association and the Exploring Company Ltd.

Strategic aims Aims intended to gain military or economic security for a state.

Boer War 1899–1902 Fought between the two Boer states of Transvaal and the Orange Free State and the British Empire.

Summarise in your own words the message in Source B. Compare Source B with Source A on page 8. Which of the two sources is the more useful in explaining the new imperialism?

SOURCE B

From a speech by Lord Rosebery, Liberal Prime Minister, 1895–96, to the Royal Colonial Institute in March 1893.

It is said that our Empire is already large enough and does not need extension. That would be true enough if the world were elastic but unfortunately it is not elastic and we are engaged at the present moment, in the language of mining, in 'pegging out claims for the future'. We have to consider not what we want now, but what we shall want in the future. We have to consider what countries must be developed either by ourselves or by some other nation, and we shall have to remember that it is part of our responsibility and heritage to take care that the world, so far as it can be moulded by us, shall receive an English-speaking complexion and not that of other nations … and we should in my opinion grossly fail in the task that has been laid upon us, did we shrink from responsibilities and decline to take our share of the partition of the world which we have not forced on but which has been forced on us.

KEY TERMS

Wahabbist Referring to a fundamentalist Islamic reform movement founded by Muhammad Ibn Abd al-Wahhab (1703–92).

Mahdi Arabic word meaning the redeemer of Islam. The Sudanese sheikh, Muhammad Ahmad (1845–85), claimed to be the Mahdi.

Power vacuum Territories left undominated by another state after the withdrawal or collapse of the original ruling power.

KEY FIGURES

General Gordon (1833–85) British general and Governor General of the Sudan.

Lord Salisbury (1830–1903) Conservative leader and three times British Prime Minister.

General, Lord Kitchener (1850–1916) Defeated the Mahdi in the Sudan and played a key role in the Boer War. Secretary of State for War in 1914–16.

The Upper Nile and Fashoda crisis

Thanks to its control of Egypt, Britain was also responsible for its possessions in the Sudan. In the early 1880s a **Wahabbist** revolution had taken place in the Sudan and the **Mahdi**, its leader, was determined to drive the British out. In this he was largely successful. He massacred 10,000 Egyptian troops under a British commander at the battle of Obeid in November 1881, and the following year defeated another Anglo-Egyptian force under **General Gordon**, which had been sent to relieve Khartoum. The consequence of this was that a **power vacuum** was created, which the Mahdi's army, the Ethiopians, the French and the Italians all competed to fill. In 1886, when Italy was defeated in its attempt to conquer Ethiopia at Adowa, the Mahdi immediately attempted to exploit the situation to attack the small Italian colony of Kasala. In response to appeals for help the British moved troops from Egypt some 200 miles (320 km) up the Nile to threaten the Mahdi's troops in Dongola, the capital of northern Sudan.

The French government saw this as the first step in the British reconquest of the Sudan, and ordered a small military expedition under Colonel Marchand to proceed from the French Congo to the Upper Nile. The French were convinced that occupation of the Upper Nile would enable France to build a huge dam in the swamps of Fashoda, which would control Egypt's vital water supplies and therefore give them effectively the power of life or death over the Egyptian economy. In response **Lord Salisbury** ordered **General Kitchener**, the commander-in-chief of the Egyptian forces, to reconquer the Sudan. Kitchener destroyed the Mahdi's forces at Omdurman in September 1898. However, Marchand had already reached the Upper Nile and hoisted the French flag at Fashoda.

Kitchener immediately sent five gunboats down the Nile to challenge him. An armed clash that could have led to war was avoided when he decided not use force to eject the French. Instead, it was left to the two governments to find a diplomatic solution (see page 20). France, lacking any support from the other powers, had little option but to concede totally to British demands in the Sudan.

ACTIVITY 

Re-read pages 3–12. In relation to Africa in 1870 to 1900, what had changed and what had remained unchanged? What problems did the changes cause?

What caused the scramble for Africa?

The explanations for the 'scramble for Africa', which was by far the most dramatic development of the 'New Imperialism' have been the subject of continuous disagreement and debate by historians and economists almost from the time that it occurred.

Until the early 1950s the view put forward by the early twentieth-century liberals and socialists was that it was mainly economic factors that triggered the scramble for Africa. They were convinced that the imperialist powers were driven into annexing African territory in order to secure guaranteed export markets. The most influential of these writers was **J.A. Hobson**, whose arguments influenced not only **Lenin** and the political left, but also a much wider group of historians and economists.

Some 50 years later it was argued that the scramble for Africa could be explained by the global extension of European rivalries. In 1953 Ronald Robinson and Jack Gallagher in their influential book, *Africa and the Victorians*, put forward the view that the scramble for Africa was caused by the dual crises in Egypt and South Africa. Both the Egyptian nationalist uprising led by Colonel Arabi and the growing hostility of the Boer republics in South Africa threatened British power in key territories guarding the route between Britain and British India – the Suez Canal and the Cape. This argument broke decisively with the notion that the scramble was caused by economic and political factors originating in Europe. Instead the catalyst for the scramble originated in Africa itself.

This argument that the scramble for Africa was essentially a consequence of the problems in Egypt and South Africa has met with much criticism. Some more recent historians argue that:

- it was French policies rather than British which triggered the scramble
- or economic factors were after all important
- or individuals like Cecil Rhodes, Carl Peters or King Leopold of Belgium played key roles that triggered the scramble.

KEY FIGURES 

J.A. Hobson (1858–1940)
An English socialist, economist and journalist.

V.I. Lenin (1870–1924)
Leader of the Russian Bolshevik Party from 1903. In 1917 the Bolsheviks seized power but were then faced with a bitter civil war, which they won under Lenin's leadership. In 1922–23 Lenin suffered a series of strokes and power passed to Stalin, Zinoviev and Kamenev.

Clearly the scramble for Africa was a complex event caused by many factors, including:

- economic considerations
- the ambition of local European traders or soldiers
- the sudden interest of Italy and Germany in acquiring African territory
- the desire to convert Africans to Christianity
- popular backing for imperialism
- local developments in Egypt, South Africa and the Congo
- the vast technical superiority of the Europeans over the Africans.

There are many detailed studies of these individual factors, but all these need to be brought together to understand the reasons for the scramble. An effort to plug this gap this has been made by Thomas Pakenham in his massive book, *The Scramble for Africa* (1991), in which he emphasizes initially the 'three Cs': commerce, Christianity and civilization. To this he added a 'fourth C' – conquest, which eventually became the most important of the lot.

ACTIVITY 

Produce a presentation to show and to explain the reasons for the 'Scramble for Africa'.

Reasons for and the extent of domestic support for overseas expansion in Britain, France and Germany

ACTIVITY 

In groups, decide how much support there was for imperialism in Britain, France and Germany, and why.

Increasingly in the last two decades of the nineteenth century, European governments, backed by public opinion, began to believe that their states could remain great nations only if they had colonial empires, which could provide trade and raw materials. By 1900 imperialism had developed in what the historian Norman Riches called 'a mass cult'. The imperial idea was popularized by patriotic and colonial societies and the new nationalist press. It did, too, provide excitement and the feeling that one's country was superior to other people and races.

Britain

In December 1884, Lord Derby, the Colonial Minister, wrote to Gladstone, the Prime Minister, that 'the British public is just now in a very aggressive and inquisitive mood'. Over the next twenty years the British public's support for what was called the 'New Imperialism' became ever louder. Some historians argue that this was essentially a 'defensive' reaction since Britain was facing growing economic and political challenges, particularly from Germany and the USA. In other words, the 'New Imperialism' trumpeted the might of the British Empire just at a time when it was in the early stages of economic decline. There are other reasons for its popularity:

- For many, whose lives were determined by routine work in offices or back-breaking labour in factories, it was above all exciting. The discoveries of the explorers and the colonial wars, which involved a small professional army, were covered in detail in the press.
- The new popular press, particularly the *Daily Mail*, took a strong imperialist line, which to judge by its rapidly rising circulation figures must have been a popular topic.
- As the historian Niall Ferguson has written: 'no medium was safe' from the 'New Imperialism': popular adventure books on the Empire were published, for example, and it was a constant theme in advertisements.
- The application of a distorted view of **Charles Darwin's** ideas to politics and humanity, which advanced the arguments that Britain, the northern European nations and the USA were superior races with a unique right and duty to govern Africa and much of Asia.

KEY FIGURE

Charles Darwin (1809–82) An English geologist and biologist, who in his *On the Origin of Species*, argued that the evolution of life was the result of natural selection or the survival of the fittest.

SOURCE C

Extract from a speech by the British Prime Minister, Lord Salisbury, on 4 May 1898 to the Primrose League at the Albert Hall, London.

You may roughly divide the nations of the world as the living and the dying. On the one side you have great countries of enormous power, growing in power, every year, growing in wealth, growing in dominion, growing in the perfection of their organisation … By the side of these splendid organisations there are a number of communities, which I can only describe as dying. For one reason or another – from the necessities of politics or under the pretence of **philanthropy** *– the living nations will gradually encroach on the territory of the dying, and the seeds and causes of conflict among civilised nations will speedily appear … These things may introduce causes of fatal difference between the great nations whose mighty armies stand opposite threatening each other…*

Summarise in your own words the message in Source C. How useful is Source C as an explanation of imperialism?

KEY TERMS

Philanthropy The desire to help humanity.

Anthropologist Someone who studies human beings and their societies, customs and beliefs.

Critics of the 'New Imperialism'

While support for the New Imperialism in Britain was widespread, there were a number of groups and influential people who did not hesitate to criticize some of its characteristics and policies. Most Christian missionaries, for instance, were committed to improve the life of the African and therefore saw the Empire as a civilising rather than conquering force. **Anthropologists** were also beginning to study the customs of African tribes on their own terms rather than viewing them as an inferior species.

The strongest critics of the New Imperialism were the radical wing of the Liberal Party and members of the ILP (Independent Labour Party), but they accepted the Empire as a fact, and sought to reform it in the interests of its subject peoples. India and Egypt were in time to be given limited self-government, but they did not think that Africa was yet ready for self-government, although they thought that the colonial powers should respect the human rights of the Africans and their own laws.

When the Boer War (see page 9) broke out in 1899, it was welcomed with enormous enthusiasm by the supporters of the 'New Imperialism'. The critics of the war, branded as the 'pro-Boers', were soundly defeated in the general election of 1900. However, the war did not lead to a speedy British victory. Instead the Boers waged a guerrilla war, which lasted until 1902. To defeat the guerrillas, the British interned Boer farmers and their families in concentration camps, where through bad food, poor sanitation and overcrowding, on average almost 117 per 1000 perished. When the press revealed the **Concentration Camp scandal** there was a revulsion against the **jingoism** of the 'New Imperialism' and it was one of the factors that led to the sweeping victory of the Liberal Party in 1906.

KEY TERMS 

Concentration Camp scandal In the final stages of the Boer War (1899–1902), in order to defeat the guerrilla tactics of the Boers, the British relocated the civilian population in concentration camps where a large proportion died of disease.

Jingoism Extreme patriotism supporting an aggressive foreign policy.

SOURCE D

The Barberton camp in a photo taken in 1901. Altogether there were 45 tented camps for Boer internees and 64 for black Africans.

How far do pictures such as Source D, together with explanatory reports in the press, explain why public opinion in Britain turned against the Boer War?

France

One of the key reasons for the creation of the French colonial empire was to overcome the legacy of humiliation left by defeats at the Battle of **Waterloo** in 1815 and at **Sedan** in 1870. The conquest of an empire ensured that France and French culture had a global role, and, as the historian Robert Tombs observed, was a 'remedy for self-doubt' in that it awakened national pride and appeared to make France great again. However, some French nationalists, like **Paul Déroulède**, argued that France's attention would better be concentrated in Europe on regaining from Germany the lost provinces of Alsace and Lorraine (see page 17).

KEY FIGURE 

Paul Déroulède (1846–1914) French politician and founder of the League of Patriots.

Imperialism's most enthusiastic supporters were found in the French **elite** – army officers, the Colonial Group of deputies in parliament, and members of the various **pressure groups** and geographical societies outside parliament – but how much support for the empire was there in France as a whole? The press and parliament swung between resentment at the costs of

KEY TERMS 

Waterloo In 1815 the British defeated Napoleon in the Battle of Waterloo.

Sedan The location of the traumatic defeat of the French by the Prussians in September 1870.

Elite The ruling class.

Pressure groups Associations formed to promote a particular interest by influencing government policy.

expansion and outbursts of jingoism and rage when France was outwitted by a rival power, as by Britain at Fashoda in 1898 (see page 10). The politician **Jules Ferry** remarked in 1889 that 'all that interests the French public about the empire is the belly dance'. On the other hand, apart from anti-militarists and **anarchists**, the majority of the French accepted that the empire was a national asset. Even the socialist leader Jean Jaurès, while rejecting the wars of conquest, stressed that the Socialist Party 'have always supported the peaceful expansion of French interests and civilization'. The French imperial mission was fully supported by Catholics, whose missionaries in Africa looked to the French authorities for assistance and protection. In schools throughout France children were taught about the benefits of French imperialism, but how much impact this had is again hard to judge. It proved difficult to recruit efficient civilian colonial administrators and, of those appointed between 1900 and 1914, hardly 50 per cent had any secondary education. The French public may have generally approved of the empire, but according to the historian Robert Tombs it had 'little knowledge or concrete interests in the colonies'.

Germany

Domestic support for imperialism in Germany was more widespread than in France (see Source G). To a certain extent it was a development of German nationalism from earlier in the nineteenth century. German imperialism began to take shape as an **ideology** when two important books were published: Friedrich Fabri's *Does Germany Need Colonies?* and Wilhelm Hübbe-Schleiden's *German Colonisation*. Both books stressed how important it was for Germany to spread its culture globally through the acquisition of colonies and to ensure that it, too, had a colonial empire in a world that would increasingly be ruled by great empires. The ideas in these books led to the formation of the German Colonial Union, which did much to make the prospect of a German colonial empire popular.

It was Bismarck, of course, who at a stroke created most of this empire (see page 7), mainly for foreign political reasons, but as a wily politician he also knew that support for imperialism was building up among the German public. In 1884–85 the German newspapers reported that 'a real fever' for colonies existed among the German public. Ten years later imperialism was supported not only by German intellectuals like **Max Weber** and the German political parties, with the partial exception of the German Social Democratic Party, but it also began to emerge as an aggressive populist mass movement promoted by such nationalist organizations as the **Pan-German League** and the **Navy League**. These demanded that Germany should acquire new colonies and have its 'place in the sun'. Germany was a new power, which had only been united in 1871. Behind the German imperialism of the 1890s lay the desire for recognition of Germany as a great global power by the other European states.

KEY FIGURES 

Jules Ferry (1832–93)
French politician and Prime Minister and strong supporter of French colonial expansion.

Max Weber (1864–1920)
An eminent German sociologist and philosopher.

KEY TERMS 

Anarchist A supporter of anarchism, a political theory advocating small self-governing societies.

Ideology A system and set of ideas and theories.

Pan-German League A German political society that believed that Germany should extend its frontiers to include all Germans – in Poland, Switzerland and Austria.

Navy League A German pressure group which agitated for a large German navy.

SUMMARY DIAGRAM

Why was imperialism a significant force for late nineteenth-century Europe?

ACTIVITY

Look again at the key political terms in Section 1, Chapter 1 (pages 3–16) and then write a definition of the following terms in your own words: ideology, pressure groups, jingoism, philanthropy, social imperialism, Khedive, New Imperialism, tariffs.

Its causes
- Economic and political
- Strategic and ideological rivalry
- Nationalism
- Christian missionaries
- Technological superiority of the West

Together these created the 'New Imperialism'

Impact of New Imperialism on Africa
- British occupation of Egypt intensified Anglo-French rivalry in Africa
- German intervention and Berlin Conference on the Congo, which accelerated the partition of Africa

↓

Anglo-French rivalry in west Africa (1885–1900)

↓

Anglo-German race for territory in east Africa (1885–1890)

↓

Tension between Britain, Germany and the Boers in South Africa (1888–1902)

↓

British annexation of the Sudan 1898

Domestic reaction to the New Imperialism
- General belief that colonies were essential for a great power
- But some dissent in Britain and a degree of apathy in France

2 What was the impact of imperial expansion on international relations?

The impact of the growth of overseas empires on relations between European nations

Relations between all four of the leading European states were influenced by the growth of their overseas empires.

The impact of the German overseas empire on international relations

German unification in 1871 after the defeat of France had created a strong power with immense economic and military potential in the middle of Europe. Bismarck's aim until his resignation was to isolate France and avoid a major war on the continent of Europe. It was thus vital to prevent the outbreak of an Austro-Russian war over the future of the **Balkans**, which might rapidly spread to the rest of Europe and provide France with an opportunity to put pressure on Germany to hand back Alsace-Lorraine. This task became increasingly difficult as the accelerating decline of Turkish power opened up the prospect of the collapse of the Turkish Empire in the Balkans.

KEY TERMS 

Balkans A geographic area in south-eastern Europe; the principal states in 1913 were: Serbia, Romania, Bulgaria, Albania and Greece.

Russo-Austrian Bulgarian war scare In 1885 the Russians kidnapped the ruler of Bulgaria because he refused to become a Russian puppet. This risked war with Austria, which wished to minimize Russian influence in Bulgaria.

Charismatic Inspiring great enthusiasm and loyalty.

The Balkans

The accelerating decline of the Turkish Empire in the Balkans left a power vacuum which both Austria and Russia competed to fill. This nearly led to war in 1878 and again in 1885–87. Bismarck feared that an Austro-German war might quickly escalate into a European war and give France an opportunity to regain the territory (Alsace-Lorraine) it had lost to Germany in 1871. By 1913 Turkey had lost virtually all its Balkan empire.

Bismarck consequently did not hesitate to exploit colonial tensions to strengthen Germany's position in Europe. He made no secret of the fact that he wished to encourage France to seek compensation for the loss of Alsace-Lorraine by building up a colonial empire in Africa. This would both distract France from seeking revenge against Germany and create tension with the other colonial powers, particularly Britain. This was his main reason for supporting France in its quarrel with Britain over Egypt (see page 7). However, Franco-German co-operation was short-lived. The threat of a **Russo-Austrian Bulgarian war scare** in 1885 and the coming to power of a new French government, whose **charismatic** Minister of War, General Georges Boulanger, believed that it was his mission to prepare for war against Germany caused Bismarck abruptly to end his colonial policy in Africa and once more focus on Europe. For Bismarck the continent of Europe, not Africa, was his priority. He once told a German explorer that 'my map of Africa lies in Europe. Here is Russia, and here is France.'

KEY FIGURE 

General Georg von Caprivi (1831–99)
German general and Reich Chancellor, 1890–94.

KEY TERM 

Alliance system The German–Austrian alliance of 1879 was opposed by the Franco-Russian alliance of 1894.

When Bismarck resigned in 1890, his successor **General von Caprivi** decided to work for a new **alliance system**, or 'New Course', which would ally Britain with Germany's two other allies, Italy and Austria, and so hold in check both Russia and France. In an attempt to achieve this, Caprivi was ready to settle any outstanding colonial disagreements in east Africa (see page 9). However, the problem for the Germans was that, while the British government was ready to settle colonial disputes with them, as eventually it also did with France and Russia (see pages 20 and 21), it was not prepared to negotiate binding alliances. Berlin refused to believe this and remained convinced that sooner or later French and Russian pressure on Britain's large and vulnerable empire would end in war and force Britain to turn to Germany for help.

Consequently, in a series of colonial disputes involving the Samoan islands, the boundaries of the Sudan and more importantly the Transvaal in South Africa (see page 27), the Germans took a strongly anti-British position in the hope that Britain would draw the conclusion that it was better to have Germany as a friend rather than an enemy. Ultimately, however, this was wishful thinking, and the British were determined not to join the Triple Alliance, because, as Lord Salisbury, the British Prime Minister, observed, the 'liability of having to defend the German and Austrian frontiers against Russia is greater than that of having to defend the British Isles against France'.

After the crisis with Britain over the Transvaal in 1896, the German government drew two conclusions:

- Imperialism was popular with much of the German public (see page 15) and was therefore a way of winning support for the government.
- However, to gain the size of empire which a growing number of Germans thought was their due, Germany would have to build a fleet of warships to challenge the supremacy of the British navy. This decision was to have a decisive impact on Anglo-German relations.

Until this fleet was constructed German colonial policy could only be opportune. As the historian Mathew Seligmann (2000) put it, 'The fact that German diplomats were always hovering near the world's trouble spots looking to gain territorial compensation out of any unfortunate incident quickly alienated the other powers.' The two Moroccan crises of 1905–06 and 1911 were to illustrate this (see page 20).

SOURCE E

A chart drawn in 1897 by Kaiser Wilhelm. He heads the chart with 'Germany's new ships [planned and approved since 1893]'. Below, in the right-hand corner, he notes how many ships France (Frankreich) and Russia (Russland) had built during the same period.

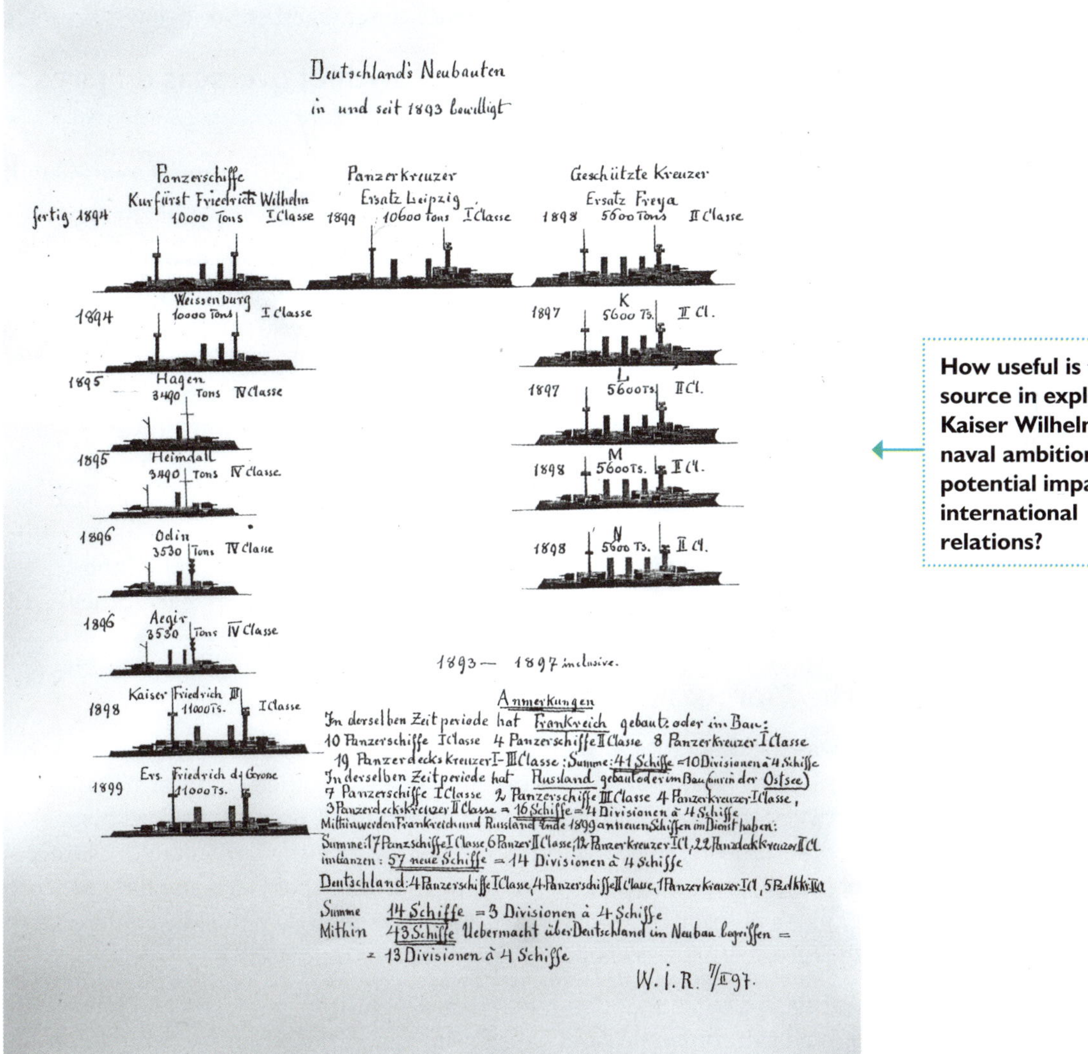

How useful is this source in explaining Kaiser Wilhelm's naval ambitions and potential impact on international relations?

The impact of the growth of overseas empires on France's relations with the other European nations

France had two enemies. In Europe it was Germany, elsewhere it was the British Empire. In the 'scramble for Africa', in Burma, Siam and the Pacific islands, there was intense Anglo-French rivalry. At Fashoda in the southern Sudan the two countries came near to war (see page 10). Yet the realization that France was powerless to challenge Britain's position in Egypt and the

KEY FIGURE 

Théophile Delcassé (1852–1923) French Foreign Minister, 1898–1906. He was forced to resign by the Germans in 1905, but in 1911–13 he was Naval Minister and Foreign Minister again 1914–15.

KEY TERMS 

Entente A friendly understanding between states rather than a formal alliance. The Anglo-French *Entente* was sometimes called the *Entente Cordiale* because it led to the restoration of good Anglo-French relations.

Protectorate A territory that is controlled and protected by another state.

Imperial overstretch Term describing the point when an empire has been overextended.

Sudan persuaded **Delcassé**, the French Foreign Minister, to negotiate a far reaching ***entente*** with Britain in 1904, the so-called *Entente Cordiale.* The essence of this agreement was that France would recognize Britain's position in Egypt if, in return, it would not object to France maintaining law and order in Morocco and at some future date establishing a **protectorate** there. The *Entente* was not an alliance, but forceful German intervention in the Moroccan question was to drive Britain and France closer together (see below).

The impact on Britain of the growth of overseas empires of the other European states

The British Empire suffered from what historians call '**imperial overstretch**'.

Britain's huge empire and worldwide interests made it vulnerable to German, French and Russian pressure and its potential weakness was shown by the fact that it took Britain three years to win the Boer War (see page 28). Once its vital interests in India, Egypt and South Africa were safeguarded, it was ready to negotiate agreements and '*ententes*' to ease the pressure on its huge empire. In 1902 the Anglo-Japanese alliance protected it from a hostile alliance of the European powers in east Asia (see page 35). An agreement with France would also remove a major source of worldwide pressure on the Empire. Negotiations began in 1903 but were speeded up by the outbreak of the Russo-Japanese war, as both states wanted to avoid what the historian John Lowe has called the 'nightmare scenario of Britain and France having to fight each other as the "seconds" of their allies'.

The Moroccan crises of 1905 and 1911

It was the dramatic German interventions in Morocco in 1905 and 1911 that turned the *Entente* into what amounted to an unofficial or informal alliance between the two countries. In March 1905 the Kaiser interrupted his Mediterranean cruise to land at Tangier. By greeting the Sultan of Morocco pointedly as an independent ruler, he indicated that Germany did not accept France's position in Morocco. The Germans then demanded a conference on the future of Morocco and the resignation of Delcassé.

At first it seemed that Berlin had won a significant success. The French agreed to a conference and Delcassé resigned, but when the conference opened at Algeçiras in January 1906, the majority of states, including the USA (see page 44), agreed that France had a special economic and security interest in Morocco. Together with the Spanish, the French were therefore entrusted with the supervision of the Moroccan police and the country's finances, although the Germans did win the concession that all the powers should enjoy equal economic rights within Morocco. The first Moroccan crisis was, as the historian A.J.P. Taylor has stressed, 'a true crisis, a turning point in European history'. For the first time since 1870 a Franco-German war seemed a real possibility. After it the German high command developed the **Schlieffen Plan** and began to prepare for a European war on two fronts while the British and French military staffs also began seriously to discuss what action should be taken if Germany invaded France.

SOURCE F

Lloyd George recalls in his memoirs that he went to visit the Liberal elder statesman, Lord Rosebery, on the day the *Entente* was announced:

His first greeting to me was: 'Well, I suppose you are just as pleased as the rest of them with this French agreement?' I assured him that I was delighted that our snarling and scratching relations with France had come to an end at last. He replied: 'You are all wrong. It means war with Germany in the end!'

Read Source F. What is Lord Roseberry's view on the Anglo-French *Entente*? Re-read pages 21–22 and then assess the accuracy of his comment.

In May 1911 Germany made a second attempt to assert its influence in Morocco when it became clear that France, contrary to the agreement of 1906, was going to occupy Morocco. A German gunboat, the *Panther*, was despatched to Agadir. The hope was, as Kiderlen-Wächter, the German Foreign Secretary, expressed it, that 'By seizing a [territorial] pawn, the imperial government will be placed in a position to give the Moroccan affair a turn which should cause the earlier setbacks of 1905 to pass into oblivion'. Again, this led to a decisive intervention by the British government, which made clear that it would not tolerate German influence in Morocco, as it feared that the Germans would build a naval base there, which would be a threat to British sea power. It further strengthened Britain's ties with both France and Russia (see below) and Germany became more isolated.

KEY TERMS 

Schlieffen Plan It envisaged a **two-front war** against France and Russia. France was to be defeated within a month by a flanking movement through Belgium, Holland and Luxembourg and then the mass of the German army would move eastwards to deal with Russia. The plan was later revised to omit Holland.

Two-front war A war in which fighting takes place on two geographically separate fronts.

Triple *Entente* An *entente* between three powers.

The impact on Russia of the growth of overseas empires of the other European states

The Russian defeat by Japan in 1905 (see page 36) and the weakening of its position in east Asia had a significant impact on its relations with the European powers. Above all it made a colonial agreement possible with Britain. The British had long wished to negotiate a compromise that would take Russian pressure off Afghanistan and northern India. Russia had little option but to improve relations with London if it was to maintain its alliance with France, who now enjoyed increasingly good relations with Britain. The Anglo-Russian agreement was signed in August 1907. Like the Anglo-French agreement, it was concerned only with colonial matters:

- The Russians gave up all claims to Afghanistan and recognized British interests in Tibet.
- Persia (present-day Iran) was divided into zones of influence: the north went to Russia, the south to Britain, with a neutral zone in between.
- Both empires recognized Chinese sovereignty over Tibet.

ACTIVITY 

Re-read pages 20–21 and write a paragraph about the Moroccan crises. Make sure you include a supported judgement about their significance.

The Anglo-Russian agreement, together with the *Entente Cordiale*, formed a **Triple *Entente***. Although it was not a formal alliance system, it did mark a shift in the balance of power in Europe. No longer could the Germans assume that an Anglo-Russian war would break out that would enable them to force Britain – or Russia – into becoming a subordinate ally. Russia's defeat in east Asia by Japan also refocused its attention back to the Balkans and the European continent.

Imperial rivalries and the outbreak of the First World War

For Germany, France, Russia, Austria and even Britain, the causes of the First World War were primarily European, even though in Britain's case, especially, colonial rivalry with Germany had aggravated relations. Russia's defeat by Japan forced Russia to turn back to Europe and focus on the Balkans. Germany's clumsy attempt to break up the *Entente* by intervening in Morocco, and its construction of a battle fleet to rival the Royal Navy, clearly emphasized the danger of the German challenge to Britain and made it more determined to stop the German domination of Europe.

KEY TERMS 

South Slavs Formed the main ethnic group in Bosnia and Herzegovina, which Austria occupied in 1878.

Alliance system The German–Austrian alliance of 1879 was opposed by the Franco-Russian alliance of 1894.

By early 1914, with the collapse of the Ottoman Empire within Europe, Serbia backed by Russia emerged as a major threat to Austria as its intention was to liberate the **South Slavs** from Austrian control. The assassination of Franz Ferdinand, the heir to the Austro-Hungarian throne, at Sarajevo on 28 June 1914 by Serb terrorists gave Austria the chance to counter this threat by declaring war on Serbia. This step was, however, fraught with danger as it could all too easily cause a European war by triggering the **alliance system**. The assassination brought together all the explosive tensions in Europe, which thanks to the alliance system resulted in the outbreak of the First World War.

The outbreak of the First World War in 1914

The crucial events leading to war were as follows:

- Germany gave Austria its unconditional support against Serbia on 5 July.
- Austria sent an ultimatum to Serbia demanding that Austria should supervise counter-terrorist measures to be taken by the Serb police. When this was rejected by Serbia, Austria declared war on 28 July.
- Russia began to mobilize its army in support of Serbia.
- Germany could not allow its only reliable ally, Austria, to which it had been allied since 1879, to be humiliated by Serbia and Russia, and declared war on Russia on 1 August.
- Once Germany declared war on Russia, France, which was allied to Russia, could not stand back and see Russia defeated. The Germans, anticipating this, declared war on France on 2 August, and invaded Belgium on 4 August.
- Britain, despite initial hesitations, could not afford to run the risk of a German victory and declared war on Germany on 4 August.

ACTIVITY

Re-read pages 16–22. Draw a spider diagram to show how the growth of overseas empires influenced relations between the European nations.

Disputes with China over imperial expansion

The opening up of China to Western influence

A major step in opening up China to Western influence was the Treaty of Nanking of August 1842. The British forced the Chinese not only to import opium from India, but also to cede them the island of Hong Kong and to open up five coastal cities to foreign traders. Over the next 50 years further concessions were forced out of the Chinese. For instance, by the Peking treaties of October 1860, eleven more treaty ports were opened up.

Russian expansion into China

As in Africa, great power rivalry in China was determined by a mixture of political, economic and strategic factors. By 1860 Russia had become a Pacific power by expanding into the Chinese Amur and Maritime provinces and wished to round off these gains by annexing Manchuria, opening up its market to Russian imports and acquiring an **ice-free port** in Korea, which China still theoretically controlled.

KEY TERM

Ice-free port A seaport that is free of ice in the winter, so that it can be used throughout the year.

Inevitably these moves were opposed by Britain, which up to this point through its superior sea power had been able to dominate China's trade. The construction of the Trans-Siberian railway by Russia, which commenced in 1891, completely changed the situation as Russia would now be able to

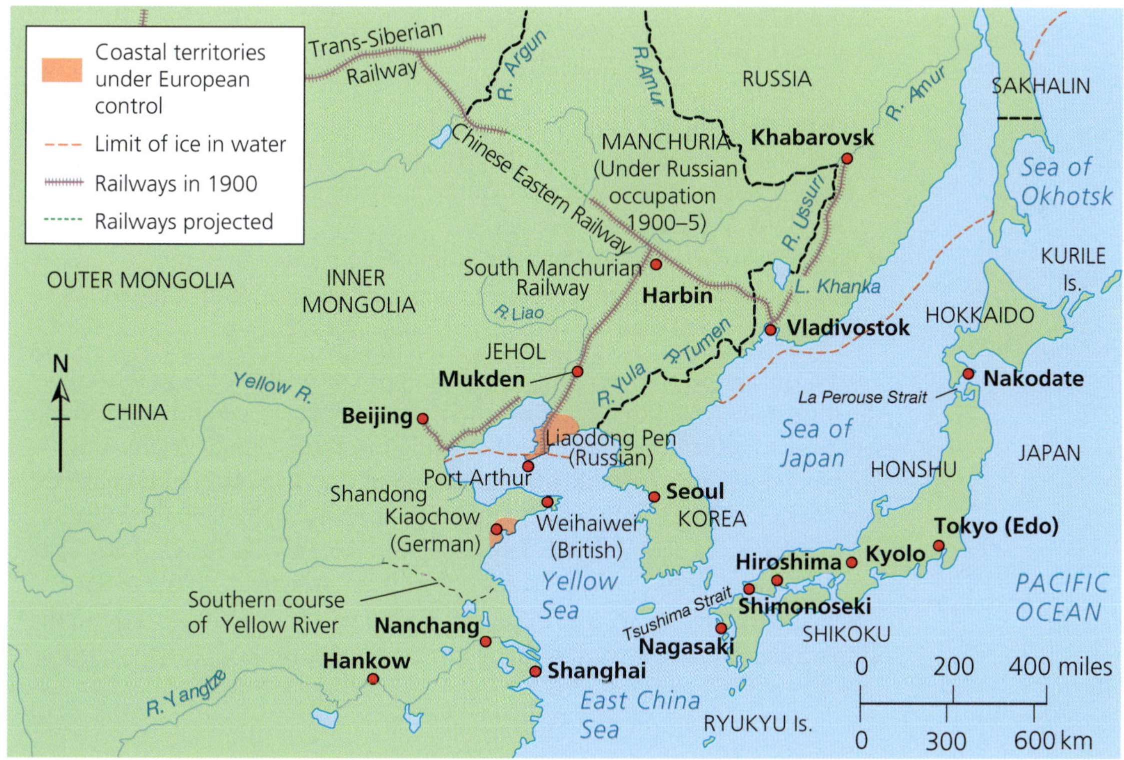

Figure 1.2 Map of northern China, Manchuria and Japan and the growth of the railways by 1900.

deploy troops to back up its demands. In China, unlike in Africa, Britain faced the prospect of a challenge to its commercial position from a major military land power. Russia could usually rely on the backing of France and Germany in China, while Britain's only potential ally was Japan, which saw Russian expansion into Korea and Manchuria as a threat to its own security.

Japanese and Russian expansion in China and its impact on international relations

Like Britain, Japan was opposed to the growth of Russian influence in Manchuria and Korea. Its chance to strengthen its position in Korea came in 1894 when a rebellion broke out against the Korean government, which theoretically owed loyalty to the Emperor in Beijing. Both China and Japan sent troops, which rapidly crushed the revolt. However, when it became clear that Tokyo was not going to withdraw its forces, China declared war on Japan, but was quickly defeated and forced to accept the Treaty of Shimonoseki (1895), which effectively set up Japanese protectorates in Korea, Taiwan (Formosa), the Pesdadores and the Liaodong peninsula where the important port of Port Arthur lay.

Britain welcomed the treaty as it created a buffer between its interests in southern China and Russia's expanding sphere of influence in the north. To the Russians, however, it was a serious blow to their ambitions for acquiring an ice-free port in Korea and terminating the Trans-Siberian railway at Port Arthur. They therefore organized a joint European protest to force the Japanese to renegotiate the treaty. Not surprisingly, the British remained aloof, but the Germans immediately supported the Russians, calculating that this would strengthen their position in Europe because it would:

- encourage Russia to become involved in China rather than the Balkans
- make a Russo-British war over China more likely and both sides would then look to Germany for support
- force France to support Russia in China even though the French government wanted to refocus Russian interest away from China back to Europe.

KEY TERM 

Triplice An agreement between three powers to work together.

As the Germans intended, the French supported the Russians to form what the diplomats called the 'Far Eastern Triplice', which successfully forced the Japanese to return the Liaodong peninsula to China. The Germans and French gained little from their membership of the '**Triplice**', but it enabled the Russians significantly to strengthen their position. In 1896 they forced Japan to agree to a joint Russo-Japanese protectorate over Korea. They also signed a treaty with China promising it military assistance in the event of being attacked by Japan, and in return were given permission to extend the Trans-Siberian railway across Manchuria to Vladivostok.

The 'scramble for China'

The chief consequence of the Japanese victory was to encourage the other imperial powers to demand more concessions from China for themselves.

As in Africa, Germany was not prepared to play a passive role in China. Like the other European powers, it was attracted by the potential of the huge Chinese market of 450 million people. The murder of two German missionaries in Shantung in 1897 provided Berlin with a convenient pretext to seize **Kiachow** as a site for a **coaling station** and naval base. This then triggered a chain reaction, and it looked as if partition of China was about to begin:

- The Russians led the way by seizing Port Arthur and Dalian on the Liaodong peninsula in December 1897 and forcing China to grant them a 25-year lease.
- The British insisted on a similar lease on Weihaiwei, which was to run as long as the Russian lease on Liaotung.
- The French then demanded a 99-year lease on the Kwang Chowan peninsula in southern China.

The Boxer Rebellion

Not surprisingly these demands led to an anti-Western backlash in China, and in the summer of 1900 the **Boxer** Rebellion broke out. The Boxer movement was essentially a patriotic and populist reaction to the increasing foreign domination of China. The Boxers were particularly hostile to the Christian missionaries, of whom there were nearly 2000 in China by 1900, as they perceived them to be undermining the traditional Chinese way of life.

The 'Boxers United in Righteousness', as they called themselves, first appeared as a force in the spring of 1898 in the Shandong province. The following year their numbers were swollen by drought and famine for which they blamed the Christians. Armed bands of Boxers advanced towards Beijing, massacring missionaries and Chinese Christian converts on the way. The initial reaction of the **Treaty Powers** was ambivalent. Britain could not make its mind up whether to negotiate or use force; the Russians advised the Chinese Emperor not to intervene. The Japanese suspected that the Russians wanted to see the north of China devastated as they would then have an excuse to intervene and restore order and so strengthen their grip on China.

On 20 June the Chinese government, emboldened by the patriotism and loyalty of the Boxers, itself declared war on 'the foreigners' and laid siege to the **legation quarter**. In response, at the beginning of August eight countries – Russia, Japan, Britain, France, Germany, Italy, Austria and the USA – assembled a force of 54,000 soldiers and within two weeks occupied Beijing, while Russia also marched into Manchuria. China was now at the mercy of the Treaty Powers.

KEY TERMS 

Kiaochow In 1897 the Germans seized Kiachow in revenge for the murder of two missionaries. They also secured mining rights in the neighbouring province of Shantung.

Coaling station A base where steamships can be fuelled with coal.

Boxer A secret Chinese patriotic and nationalist organization. The literal translation of 'Boxer' is 'the Righteous and Harmonious Fists'.

Treaty Powers Those powers which had signed treaties with China giving them territorial concessions and commercial privileges.

Legation quarter The area in Beijing where foreign diplomats, businessmen, etc., and their families lived.

SOURCE G

'The Germans to the Front', a painting by Carl Rochling in 1900. The title refers to a remark by a British admiral when the international force, which included German troops, marched on Beijing. The picture was very popular and often hung in the more nationalistically inclined households in Germany before the war.

Who do you think is the intended audience for Source G?

Peace negotiations: the Boxer Protocol

Once the Boxer revolt was defeated, the Emperor was forced to agree to foreign troops being stationed on the approaches to Beijing and to pay a large (by the standards of the time) indemnity of £67 million over 39 years at 4 per cent interest. Paradoxically this guaranteed Chinese unity, since the victorious powers would get less of this money if China were partitioned. It was in fact much more economical to continue the treaty port system, which gave the Treaty Powers a key position in the major cities at minimal cost. In other words, they could dominate China without having to pay to police and administer large unwieldy colonies. After the defeat of the Boxer Revolt, 25 concessions and leases were scattered along the Chinese coast from Manchuria to Guangdong.

The impact of Russian expansion in China on international relations

ACTIVITY 

In groups decide what were the main reasons for the scramble for China. Then try to put the points in order of importance. If you disagree, try to work out why.

In October 1900, Britain, worried about the possible partition of China, negotiated the Yangtze Agreement with Germany. The two powers agreed that Chinese unity must be preserved and that China must remain open to foreign trade – the so-called 'open door' policy. The agreement, however, was threatened by the Russian refusal to withdraw from Manchuria. As the Germans were unwilling to put pressure on Russia to withdraw because they had no wish to make an enemy of Russia in Europe, Britain had no means of opposing Russian encroachments in northern China. Effectively Britain was now isolated in China as Germany, France and Russia had formed the Far Eastern Triplice (see page 24) and were able to work together, and the USA pursued its own independent policy. It appeared that Russia would now be free to pursue its ambitions in Manchuria, Korea and northern China, but these were to be dramatically checked by the conclusion of the Anglo-Japanese alliance in January 1902 (see page 35).

Tension between Britain and Germany in South Africa

South Africa was vital for the security of the British Empire, as it lay on the route to India. Initially the main challenge to British power in South Africa came from the former Dutch settlers, the **Boers**. They resented Britain's annexation of Cape Colony from the Dutch in 1814, and to escape British control a large number migrated between 1836 and 1840 in what was called the 'Great Trek' to found new settlements, which later became the Orange Free State and the Transvaal (see map, page 4). In 1877 both states, which were threatened by the Zulus, agreed to annexation by the British. However, once the Zulus were defeated at the battle of Ulundi, the Boers began to agitate for independence. This led in 1880 to the first Boer War. The Prime Minister, **William Gladstone**, sympathized with their demands and in the Convention of Pretoria, August 1881, recognized their freedom to run their own affairs, although London was still theoretically responsible for their foreign policy.

KEY TERM 

Boers Descendants of Dutch settlers who had originally colonized South Africa.

KEY FIGURES 

William Gladstone (1809–98) Liberal politician, who served four terms as Prime Minister.

Paul Kruger (1825–1904) President of the Transvaal, 1883–1900.

ACTIVITY 

In pairs or small groups research the causes and consequences of Anglo-German rivalry in South Africa. Prepare a 5-minute presentation on this rivalry.

Germany and the Transvaal

With the German annexation of South West Africa in 1884, the British faced the threat that the Germans would try to extend their power eastwards to the borders of the Transvaal by annexing the African kingdoms of Bechuanaland and Matabeleland. Under pressure from Cecil Rhodes, the Prime Minister of Cape Colony, steps were taken to prevent this. In 1889 the British government gave the right to Rhodes' British South African Company to colonize and govern the whole area north of the Transvaal and between Mozambique, German South West Africa and Angola, which was duly renamed Rhodesia in May 1895 (see page 4).

The discovery of gold in the Transvaal

The economic significance of the Transvaal was transformed by the discovery of gold there in 1886. Over the next five years large numbers of British prospectors and adventurers poured in. Inevitably this posed a challenge to the supremacy of the Boer population, and **Paul Kruger**, the President of the Transvaal, began to look to Germany to prevent the absorption of the Transvaal into the British Empire. By 1894 the economy of the Transvaal was dominated by the Germans. German bankers controlled the Transvaal's National Bank and some 20 per cent of the foreign investment in the state came from Germany.

The Jameson raid and the German response

KEY TERM

Jameson raid Armed intervention in the Transvaal led by the British politician in Cape Colony, Leander Starr Jameson, over the New Year weekend of 1895–96.

At the end of 1895 Cecil Rhodes launched a badly planned and unsuccessful attempt to overthrow the Boer government in the Transvaal, the so-called **Jameson raid**. The Germans could hardly remain indifferent to such a naked act of aggression. The Kaiser at first wanted to declare the Transvaal a German protectorate, send military aid to Kruger, and then summon a congress in Berlin, which would redraw the map of South Africa, but in the end he was persuaded by his own diplomats that, because of British sea power, these were just empty threats. Instead he sent a telegram to Kruger congratulating him on preserving the independence of his country against attack. This caused intense resentment in Britain as it was perceived to be Germany meddling in the private affairs of the British Empire. Windows belonging to German-owned shops were smashed and for the first time popular anti-German feeling became widespread and intense.

Rewrite Source H in your own words so that its meaning is clear. Study Sources B (page 10) and H. How far does Source H indicate the possible consequences of Lord Rosebery's policy as outlined in Source B?

SOURCE H

The so-called Kruger telegram, which was drafted in early January by the German Foreign Office in an effort to tone down the Kaiser's warlike language.

I wish to express my sincere congratulations that you, and your people without asking the help of friendly powers, have succeeded in restoring peace through your own actions against the armed bands which invaded your country as disturbers of the peace, and in preserving the independence of your own country against attack from without.

The Boer War and Germany's inability to intervene

Four years later Kruger, who had rebuilt the Boer army and equipped it with modern German artillery, declared war on Britain believing that France, Germany and Russia would intervene and force Britain to make concessions. 'There could never be', as the historian A.J.P. Taylor (1954) observed, 'a more favourable opportunity, in theory, for the Continental Powers to exploit British difficulties.' Public opinion in France, Russia and Germany was decidedly pro-Boer (see Source D), and Delcassé attempted to secure a joint intervention by these three powers. Why was he not successful? Again, to quote Taylor, 'the British navy decided the issue' in that it made large-scale military intervention physically impossible. Yet if the three powers had set up a Continental League or alliance, they might have been able eventually to force Britain to agree to mediation or a congress.

In practice, however, neither France nor Russia were ready to intervene against Britain unless they had German backing, but the Germans would only intervene if all three powers guaranteed the frontiers of each other's states. France was unwilling to agree to this as it refused to recognize the German annexation of

Alsace-Lorraine, and Russia was too distracted by the situation in the Far East (see above) to undertake fresh commitments in Europe. Britain was therefore able to defeat the Boers in a long, drawn-out war, which ended only in 1902.

Attempts to resolve tensions between imperial nations

Traditional diplomacy

Until the formation of the League of Nations in 1920, there was no international organization which could solve disputes between the imperial nations, as they were fully **sovereign** and not bound by **international law**. Nevertheless, there were often successful efforts to reduce and resolve tensions arising from colonial rivalries.

Each great power (and minor power too) had an ambassador backed up by an embassy in the capital of every independent state in the world. There was what one historian has called a 'universal system of liaison'. This meant that ambassadors could consult and inform each other about their countries' policies. A good ambassador, like France's **Paul Cambon** in London, could discreetly advise on solving problems between his own country and the country to which he was posted. However, ambassadors were agents of their governments and alone could not take the initiative in resolving international tensions. Essentially it was up to the governments through their foreign offices and ambassadors to attempt to resolve the tensions that frequently arose between them.

KEY TERMS 

Sovereign Self-ruling, fully independent.

International law Law concerning international relations – relations between states.

KEY FIGURE 

Paul Cambon (1843–1924) French ambassador in London, 1898–1920, and a key figure in negotiating the *Entente Cordiale*.

International conferences

When complex problems involving more than one of the great powers were incapable of solution by simple treaties or agreements, the powers would summon a congress or conference. These acted, to quote the historian Alfred Zimmern, as a 'safety valve' when there was a particularly acute crisis. Their decisions were published in formal documents known as treaties, agreements, Final Acts or conventions. Once the issues had been solved, even if only temporarily, the conference/congress was dissolved, and there was no permanent organization with its own secretariat to prepare for the calling of another.

The Berlin West African Conference, 1884

In 1884 the Berlin West African Conference was held in Berlin to regulate the complex situation in the Congo (see page 6). Both France and the International Association of the Congo (IAC) under the presidency of King Leopold suspected that the newly signed Anglo-Portuguese Treaty, which recognized Portuguese control over the lower Congo, was merely an attempt by Britain to exploit Portugal's weakness to increase its own influence in the Congo. In 1884 Germany and France were able to co-operate and override British objections to calling an international conference in Berlin of 15 countries, including the USA and Turkey, to decide on the future of the Congo. It was decided that this was to be administered by Leopold's IAC and Portuguese control was to be limited to Angola. The conference also agreed on a treaty which laid down some important ground rules for a huge belt of central African territory stretching from the Atlantic to the Indian Ocean:

- The entire area was to be a free trade zone and all states were to have free access to the rivers and ports of this region for their trade.
- Religious missions and scientific research were to be protected.
- The slave trade was to be banned in the area and the powers committed themselves 'to bringing home the blessings of civilization'.

They also agreed that rules should be set defining 'effective occupation' and informing the other powers when this had taken place, although this initially only applied to coastal districts.

Rewrite Source I in your own words so that its meaning is clear. How far did Source I influence the 'scramble for Africa' after 1885?

SOURCE I

Article 34 of the Conference's final 'General Act' declared:

Any power which henceforth takes possession of a tract of land on the coasts of the African Continent outside of its present possessions, or which being hitherto without such possessions, shall acquire them and assume a protectorate … shall accompany either act with a notification thereof, addressed to the other Signatory Powers of the present act, in order to enable them to protest against the same if there exists any grounds for their doing so.

The Hague Conferences, 1899 and 1907

It was only in 1898 that the great powers began to consider the creation of a more permanent organization for dealing with disagreements between different states. That year the Tsar of Russia proposed an international conference to consider disarmament and the peaceful settlement of international disputes. When it met in 1899, there was little agreement on disarmament, but considerable progress was made in resolving future tensions between states through making arrangements for commissions of inquiry and **arbitration**. A permanent court of arbitration was set up to be composed of judges nominated by the states, which had signed the arbitration agreement. Its greatest success was the settling of a dispute between Britain and Russia when Russian warships on the way to fight the Japanese (see page 36) fired on British trawlers on the Dogger Bank. The second world conference at The Hague in 1907 achieved little apart from banning countries from using force to collect international debts from states delaying or refusing payment. Provision was made to call a third conference in 1914, but the war intervened.

KEY TERM

Arbitration A form of resolving disputes through mediation by a third party.

SUMMARY DIAGRAM

What was the impact of imperial expansion on international relations?

Africa and China became the focus for great power rivalries

Africa

- Bismarck exploited Anglo-French quarrel over the Sudan to reconcile France to loss of Alsace-Lorraine
- Britain put under pressure in east Africa by Germany and forced to abandon Anglo-Portuguese Treaty
- German support for Boers in South Africa
- 1898 Britain and France on verge of war over Fashoda
- Berlin Conference does not resolve imperial tensions

China

- Theatre of rivalry between five imperial powers: Britain, Germany, Russia, France, Japan
- Britain is isolated after collapse of Yangtze Agreement, 1900. Failure of Germany to exploit British isolation to force Britain into an alliance (the 'New Course')
- Anglo-Japanese alliance of 1902 made Britain independent of Germany in China
- Russia's defeat by Japan in 1905 made Russia less of a threat to British interests
- Franco-British Agreement of April 1904 over Morocco ended Anglo-French hostility over Egypt
- Germany unable to help Boers during Boer War through lack of sea power

Consequences

- Russia refocused on the Balkans
- German reaction to Anglo-French Agreement drives France and Britain closer

ACTIVITY

For each of the factors shown on the summary diagram explain how they led to Africa and China becoming the focus of great power rivalry.

ACTIVITY

Re-read pages 29–31 and then copy this chart to briefly summarize, as indicated, efforts to resolve disputes between the imperial nations, 1885–1914.

Conferences	Decisions taken	How effective

Now write a concluding paragraph explaining progress (or lack of progress) made in resolving disputes between the imperial nations.

Why did Japan emerge as a world power and what was the impact on international relations?

Reasons for rapid modernization and military development

Since the early seventeenth century Japan had been ruled by the Tokugawa dynasty, which did its utmost to isolate Japan from the rest of the world and to preserve a rigid class system. However, by 1850 there was increasing demand for change from many of the Japanese nobility, the merchant class and the poverty-stricken peasantry.

'The unequal treaties'

Significantly there was also a growing awareness that Japan's traditional isolation was threatened by the expansion of the Western powers into China (see page 23). These fears were confirmed when the USA sent a naval squadron under Commodore Perry to Japan in 1853 to demand the opening up of two ports to international trade and also their use by the US navy. Japan had little option but to agree, and soon similar privileges were extended to Britain, France and Russia. They were based on the treaties which the Western powers had made with China, and because they gave the Americans and Europeans such privileges, they were quickly named 'the unequal treaties'. Foreigners were allowed to live and trade under the laws of their own countries administered through **consular courts** in specially designated ports. To encourage trade, tariffs were to be kept at a very low level.

The Meiji restoration

In 1868 a political revolution broke out, which resulted in the restoration of the power of the emperor – the so-called Meiji restoration. This marked the victory of the '**Westernizers**' and modernizers, who in the course of the next 30 years began to transform Japan into a modern state:

- A central administration was created, which controlled the local authorities and ensured that an effective tax system could be introduced to provide the government with money. A legal system based on Western practice was introduced and in 1890 a new constitution was drawn up with an elected house of representatives and a cabinet.
- A modern army was created with a three-year **universal conscription**. By 1883 it had wartime strength of 200,000 and a **general staff** on the

KEY TERMS 

Consular courts A court presided over by foreign officials to protect the interests of their countrymen, who were trading or working in a country such as Japan or China. These courts were recognized by treaty.

Westernizers Those who believed that the Japanese state should modernize along European lines.

Universal conscription The law by which all young males – and nowadays young females – have to serve for a period in the armed services.

General staff A group of officers responsible for planning operations and administering an army.

German model. At the same time progress was made in constructing a navy. By 1894 the Japanese navy had 28 warships and 24 torpedo boats.
- Successful efforts were also made to modernize the Japanese textile industry and to introduce steam-powered factories.

International recognition of Japan as a world power: wars with China (1894–95), Russia (1905) and the treaty with Britain (1902)

After 1878 the main aim of Japanese foreign policy was to negotiate the modification of the so-called 'unequal treaties' of 1853, in particular the clauses which prevented Japan from setting its own tariffs and allowed foreigners working in the treaty ports to be independent of Japanese law (extra-territoriality). The negotiations were long and drawn-out and frequently their lack of success led to outbursts of nationalism in Japan. Only in 1889 was 'extra-territoriality' abolished, but Japan did not obtain complete freedom to set its own tariffs until 1911.

War with China, 1895

Up to 1884, while Japan was still building up its economic and military strength, it pursued a conciliatory policy with its neighbours. The status of Korea was, however, an issue that was eventually to cause conflict with China. Japan perceived Korea to be a Japanese satellite even though China claimed to exercise ultimate power over it. In 1876 Japan forced Korea to open its ports to Japanese traders and in defiance of China's claims negotiated a treaty with Korea which recognized it as a state independent of China.

In December 1884 Korean modernizers, who wanted their country to look more to Japan than to China, attempted to seize control of Korea. Potentially this could have caused a Sino-Japanese war, but neither power was yet in the position to risk conflict. By the Convention in 1885 of Tientsin, both powers agreed not to change the status of Korea, but mutual distrust still continued. The Japanese, for instance, were suspicious of China's efforts to increase its trade with Korea.

Growing economic and military strength led to a change of Japanese policy towards Korea. Japan's chance to strengthen its position in Korea came in 1894 when the **Tong-haks** attempted to overthrow the Korean government. The King of Korea immediately turned to China for help to crush the revolt. Chinese troops were sent, but Japan argued that this broke the Tientsin Treaty and also sent a military force to protect its own position in Korea. Under pressure from the army, the political parties and patriotic activists the Japanese government was ready to challenge China. The Prime Minister, **Itō Hirobumi**, was also convinced that the political and economic gains from war far outbalanced the international risks.

ACTIVITY 

Using the further reading section, find out more details about the Sino-Japanese war of 1896.

KEY TERM 

Tong-haks A nationalist movement that was strongly opposed to Western culture and domination.

KEY FIGURE 

Itō Hirobumi (1841–1909) Japanese Prime Minister, who played a key role in the modernization of Japan.

When Japan refused to withdraw its forces, China declared war. Although the Japanese army was smaller than the Chinese, it was better motivated and organized, as well as possessing more modern weapons. The Chinese were defeated at Pyongyang in north Korea and their fleet destroyed in the mouth of the Yalu River. The Japanese then went on to seize the Pescadores Islands and Taiwan. In April the Chinese had little option but to accept the Treaty of Shimonoseki. By this treaty China recognized Korea's independence and ceded to Japan Taiwan, the Pescadores and the Liaodong peninsula where the important port of Port Arthur lay. Shimonoseki, however, provoked a humiliating intervention by Russia, France and Germany (see page 23) and forced Japan to return the Liaodong peninsula to China (see maps, pages 23 and 211).

Japan under pressure, 1895–1902

At home these concessions were met with bitterness as they indicated that Japan was still not in a position to ignore pressure from the great powers. The government therefore decided at considerable financial cost to accelerate its armaments programme: the fighting strength of the army was doubled and the navy greatly increased in size.

Until this programme was complete, it faced further challenges from Russia and the other Western powers in China:

- In Korea Russia had supplanted China as the main challenge to Japanese influence. Another unsuccessful attempt by Tong-hak groups to seize power led to the murder of the Korean queen and the flight of the king to the Russian **legation**. This enabled the Russians to increase their influence in Korea and gave them the excuse to send a **military mission** to Seoul, but in 1898, through the Nishi-Rosen agreement, both countries agreed not to interfere in Korean politics.
- In China, the French, British, Germans and Russians were all expanding their power and creating spheres of influence (see page 25), which threatened to exclude Japan. Russia was building up her power in Manchuria and took over Port Arthur in Liaodong, which Japan had been prevented in 1895 from doing.
- In response to the Boxer Revolt (see page 25), Japan demonstrated its interest in the future of China by providing the largest contingent of troops to the international force sent to relieve the Beijing legations. However, when Russia used the revolt as an excuse to strengthen their forces in Manchuria, Japan faced a major challenge to its ambitions in Korea.

KEY TERMS

Legation Embassy.

Military mission A small military presence sent to advise on military matters.

The Anglo-Japanese Treaty of 1902

By the autumn of 1900 it was becoming clear that to defend its interests in China and Korea Japan would either have to align itself with France, Germany and Russia, or with Britain. Both choices would create problems for Japan. A British alliance would tie Japan to supporting the policy of the 'open door' in China, which aimed to preserve free trade in the Chinese Empire, whereas Japan preferred to carve out its own sphere of influence. On the other hand, co-operation with Russia would be possible only at the cost of accepting Russian domination of Manchuria, Korea and northern China. As this would seriously challenge Japan's interests in Korea, it turned to Britain with a proposal for an alliance.

To protect their interests, Japan and Britain negotiated a defensive alliance. Japan recognized Britain's interests in China, while Britain accepted that Japan was 'in a peculiar degree politically as well as commercially and industrially' interested in Korea. Both powers then went on to agree in January 1902 that if these interests were threatened, each power should be free to take the necessary action to protect them. In the event of war between Japan and another country, Britain would remain neutral unless a third power came to that other country's assistance. Similarly, if Britain were involved in a conflict in the Far East, Japan would only intervene if a third power declared war against Britain. The advantage to Japan of this agreement was that in any future conflict with Russia, the alliance with Britain would deter intervention by Germany or France.

SOURCE J

The Anglo-Japanese agreement, 30 January 1902.

The Governments of Great Britain and Japan actuated solely by a desire to maintain the status quo and general peace in the extreme east, being moreover specially interested in maintaining the independence and territorial integrity of the Empire of China and the Empire of Korea, and in securing equal opportunities in those countries for the commerce and industry of all nations, hereby agree as follows:

Article I *The High Contracting Parties having mutually recognized the independence of China and Korea, declare themselves to be entirely uninfluenced by the aggressive tendencies in either country. Having in view, however, their special interest, of which those of Great Britain relate principally to China, while Japan, in addition to interests which it possesses in China, is interested in a peculiar degree, politically as well as commercially and industrially in Korea, the High Contracting parties recognize that it will be admissible for either of them to take such measures as may be indispensable in order to safeguard those interests if threatened either by the aggressive action of any other Power, or by disturbances arising in China or Korea, and necessitating the intervention of either of the High Contracting parties for the protection of lives and property of its subjects*

Article II *If either Great Britain or Japan, in the defence of their respective interests as above described, should become involved in war with another power, the High Contracting Party will maintain a strict neutrality, and use its efforts to prevent either Powers from joining in hostilities against its ally.*

Article III *If in the above event, any other Power or Powers should join in hostilities against that ally, the other High Contracting Party will come to its assistance, and will conduct war in common, and will make peace in mutual agreement with it.*

Summarize the key points of Source J. What is the real message of the source? What additional knowledge could you use to understand the significance of the source?

The Russo-Japanese war, 1904–05

When it became clear by 1904 that Russia would not withdraw troops from Manchuria and cede to Japan a dominant position in Korea, the Anglo-Japanese Treaty enabled Japan to launch a surprise attack on Port Arthur. The subsequent Russo-Japanese war was fought in isolation. Neither France, which had just signed a colonial agreement with Britain, the *Entente* (see page 20), nor Germany, wanted to fight Britain, and each feared that its involvement in a Far Eastern war would make it vulnerable to an attack in Europe. Both Britain and the USA gave Japan loans to finance the war provided there was a firm Japanese commitment to the 'open door' in China.

The Japanese victory in the Russo-Japanese war marked Japan's emergence as one of the imperial powers. It showed that it could defeat a European rival. Initially there was fighting in Korea and along the coast in the direction of Liaotung (see map, page 23). In April a Japanese naval victory outside Port Arthur gave Japan control of the seas and enabled it to move troops by ship to north Korea where they crossed the Yalu River and advanced into Manchuria in May. A second Japanese army landed in the Liaotung peninsula and laid siege to Port Arthur, which fell in January 1905. The way was then clear for a Japanese advance towards Mukden. After the defeat of the Russian fleet at Tsushima, which had been forced to sail half way round the world by Britain's refusal to allow it through the Suez Canal,

ACTIVITY 

Prepare a presentation on Japan's foreign policy 1895–1905. Then write a couple of paragraphs to show the similarities and differences in its victories of 1895 and 1905.

SOURCE K

Sinking of the Russian battleship *Knyaz Suvorov*, 27 May 1905.

Study Sources J and K. How far do these sources explain Japan's victory over Russia in 1905?

and of the Russian army at Mukden, the Russians, paralysed by large-scale unrest at home, agreed to mediation by the US President in August 1905.

By the terms of the Treaty of Portsmouth (New Hampshire), Russia ceased to be an immediate threat to either Britain or Japan in the Far East and withdrew from Korea and Manchuria. Russia gave Japan a free hand in Korea, and Japan also took over the Russian lease of Liaodong and the railway that linked it to Harbin (the South Manchuria railway) (see map, page 23).

What were the reasons for Japan's victory?

- By initially agreeing to the 'unequal treaties' and then acting cautiously until the 1890s when it was strong enough to assert its independence, it avoided the fate of China – domination by the imperial powers.
- It built up its armed forces and a modern financial and industrial infrastructure.
- It had also inherited the ancient Japanese traditions of loyalty to the Emperor and state. In 1889 both the Meiji Constitution and the Imperial Rescript (Proclamation) on Education emphazised that subjects of the Japanese Emperor should in an emergency 'offer themselves courageously to the state'. A British observer of the Russo-Japanese war, General Sir Ian Hamilton, attributed their success to the fact that they 'have behind them the moral character produced by mothers and fathers, who again are the product of generations of mothers and fathers nurtured in ideas of self-sacrifice and loyalty…'

Japanese policy in Korea, Manchuria and China, 1906–14

After the victories of 1905 the Japanese government came under increasing pressure from the patriotic societies, particularly the **Black Dragon Society**, to pursue much more aggressive policies, not only in Korea, Manchuria and China, but also to occupy Mongolia and Siberia. These ideas appealed to the officer corps, who believed that Japan should at all costs preserve its gains from the Treaty of Portsmouth. In 1906 the government rejected the army's demands that in return for a military withdrawal from Manchuria, Japan should retain a number of administrative rights there, which would in fact ensure its dependence on Japan. The government believed that it was more important to cultivate trade with China and keep good relations with the USA and Britain. This tension between the army and civilian ministers was to become more acute after the end of the First World War (see pages 206–8).

KEY TERM 

Black Dragon Society (or the Kokuryukai or Amur Society) Founded in 1901 with the aim of extending Japan's 'imperial mission' to Manchuria, Mongolia and Siberia. It had close contacts with the Japanese officer corps.

Even if it had failed to convince ministers in 1906, it continued with some success to press its arguments on the government, and as a result, in the years up to the outbreak of the First World War Japan steadily strengthened its position in both Manchuria and Korea. In 1910 a secret agreement between Japan and Russia divided Manchuria into Russian and Japanese spheres of interest: Russian in the north and Japanese in the south. The reason for this was that neither country wanted to open up trade in Manchuria to the other powers. In 1910 Japan also annexed Korea outright. Initially in 1906 the Japanese had allowed the Koreans self-government, subject to overall control from Tokyo, but in the face of growing nationalist opposition, and attempts to regain its independence, it annexed Korea outright.

The army and the cabinet disagreed about how to react to the Chinese revolution of 1911–12 (see page 174). The army, backed by the Black Dragon Society, wanted to exploit the chaos of the revolution to create an independent Manchuria under a puppet ruler, as indeed it was to do in 1932 (see page 209). The Japanese government was more cautious and, once the Chinese politician Yuan Shikai (see page 177) was able to establish what promised to be a more stable regime in China, Japan followed Britain's and the USA's lead in supporting it. The reason for this cautious policy was that Japan had built up a considerable economic stake in China. By 1914 some 20 per cent of its exports went there and it wanted to safeguard this trade.

Japan's role in the First World War and global position by 1918

ACTIVITY 

Re-read pages 32–39. In relation to Japan's international position what was different in 1919 as compared to 1853? Were any of the problems facing Japan the same? What had changed?

The terms of the Anglo-Japanese Treaty did not require Japan to enter the war as an ally of Britain, but Japan declared war on Germany on 23 August 1914 in order to seize the German concessions in Shandong in China and annex the German Pacific islands. Japan refused to send any troops to Europe, but its navy helped Britain ensure the security of the Pacific Ocean. Japan's primary interest was to strengthen its economic and political hold on China while its rivals were distracted by the war in Europe. In January 1915 China was presented with 'the Twenty-One Demands' by the Japanese government, which would grant Japan privileged territorial and economic concessions as well as the right to appoint military, financial and police advisers to the Chinese government. In the face of Chinese hostility Japan dropped its demands for appointing advisers, but through an ultimatum gained the rest of their demands:

- Japan's seizure of the German concessions in Shandong province was confirmed.
- Japan was also able to extend its lease on the South Manchuria Railway Zone to 99 years and to gain control of the Hanyeping mining and metallurgical plants, which already owed Japan vast sums of money.
- China agreed not to grant any more coastal or island concessions to any other power but Japan.

KEY FIGURES 

Duan Qirui (1865–1936) Chinese warlord and Prime Minister of China intermittently 1913–18.

Nishihara Kamezo (1873–1954) Businessman sent as personal envoy by the Japanese Prime Minister to negotiate loans to Duan Qirui.

Further economic concessions were acquired in exchange for a series of loans made to China in 1917 and 1918. In the short term it was hoped that the loans would consolidate the power of the pro-Japanese Prime Minister, **Duan Qirui**, and enable him to defeat his rivals. However, the ultimate aim was, in the words of the Japanese businessman **Nishihara Kamezo**, who negotiated the loans: 'to develop the limitless resources of China and the industry of Japan by co-ordinating the two, so as to make possible a plan for self-sufficiency under which Japan and China would become a single entity'.

By 1918 Japan was the leading power in east Asia. Russia by a secret treaty in 1916 recognized its growing mining and railway interests in Manchuria, while Britain, France and Italy recognized its claims to Germany's former rights in Shandong and the Pacific islands. When the USA entered the war in 1917 it recognized that Japan's geographical position gave it a special position in China which it was entitled to protect.

SUMMARY DIAGRAM

Why did Japan emerge as a world power and what was the impact on international relations?

Reasons for emergence as a world power
- With the Meiji restoration the modernizers were in control
- Acted unprovocatively until the unequal treaties were abolished
- Military and economic strength built up
- Effective central administration and tax system created
- Could count on loyalty of its subjects

Road to becoming a world power
- Defeat of China, 1895
- Anglo-Japanese Treaty of 1902
- Defeat of Russia, 1905
- Declaration of war on Germany in 1914 and seizure of its far Eastern possessions
- Twenty-One Demands to China
- Attends Paris Peace Conference as a major power

Why did the USA emerge as a world power and what was the impact on international relations?

Impact of the closing of the frontier on US foreign policy

Since gaining independence from Britain in 1783, the energies of the USA had been for the most part concentrated on extending its frontiers westwards at the expense of the Native Americans. By the mid-1890s this process was virtually complete: a network of railroads extended from east to west and some 8 million acres of territory, which had originally been designated as 'Indian territory', was opened to US settlers. In 1890 the US Census Bureau declared the frontier was now 'closed'. By that it meant that there was no longer a frontier line beyond which the population density was less than two persons per square mile.

Some historians argue that the 1890s marked a turning point in US foreign policy. Like the European powers, between 1898 and 1914 the USA began to acquire colonies and protectorates – in Puerto Rico, Cuba and the Philippines, for example – and show an interest in establishing spheres of interest in China.

KEY TERMS

Jingoism Extreme patriotism supporting an aggressive foreign policy.

Psychic crisis A crisis caused for an individual by outside events, which he or she is unable to come to terms with.

Others, on the other hand, argue that US foreign policy in the 1890s was merely a logical development from past trends. What cannot be denied, however, is that the 1890s witnessed, as in Britain, an outburst of '**jingoism**' in the USA, which was caused by both pride in American achievements and foreboding about the future. In the eyes of some contemporary commentators, the closing of the frontier marked the emergence of the American nation, which according to the Kentucky journalist, Henry Watterton, was 'destined to exercise a controlling influence upon the actions of mankind and to affect the future of the world'.

KEY FIGURE 

Frederick Jackson Turner (1861–1932) American historian who taught at the universities of Wisconsin and Harvard. The focus of his work was on the US Midwest.

An impressive exhibition – the Columbian exposition – was held in Chicago in 1893 to mark the nation's coming of age after Columbus' 'discovery' of America 400 years earlier. At the exhibition a contemporary historian, **Frederick Jackson Turner**, gave a lecture, which was later published under the title 'The Significance of the Frontier in American History' that caught the imagination of the public. He argued that US democracy had been shaped by the availability of land beyond the frontier in the west, which had enabled generations of US settlers to become sturdy self-supporting independent farmers. This became known as 'the frontier thesis'. Although it was a positive explanation of the US national character, it could also be given a more pessimistic interpretation by raising the question whether the closure of the frontier would undermine the country's unique values and character.

These fears were further fuelled by threatening developments, which were both internal and external:

- The severe economic depression of 1893 created unemployment, which led to a wave of demonstrations and strikes that seemed to threaten revolution.
- There were also threats from abroad with the emergence of Japan and Germany as imperial powers, while the scramble for Africa and the threat to China showed the dynamism and aggression of European imperialism.
- It was feared that the influx of immigrants from the Mediterranean countries and eastern Europe would dilute the 'traditional' ethnic composition of the USA.
- The rapid growth of great cities with their social problems and slums also led to the creation of a new world very different from 'frontier America'.

The historian Richard Hofstadter has described with some exaggeration the 1890s as a time of '**psychic crisis**' for American society from which Americans sought escape by supporting an aggressive foreign policy. This interpretation would seem to be backed up by an observation by the

Massachusetts Senator, **Henry Cabot Lodge**, that this assertive foreign policy could 'knock on the head … the matters which have embarrassed us at home'. Yet, while the 1890s were indeed an unsettling time for Americans, which the 'closing of the frontier' came to symbolize, there were other factors which also determined US foreign policy during this decade.

KEY FIGURES 

Senator Henry Cabot Lodge (1850–1924) Republican Congressman.

Captain Alfred Mahan (1840–1914) A US naval officer and naval historian, whose book *The Influence of Sea Power upon History* was very influential in both Europe and the USA.

Economic growth and the need for trade in the late nineteenth century

By 1890 the USA had a developed industrial economy as well as a large agricultural sector. Like their counterparts in Europe, American industrialists and farmers needed markets for their goods and produce. The situation was made even more acute by a series of economic crises in the mid-1880s, which peaked in the Great Depression of 1893–97. The historian William A. Williams argued that the American government was convinced that 'America's domestic well-being depends upon … ever increasing overseas economic expansion' for both industrial and agricultural products. Manufacturers and industrialists stressed the need both to safeguard traditional markets in South America and open up new ones. In China, for instance, the US government, together with Britain, supported the 'open door' policy (see page 26) that would open up the internal Chinese market to American and European trade.

SOURCE L

Extract from the American business periodical, *The American Exporter*, in May 1881.

No greater field for commercial enterprise can be found in the vast and underdeveloped markets of China for our manufacturers and farmers … its vast rivers and canals present unrivalled scope for our steam navigation, and its wide plains and valleys offer matchless facilities for railways … It stands upon the threshold of the New World and offers to America the greater share of a trade which has enriched every community which has been able to command it.

How useful is Source L in explaining why the USA emerged as a world power? What additional information is needed to assess this source? (Re-reading pages 23–27 and 40–46 will help you to answer this.)

Public opinion and the government were also swayed by **Captain Alfred Mahan**'s influential book, *The Influence of Sea Power upon History*, which was published in 1890. This argued that the USA must abandon its '**continentalist strategy**' and instead build up a large navy and **merchant marine** to compete for world trade and acquire colonies for raw materials and bases. In the 1890s the US government followed this advice and began to construct a formidable navy, which gave it the ability to project its power globally. Between 1898 and 1913 the fleet expanded from 11 battleships to 36, and special gunboats, for example, were designed to protect US concessions in China.

KEY TERMS 

Continentalist strategy A policy that was primarily concerned with the North American continent.

Merchant marine A fleet of cargo vessels.

Despite the fears or 'psychic crisis' of the 1890s, by 1912 the USA was a major trading power. Its national wealth doubled between 1900 and 1912, and its investments abroad rose from $700 million in 1897 to $3.5 billion by 1914. It was also a leading global power in technology and manufacturing and had pioneered modern mass industrial production.

Reasons for, and the impact of, the Spanish-American war

The historian George Herring has called the Spanish-American war 'the pivotal event of a pivotal decade' which marked the USA's emergence as a world power.

The situation in Cuba

The war was caused by a revolution in the Spanish colony of Cuba. In 1890 a free trade treaty between Spain and the USA caused a short-lived economic boom on the island, but it ended abruptly in 1894 when the USA introduced a tariff which discriminated against Cuban sugar, the island's main product. This caused widespread economic devastation and political unrest, which was quickly exploited by Cuban exiles in the USA. In 1895 **José Marti** returned to stir up a revolt against the Spanish. This led to a prolonged and brutal struggle between the Spanish and the rebels, which by 1898 had resulted in a stalemate.

KEY FIGURES 

José Marti (1853–1895) One of the leading Cuban revolutionaries, who was killed by Spanish troops in the battle of Dos Rios.

William McKinley (1843–1901) Republican President of the USA, 1897–1901; assassinated in September 1901.

Causes of US intervention

Historians argue over whether the war was an 'aberration' and caused by sensationalist reports in the '**Yellow Press**', which put irresistible pressure on a supposedly weak president, **William McKinley**, or whether it was the consequence of deliberate US intentions to pursue a more assertive and global foreign policy.

KEY TERM 

'Yellow Press' The new popular press, which published jingoistic and sensational reports.

The USA could not afford to ignore the situation in Cuba as it had important trading interests on the island. In 1897, 87 per cent of Cuba's exports went to the USA, and the value of US investments and trade with the island was $150 million (approximately $ 2.5 billion in today's prices). The war also threatened US-owned sugar estates, mines and ranches as well as the safety of US citizens in Cuba. The 'Yellow Press' undoubtedly whipped up hostility towards Spain as it depicted the Spanish as the most brutal of oppressors, but it alone did not cause US intervention. A complex mixture of factors were in play:

- The divided Democrat Party saw in US intervention a chance to unite their party.
- This in turn put pressure on the Republicans to pursue a tough line against Spain to head off Democrat opposition.
- The US elites increasingly argued that the USA as a rising world power must act to create order in its own 'back yard'.

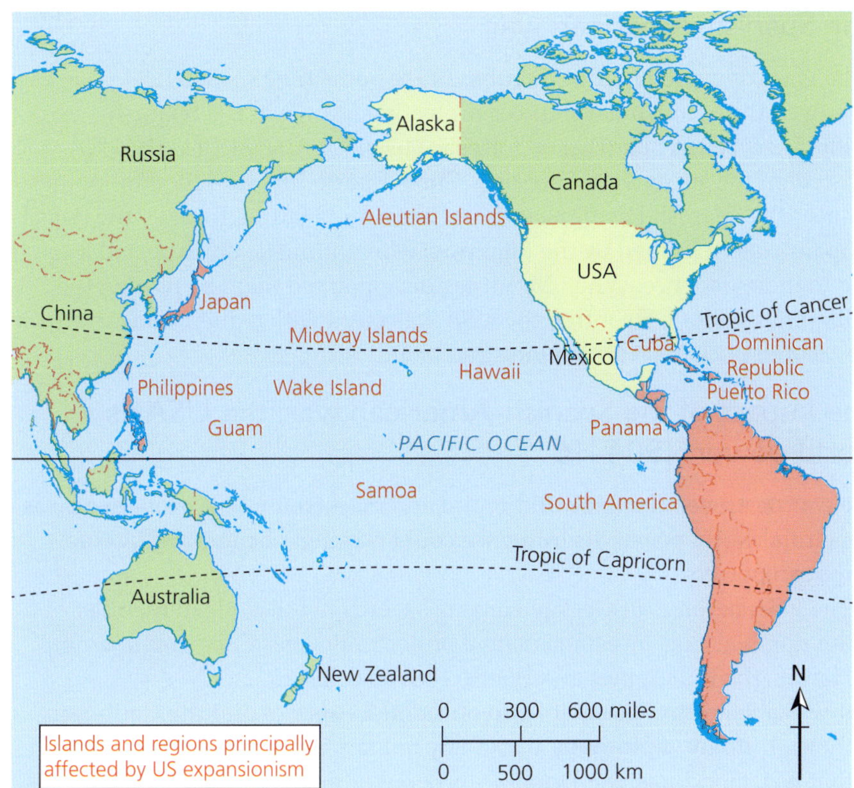

Figure 1.3 Map showing US expansion, 1890–1914.

To what extent does this map suggest that the USA had created an empire and emerged as a world power by 1914?

William McKinley, who became President in 1897, intended to drive Spain out of Cuba, but initially he hoped to do so without resorting to war. Whether this could have been done peacefully is debatable, but two incidents made war between the USA and Spain inevitable. The first was a leaked letter from the Spanish ambassador in Washington, which caricatured McKinley as a weak man seeking cheap publicity and also hinted that Spain's promise to give the Cubans greater autonomy was not seriously meant. The US press seized upon it, and one newspaper claimed that it was the 'worst insult to the United States in its history'!

A few days later the US battleship, the *Maine*, blew up in Havana harbour, killing 266 sailors. This was almost certainly the result of an internal explosion, not of Spanish aggression, but the press pinned the blame on the Spanish. 'Remember the *Maine*, to hell with Spain' became a popular slogan, and both the public and **Congress** demanded war. McKinley had little option but to send troops to Cuba, which he described as 'neutral intervention' to install a Cuban government, 'which would', as his supporters in Congress stressed, 'be of practical advantage to the United States'. The **Teller Amendment** passed by Congress specifically forbade him to annex the island.

KEY TERMS

Congress The US parliament.

Teller Amendment An amendment (or qualification) put forward by Senator Henry Teller to a joint resolution by the US Congress limiting the freedom a victorious USA would have in Cuba.

The Spanish-American war

Cuba was conquered in four months. At the same time the US fleet destroyed the Spanish naval forces protecting Manila in the Spanish Philippines. When Spain asked for peace terms in August 1898 the USA insisted on the surrender of not only Cuba, Puerto Rico and the Philippines, but also the Spanish Pacific islands of Guam and Hawaii. Initially the defeat of Spain was welcomed by the **Filipinos**, who optimistically expected it to lead to independence. When McKinley disappointed them by placing the Philippines under US control, the USA was faced with a guerrilla war, which they won only in 1904 after a long and bloody struggle.

KEY TERMS 

Filipinos The inhabitants of the Philippines.

Dollar diplomacy The furthering of diplomatic aims by using economic pressure and the offer of loans.

The impact of the Spanish-American war: the USA as a world power, 1904–16

The war destroyed the Spanish Empire and marked the USA's emergence as a potential world power. Its influence could no longer be ignored by the European powers:

- The USA became, in George Herring's words, 'a full-fledged member of the imperial club' by establishing a protectorate over Cuba and seizing Hawaii, the Philippines and Puerto Rico as colonies.
- It was able to strengthen its grip on Central America and the Caribbean through '**dollar diplomacy**' backed by military power where necessary. In that way Honduras, the Dominican Republic and Nicaragua became colonies of the USA in all but name.
- Liberia in west Africa, which had been founded as an independent state for freed slaves, was similarly subjected to 'dollar diplomacy' when its existence was threatened by civil war and foreign debts. In 1908 a US loan was arranged, a warship sent to crush the revolt and a US army officer was given responsibility for building up Liberia's frontier force.
- The USA brought pressure to bear on Columbia to surrender the Isthmus of Panama, which was effectively placed under US control so that the Panama Canal could be constructed.
- Thanks to the annexation of the Philippines, the USA also became a more powerful force in the Pacific and east Asia. It was, for example, able to mediate between Russia and Japan and persuade them to accept the Treaty of Portsmouth in 1905 (see page 37). A key motive for this intervention was fear that a total Japanese victory over Russia would make the Philippines and Hawaii vulnerable to Japanese sea power.
- In 1905 **President Theodore Roosevelt,** also in an unprecedented act of US policy, intervened in European politics. Responding to an appeal from Kaiser Wilhelm of Germany to mediate in the dispute between France and Germany over the control of Morocco, he played an important role in the Algeçiras Conference (see page 20) and skilfully manoeuvred the Kaiser into accepting an agreement which favoured France.
- Even when the Democrat Woodrow Wilson was elected President in 1912 on an anti-imperialist platform, US policy did not change. Faced with

KEY FIGURE 

President Theodore Roosevelt (1858–1919) Leader of the Republican Party and US President, 1901–09.

political instability in the Caribbean and Central America he pursued a policy very similar to McKinley and Roosevelt. US troops were sent to Cuba, Panama, Hispaniola and Haiti, while Nicaragua became a protectorate.

- The USA also intervened in the **civil war in Mexico** in an attempt to restore order and to prevent a government hostile to its interests being established. In March 1916, when rebel troops actually attacked the US border town of Columbus in New Mexico, Wilson sent a 'punitive expedition' to destroy the rebel forces. Both countries came to the brink of war, but in January 1917, after tortuous negotiations, the US expeditionary force was withdrawn. Wilson could not afford a war that would need at least 500,000 troops to defeat the rebels at a time when war with Germany was imminent (see below).

KEY TERMS 

Civil war in Mexico Conflict in Mexico, 1910–20; initially a revolt against the Diaz regime and then became a multi-sided civil war.

Senate The Upper House of the US Congress.

Woodrow Wilson

1856	Born in Virginia
1890–1902	History Professor at Princeton University
1911–12	Member of the Democratic Party Governor of New Jersey
1913–21	President of the USA
1924	Died

Wilson was an academic who had been President of Princeton University. He entered national politics in 1912 and was elected President of the USA in 1912. He pursued a policy of strict neutrality in the First World War and in 1916 was re-elected on the slogan 'Keep us out of the war'. The USA was, however, forced into the war in April 1917 by the resumption of unrestricted submarine warfare by Germany (see page 47). On 8 January 1918 he issued his Fourteen Points as the basis for a negotiated peace. In 1919 he was welcomed as a hero in Europe but at the Paris Peace Conference he was forced to compromise his ideas by Britain and France. His hopes that the League of Nations would eventually correct the injustices of the peace treaties were dashed by the **Senate's** refusal to ratify the treaty. He was struck down by a stroke while campaigning to win public support for the League, and was an invalid until his death in 1924.

ACTIVITY

Re-read pages 39–46. Hold a class debate about how far the USA became an imperial nation, 1890–1914. One group will argue that the USA was never an imperial nation like Britain, for example. Another will argue that it did become an imperial power. Each group should use cards with clear debating points on one side and supporting evidence on the other.

SOURCE M

'The Dragon's Choice'. American cartoon showing a firm Uncle Sam offering the Chinese Dragon a choice between war and peace at the height of the Boxer Rebellion. Cartoon by W.A. Rogers, 1900.

Who is the intended audience for Source M? What is the purpose of this source and how might this affect its reliability?

KEY TERM 

Allies Britain, France, Russia and Italy, who declared war against Germany in 1914.

Reasons for the USA's entry into the First World War and its subsequent impact

When war broke out in Europe in August 1914 (see page 22), the reaction of the majority of Americans was relief that their country was neutral. Although Wilson himself and the majority of the US elites favoured the **Allies**, many Americans did not. German Americans naturally supported their former homeland, while Irish Americans deeply distrusted Britain and Jewish Americans hated anti-Semitic Imperial Russia.

SOURCE N

President Wilson's neutrality message to the Senate, 19 August 1914.

The people of the United States are drawn from many nations and chiefly from the nations now at war. It is natural and inevitable that there should be the utmost variety of sympathy and desire among them with regard to the issues and circumstances of the conflict…

I venture therefore, my fellow countrymen, to speak a solemn word of warning to you against that deepest, most essential breach of neutrality, which may spring out of partisanship, or of passionately taking sides.

Summarise in your own words the message in Source N. How far does the source explain the reasons for US neutrality?

Growing economic links between the Allies and the USA

Nevertheless, there were powerful economic factors that were to influence the USA in favour of the Allies. Britain needed to purchase weapons, explosives and food from the USA. Given that the British naval blockade of Germany prevented the USA from trading with the Central Powers, US industry was delighted with the volume of orders which they received from Britain, and to pay for these orders US banks were ready to loan the British government millions of dollars – in May 1916 this amounted to about $10 million a day. In effect, as Wilson's adviser, **Colonel House**, admitted in the spring of 1915, the United States was 'bound up more or less' in an eventual Allied victory.

KEY FIGURE

Colonel Edward House (1858–1938) Diplomat, politician and adviser to President Wilson. 'Colonel' was a nickname.

The German U-boat threat, 1915

The only way the Germans could halt the steady flow of munitions and vital supplies from across the Atlantic to Britain was to deploy U-boats (submarines) around the British Isles to sink shipping bringing imports to Britain. For Germany this ran the risk of sinking US vessels, which could lead to eventual confrontation with Washington. On 7 May 1915, the British liner, the *Lusitania*, was sunk off the Irish coast by a German U-boat, killing 1198 people, which included 128 Americans. At first the Germans responded to Wilson's protests by pointing out quite correctly that the liner had munitions in its hold, but the German Chancellor, Bethmann Hollweg, realising that it was more important to keep the USA out of the war than to wage **unrestricted submarine warfare,** promised that no more passenger ships would be sunk without warning. It was only this assurance that kept the USA out of the war.

KEY TERM

Unrestricted submarine warfare Sinking by German submarines (called U-boats) of all merchant ships, Allied or neutral, engaged in carrying goods to or from Allied states.

US declaration of war

Bethmann Hollweg was reluctant to risk a rupture with the USA, but in January 1917, against his better judgement, he was pushed by the German high command into sanctioning unrestricted submarine warfare against all ships trading with the Allies, on the optimistic assumption that this would rapidly defeat Britain. Predictably, US shipping and commerce suffered severely from the U-boat attacks. Any remaining doubts about abandoning neutrality were removed when, in February, the British gave Wilson the text of a telegram from the German Foreign Secretary, Arthur Zimmermann, to the German ambassador in Mexico, which they had intercepted. It revealed that if the USA entered the war on the Allied side, the Germans would ally with Mexico and encourage a Mexican invasion of New Mexico, Arizona and Texas. On 6 April President Wilson declared war on the Central Powers as an '**associated power**' rather than ally of the *Entente* powers. This distinction, Wilson hoped, would enable him to pursue when necessary a policy independent of the *Entente*.

KEY TERM

Associated power The USA was not bound by any treaties with the Allies, 1917–19, and was free, if necessary, to pursue its own policies.

The USA as a belligerent

SOURCE O

President Wilson's war address to Congress, 2 April 1917.

We are glad now that we see the facts with no veil of false pretence about them, to fight thus for the ultimate peace of the world, for the liberation of its peoples – the German peoples included – the rights of nations, great and small and the privilege of men everywhere to choose their way of life and obedience. The world must be safe for democracy. Its peace must be planted upon trusted foundations of political liberty.

We have no selfish ends to serve. We desire no conquests and no dominion. We seek no indemnities for ourselves, and no material compensation for sacrifices we shall freely make.

Compare Sources N and O as evidence for the decisive change that occurred in US foreign policy 1914–17.

The US declaration of war was a development of immense importance because the manpower reserves and economic strength of the USA would now be available to the Allies. On the other hand, it would take the USA at least a year to train and equip an army that could fight in France. The Russian revolutions of February and October 1917, which resulted in Russia leaving the war, gave the Germans a window of opportunity to launch one last great offensive against the British and French in the west in March 1918. US troops under **General Pershing** played a part in halting this at the Second Battle of the Marne in July, and by September there were more than a million US troops in France. At the Battle of Argonne (26 September–11 November) they won a major victory over the Germans that hastened the end of the war.

KEY FIGURE 

General Pershing (1860–1948) Commander of US troops in France.

The USA and Russia

In Russia the February Revolution had swept away the Tsarist regime. The new **Provisional Government** initially promised to fight a '**people's war**' against the Germans. It hoped that carrying on the war under a new democratic regime would ignite a great burst of popular enthusiasm. Wilson welcomed the new regime and promised $450 million in aid, but the Russian army was in no state to fight. Its morale was low and discipline was

KEY TERMS 

Provisional Government A government in power until the holding of elections.

People's war Popular war fought by the mass of the people.

undermined by the **Bolsheviks**, who seized power in October and were determined to pull Russia out of the war. This was achieved in March 1918 when Lenin, the Bolshevik leader, signed the Treaty of Brest-Litovsk.

In a desperate but ultimately unsuccessful attempt to keep Russia in the war, the Allies and the USA tried to support the **White Russians**, who were hoping to overthrow the Bolsheviks by force with both money and small numbers of troops. To help achieve this Wilson agreed in June 1918 to send a force of 20,000 troops to Siberia. An added reason for this step was to block any Japanese plans for taking over Siberia. Allied and US intervention was to achieve little and by 1920 the Bolsheviks had won the civil war in Russia.

KEY TERMS 

Bolsheviks The Russian Communist Party.

White Russians The name given to members and supporters of the counter-revolutionary 'White' armies, which fought against the Bolshevik 'Red' Army in the Russian Civil War (1918–21).

The Fourteen Points and the Armistice, November 1911

By the early autumn of 1918 the USA had emerged as potentially the most powerful of the states waging war against the Central Powers. Wilson and his advisers were ready to exploit this position to ensure what they called 'a just peace'. On 8 January 1918, in a speech to Congress, Wilson had proclaimed that the USA wanted a peace of 'no annexations, no contributions, no punitive damages' and in the Fourteen Points outlined how this would be achieved. When on 28 September, after further military defeats in the west, the German military leadership conceded defeat, the German elite, in the words of the historian Holger Herweg, embraced the Fourteen Points 'much like a drowning person reaches for a life-line'.

To impress President Wilson that it was now a democratic country, the Germans rapidly created a parliamentary government, which on 4 October asked Wilson for 'an immediate armistice' on the basis of the Fourteen Points. Similar requests then came from Bulgaria, Austria–Hungary and the Ottoman Empire, all of which faced imminent defeat by Allied forces. However, Germany's immediate hopes of dividing its enemies and achieving an armistice based on the Fourteen Points were dashed when Wilson asked the Allies to draft the details of the armistice agreements. They produced tough terms, which anticipated their key aims at the coming Peace Conference and were to contradict the ideals of a Wilsonian peace (see Source O).

ACTIVITY 

List five reasons why the USA went to war. Then choose the reason you think is the most important and be ready to defend your choice in a class discussion.

SOURCE P

Extract from Wilson's Fourteen Points.

1 *Open covenants [agreements], openly arrived at … diplomacy shall always proceed frankly and in the public view.*

2 *Absolute freedom of navigation upon the seas, outside territorial waters…*

3 *The removal, so far as possible, of all economic barriers…*

4 *Adequate guarantees given and taken that national armaments will be reduced to the lowest point consistent with domestic safety.*

5 *A free, open-minded, and absolutely impartial adjustment of all colonial claims … the interests of the populations concerned must have equal weight with the equitable claims of the government whose title is to be determined.*

6 *The evacuation of all Russian territory…*

7 *Belgium, the whole world will agree, must be evacuated and restored, without any attempt to limit the sovereignty, which she enjoys in common with all other free nations.*

8 *All French territory should be freed and the invaded portions restored, and the wrong done to France by Prussia in 1871 in the matter of Alsace-Lorraine … should be righted…*

9 *A readjustment of the frontiers of Italy should be effected along clearly recognisable lines of nationality.*

10 *The peoples of Austria–Hungary, whose place among the nations we wish to see safeguarded and assured, should be accorded the freest opportunity of autonomous development.*

11 *Romania, Serbia and Montenegro should be evacuated … Serbia afforded free and secure access to the sea; and the relations of the several Balkan states to one another determined by friendly council along historically established lines of allegiance and nationality…*

12 *The Turkish portions of the present Ottoman Empire should be assured a secure sovereignty, but the other nationalities … should be assured an absolutely unmolested opportunity of autonomous development, and the Dardanelles should be permanently open as a free passage to the ships and commerce of all nations…*

13 *An independent Poland should be erected which should include the territories inhabited by indisputably Polish populations, which should be assured a free and secure access to the sea…*

14 *A general association of nations must be formed under specific covenants for the purpose of political independence and territorial integrity to great and small states alike…*

Re-write the extracts from the 14 Points in Source P in your own words, and explain the significance of each point for the international situation.

ACTIVITY

Find evidence to support each of the points about the USA's emergence as a world power made in the summary diagram.

SUMMARY DIAGRAM

Why did the USA emerge as a world power and what was the impact on international relations?

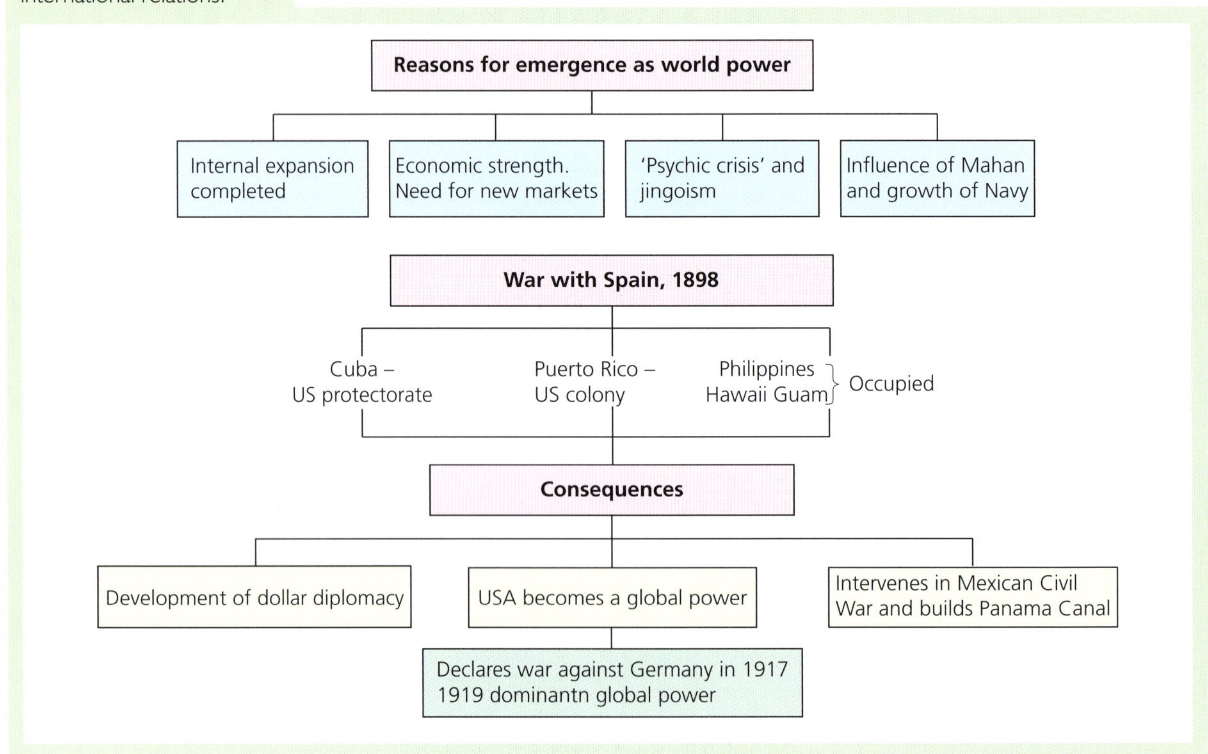

ACTIVITY 

Copy and complete this chart by putting in the relevant columns, as indicated, the events marking the USA's emergence as a world power, 1870–1919.

Date	Event	Significance

Now write a concluding paragraph explaining to what extent the US had emerged as a world power by 1919.

Chapter summary

The years 1870–1900 saw the emergence of the 'New Imperialism'. Its causes are complex: economic motives were important, but so too were political factors. Bismarck exploited Anglo-French quarrels in Africa to deflect French attentions from Europe, while France reacted to its perceived humiliation in Egypt to challenge Britain in West Africa. By the 1890s all the great powers of Europe were competing against each other to build up or extend their colonial empires. Their governments were often encouraged by jingoistic domestic support, although this was mixed with a sense of responsibility among liberals, Christians and socialists for the well-being and development of the newly colonized peoples.

The competition for empire, especially in China and Africa, inevitably influenced relations between the European powers. German intervention in South Africa, for example, led to a furious counter-reaction in the British press, while the Moroccan crises of 1904 and 1911 led to close Anglo-French co-operation. There were attempts, particularly at the Berlin West African and the Hague Conferences, to regulate international rivalries, but they were largely ineffective and were unable to prevent conflict.

The European empires were challenged by 1900 by the emergence of two new potentially powerful states: in east Asia Japan, which defeated Russia in 1905, and the USA, which by 1914 was already potentially the strongest power in the world. In 1918 its strength effectively won the First World War for the Allies.

Refresher questions

1. What economic and political motives were behind the creation of the colonial empires, 1870–1919?
2. Why did the 'scramble for Africa' take place?
3. How popular was overseas expansion in the European states, Japan and the USA?
4. How did the 'New Imperialism' affect relations between the European powers?
5. To what extent was there a 'scramble for China'?
6. How much progress was made in resolving the tensions between the imperial powers by 1914?
7. What impact did the rise of Japan have on east Asia?
8. How did Japan manage to escape the fate of China, 1870–1919?
9. To what extent did the USA create an empire, 1890–1919?
10. How true is it to say that the USA had the potential but not the will to be a great power, 1890–1918?

Paper 1 guidance: sources

Understanding and interpreting sources

In your examination for Paper 1 you will be presented with four sources and a question made up of two parts. You will have to answer both parts of the question. The first question will ask you to read two sources and compare and contrast them – see where they agree or disagree and assess how useful they are as evidence. For the second question you will need to read all four sources and consider how they support a particular view.

In the examination, you need to show key skills in approaching evidence:

- You have to interpret evidence. You need to link it to the issue in the question and decide what the evidence is saying about the issue. In the example below the issue is how far the scramble for Africa was caused by economic factors? You will need to consider how useful the evidence is. This involves thinking carefully about who wrote it, why it was written and how typical it might be.
- This really involves knowledge of all aspects of the 'scramble for Africa', but it is also important to look at the type of evidence you are dealing with. The use of knowledge is a skill that will be developed in the next two chapters. Here it is important to ask 'How is this source linked to the issue in the question?' and 'Was the person who produced this source in a position to know, and is there a reason why he or she might hold that view?'
- However, you can only move on to these questions once you are sure you understand the relevance of the sources to the question.

The activity below will help you to establish the basic relevance of the four sources. You do not need to create a table in an examination but the activity will help you with the vital first step – the skill of interpreting the sources.

Look at Sources A, B, C and D. The question is 'How far do these sources support the view that the scramble for Africa was caused by economic factors?' Think about how they explain colonial expansion. Make a copy of the table on page 53. You will see that one part has been done for you. Now fill the rest in for Sources B to D.

SOURCE A

Alex Thompson, a socialist, wrote in the *Clarion*, 1 October, 1898, a British left-wing newspaper, the following explanation:

There you have the real reason of the world's murderous turbulence. It is the excessive accumulation of capital and the insatiable greed of capital for profitable investment, that causes the bloody and ruthless scramble now threatening to set all Europe by the ears.

SOURCE B

Lord Rosebery, the Liberal Prime Minister of Britain, explains to the Royal Colonial Institute in March 1893 why Britain was still planning colonial expansion.

It is said that our Empire is already large enough and does not need extension. That would be true enough if the world were elastic but unfortunately it is not elastic and we are engaged at the present moment, in the language of mining, in 'pegging out claims for the future'. We have to consider not what we want now, but what we shall want in the future.

SOURCE C

The former German ambassador, Prince Hohenlohe, to France recalls in his Memoirs, published in 1880, Bismarck's comments on the acquisition of colonies.

In the evening [of 22 February 1880] I had dinner with Bismarck … The Chancellor refuses all talk of colonies. He says that we haven't an adequate fleet to protect them and our bureaucracy [civil service] is not skilful enough to direct the government of such territories. The Chancellor also alluded to my report on the French plans for Morocco, and though we could only rejoice if France annexed it. She would then be very occupied, and we could let her expand into Africa as compensation for Alsace-Lorraine.

SOURCE D

A speech by King Leopold of Belgium to an international group of explorers meeting in Brussels on 12 September 1876, claiming that his plans for expansion in Africa are a crusade.

To open to civilization the only part of our globe where it has yet to penetrate, to pierce the darkness which envelops whole populations, it is, I dare to say, a crusade worthy of this century of progress … Needless to say, in bringing you to Brussels, I was in no way motivated by selfish designs. Belgium is small, she is happy and satisfied with her lot. My only ambition is to serve her.

Source	What is this source saying about the key issue?	What evidence from the source shows this?
A	Indicates that the desire for profit is the motive behind colonial expansion.	'excessive accumulation of capital' and its 'insatiable greed for profitable investment'
B		
C		
D		

On the basis of what they say about economic factors in the 'scramble for Africa', group the sources. Which ones are most obviously saying that economic factors are the key and which ones suggest that it was caused by other issues?

Comparing and contrasting two sources

In the examination you may be asked to compare and contrast two sources. It is important not to just describe what one says and follow it by describing what the other says.

- There should be a point-by-point comparison (where the sources agree) and contrast (where the sources disagree).
- The comparisons should be illustrated by brief quotations from both texts.
- There should be some explanation of the differences by looking at who was writing and why.

To help practise the skill of comparing and contrasting sources and plan an answer it might be helpful to draw up a table like the one below:

Practise this skill by filling in the table for the two sources (B and C) on pages 10 and 13.

Points on which the sources agree	Parts of each source which show this	Reasons as to why the sources might agree (provenance)	Points on which the sources disagree	Parts of each source which show this	Reasons as to why the sources might disagree (provenance)

Paper 2 guidance: essay questions

In Paper 2 of your examination you will have to answer two types of essay question for two topics. The first question is a short answer essay which will ask you to explain an issue or event, the second is a long essay. Most of the advice applies to answering the long essays but there is also guidance on how to tackle the 'explain' or short essay questions.

Understanding the wording of the question

It is very important that you read the wording of the question you are answering very carefully. You must focus on the key words and phrases in the question; these may be dates, the names of leading figures or phrases such as 'How successful…?'

The first thing to do is to identify the command words, these will give you the instructions about what you have to do.

In Question (a) you will be asked to **explain** an event or why something happened.

In Question (b) you may be asked to:

- make a judgement about the causes or consequences of an event

- consider to what extent or how far a particular factor was the most important in bringing about an event
- make a judgement about a particular government or ruler.

Here are two examples:

> **'The most important reason for the rise of Japan to the position of an imperial power was its readiness to use force.' How far do you agree?**

This question puts forward one of the causes of the rise of Japan and argues that it was the most important. You must consider military factors carefully in a good paragraph on it, whether you believe them to be the main cause or not. In the other paragraphs you must look at the other factors, explaining either that they were more or less important.

> **To what extent did the growth of overseas empires damage relations between the European powers?**

This question asks you to consider the extent to which the growth of overseas empires damaged relations between these powers. You would need to consider the ways in which they did and did not damage relations between these powers. Given the wording of this question, you would not need to consider other factors that damaged relations.

Planning an answer

Once you have understood the demands of the question, the next step is planning your answer. The plan should outline your line of argument. This means that you will need to think about what you are going to argue before you start writing. This should help you to maintain a consistent line of argument throughout your answer. It also means that your plan will be a list of reasons about the issue or issues in the question which will ensure an analytical response. Simply having a list of dates would encourage you to write a narrative or descriptive answer and this would result in an unsuccessful essay.

Consider the first example above:

> **'The most important reason for the rise of Japan to the position of an imperial power was its readiness to use force.' How far do you agree?**

Your plan should be structured around the following issues:

- Why was force important for Japan?
- What other reasons were there for the increase in Japan's power?
- How important were these reasons?
- Were they more or less important than force?
- What is your overall view, having looked at the key factor and the other causes?

A plan for this essay might take the following form:

- 'Readiness to use force': the building up of its army and navy which was necessary in a world of imperial power rivalry in China and elsewhere. When did it use force to increase its power? Make the view that it was the most important factor clear by linking these ideas to events, for example, the Sino-Japanese war of 1895, the Russo-Japanese war and the seizure of German concessions and territory in 1914.
- Other factors: the Meiji restoration, which resulted in legal and financial reforms necessary for a modern state, particularly one with claims to becoming an imperial power.
- The increasing desire of the Japanese government to end the 'unequal treaties' of 1853. This was not achieved through war but diplomacy. Yet to negotiate with the Western powers Japan needed to modernize and build up its armed forces to be taken seriously by them.
- The growth of patriotism and nationalism in Japan.
- Diplomacy and a sense of realism that force was either premature or an awareness that Japan needed allies before it could be used – for example, the Convention of Tientsin, the Anglo-Japanese agreement of 1902.
- The building up of its economy and growing volume of exports to China – a peaceful extension of influence.

The conclusion should weigh up the relative importance of the readiness to use force argument and bring together interim conclusions in previous paragraphs, perhaps arguing that, while Japan was certainly ready to use force as a final weapon, it was not reckless with its use. It modernized itself, developed its economy and also used diplomacy to buy time or divide its potential enemies.

Planning answers to these questions will help you put together a structured answer and avoid the common mistake of listing reasons with each paragraph essentially saying 'Another reason for Japan's rise to an imperial power was…' Clearly 'another reason' needs to be shown to be relevant and linked to the question.

Planning an answer will help you focus on the actual question and not simply write about the topic. In the second question you might write all you know about the imperial rivalry between the great powers but not explain the extent to which it damaged diplomatic relations between them. Under the pressure of time in the examination room, it is easy to forget the importance of planning and just to start writing; but this will usually result in an essay that does not have a clear line of argument, or changes its line of argument half way through, making it less convincing.

QUESTION PRACTICE

The focus of this section has been on planning. Use the information in this chapter to plan answers to the following questions:

1 To what extent was Japanese 'aggression' before 1914 a defensive response to the claims of other powers?

2 'It was only great power rivalry that saved China from partition among the great powers.' How far do you agree?

3 How important was public opinion in the individual imperial nations in the partition of Africa?

4 To what extent was the USA an imperial power by 1918?

EXPLAIN QUESTIONS

1 Explain why the USA went to war against Spain in 1898.

2 Explain why the Berlin Conference of 1884–85 was called.

3 Explain why the Russo-Japanese war broke out in 1905.

4 Explain why Egypt was a source of Anglo-French rivalry.

CHAPTER 2

The League of Nations and international relations in the 1920s

This chapter considers the peace settlements of 1919–20 and the aims and motives of the participants. It assesses how effective these complex settlements were and what their impact, particularly on Europe and the Middle East, was. It also looks at the aims, structure and record of the League of Nations in the 1920s.

It analyzes these problems by examining the following key questions:

★ Why was there dissatisfaction with the peace settlements of 1919–20?

★ How and why did international tensions remain high in the period 1920–23?

★ How successful were attempts to improve international relations from 1924–29?

★ How successful was the League of Nations during the 1920s?

KEY DATES

1919	**28 June**	Treaty of Versailles signed with Germany
	10 September	Treaty of Saint-Germain signed with Austria
	27 November	Treaty of Neuilly signed with Bulgaria
1920	**4 June**	Treaty of Trianon signed with Hungary
	10 August	Treaty of Sèvres signed with Turkey
1921	**March**	Plebiscite in Upper Silesia
	April	German reparations fixed at 132 billion gold marks
	November	Washington Conference
1922	**April**	Genoa Conference and Rapallo Treaty between Germany and USSR
1923	**11 January**	French and Belgian troops occupy the Ruhr
	24 July	Treaty of Lausanne
1924	**August**	Dawes Plan
1925	**December**	Locarno Treaties
1926	**September**	Germany joins League of Nations
1928	**August**	Kellogg–Briand Pact
1929	**August**	The Young Plan

Why was there dissatisfaction with the peace settlements of 1919–20?

Key terms and implications of the peace treaties (Versailles, Trianon, Neuilly, Saint-Germain and Sèvres)

In January 1919 the statesmen of the victorious powers were confronted with a Europe in turmoil. The sudden and complete defeat of the Central Powers had made Europe vulnerable to the spread of communism from Russia. For much of the winter of 1918–19, Germany seemed poised on the edge of revolution. With the disintegration of the Austro-Hungarian, Ottoman and Russian empires there was no stable government anywhere east of the Rhine. Further problems were caused by the influenza **pandemic** which by the spring of 1919 had caused the deaths of millions of people, and by the near famine conditions in central and eastern Europe.

When the Paris Peace Conference opened the delegates of 27 states, which included China, attended, but in reality, power lay with the big four: Britain, France, Italy and the USA. Russia convulsed by civil war sent no delegates. The defeated states sent no representatives, which in Germany later gave rise to the bitter accusation that the Treaty of Versailles was a '**dictated peace**'.

KEY TERMS 

Pandemic An epidemic on a global scale.

Dictated peace A peace treaty that is dictated to the defeated state(s) rather than negotiated.

Covenant Rules and constitution of the League of Nations.

Reparations Compensation paid by a defeated power to make good the damage it caused in a war.

Aims of the victorious great powers

When the USA, Britain, France, Italy and Japan gathered in Paris to draw up the peace terms with Germany, each power had its own set of aims and agenda:

- President Wilson of the USA was determined to ensure that the Fourteen Points (see page 49) should be the basis for the coming peace negotiations and to anchor the **Covenant** of the League of Nations in the text of the peace treaties.
- **Clemenceau**, the French Prime Minister, was painfully aware that France, with its reduced birth rate and a total number of casualties of 1.3 million dead and another 2.8 million wounded, faced a Germany which, as a consequence of the collapse of Austria–Hungary and Tsarist Russia, was potentially stronger than in 1914. He therefore wanted to enforce maximum disarmament and **reparation** payments on the Germans, to set up strong independent Polish, Czechoslovak and Yugoslav states, and in addition an independent Rhineland state. He also wanted an alliance with Britain and the USA and to continue inter-Allied financial and economic co-operation into the post-war years.

KEY FIGURE 

Georges Clemenceau (1841–1929) A French politician whose outspokenness won him the title of 'the tiger'. As Prime Minister, he was a charismatic war leader, 1917–18, and presided over the Paris Peace Conference of 1919, but lost power in 1920. He foresaw the re-emergence of Germany as a great power and even predicted war in 1940.

KEY TERMS 

War guilt Carrying the blame for starting the war.

Dominions The British Dominions of Australia, Canada, New Zealand and South Africa were self-governing, but part of the British Empire and Commonwealth, of which to this day they are still members.

- In contrast to France, Britain, even before the great powers met in Paris, had already achieved many of its aims: the German fleet had surrendered, German trade rivalry was no longer a threat and Germany's colonial empire was liquidated. Britain's territorial ambitions lay in the Middle East, not Europe. Prime Minister Lloyd George also realized that a peaceful united Germany would act as a barrier against the spread of Bolshevism from Russia. The logic of British policy pointed in the direction of a peace of reconciliation rather than revenge, but in two key areas, reparations and the question of German **war guilt**, Britain adopted a much harder line. Lloyd George, the British Prime Minister, and Clemenceau agreed in December 1918 that the Kaiser should be tried by an international tribunal for war crimes. Under pressure from the **Dominions**, who also wanted a share of reparations, the British delegation at Paris was authorized 'to secure from Germany the greatest possible indemnity she can pay consistently with the well-being of the British Empire and the peace of the world without involving an army of occupation in Germany for its collection'.
- The Italian Prime Minister, Orlando, was anxious to convince the voters that Italy had done well out of the war, and concentrated initially on attempting to hold the *Entente* to their promises made in 1915 in the Treaty of London to give Italy the Austrian territories of South Tyrol and those along the Dalmatian coastline, as well as demanding the port of Fiume in the Adriatic.
- Japan's aims were limited to securing recognition of the territorial gains made in the war (see page 38) and having a racial equality clause inserted in the Covenant of the League of Nations.

ACTIVITY

Prepare a presentation showing what each of the victorious great powers hoped to gain from the peace negotiations.

David Lloyd George

1863	Born
1890	Elected to parliament as a Liberal
1908–15	Chancellor of the Exchequer
1916–22	Prime Minister and inspirational war leader
Oct 1922	Resigned and never again held office
1945	Died

Lloyd George was brought up in Wales, and in 1890 became a Welsh MP. He was bitterly critical of the Boer War, and in 1905 became a cabinet minister. During the First World War he made his reputation as a very effective Minister of Munitions and then 1916–18 served as an inspirational war leader, who remained in power until 1922 when he was forced to resign over the Chanak crisis (see page 81). After his fall he never returned to power, as he was distrusted by both the Conservative and Labour Parties, and died in 1945.

The Treaty of Versailles: the settlement with Germany

All the peace settlements were to a greater or lesser extent the result of compromises between the Allied powers. Versailles was no exception. Its key clauses were the result of fiercely negotiated agreements, which were often reached only when the conference appeared to be on the verge of collapse. The first 26 articles (which appeared in all the other peace treaties as well) contained the Covenant of the League of Nations (see pages 97–100) and were agreed unanimously.

German war guilt

There was universal agreement among the victorious powers that Germany was guilty of having started the war. It was this principle of war guilt which was to provide the moral justification for the reparations clauses of the treaty, as was stressed in Article 231 (see Source A).

SOURCE A

Extract from Part VIII, Section I [I], Article 231 and 232, 1919 of the Treaty of Versailles. The claim that Germany was guilty of starting the war is strongly asserted.

Article 231

The Allied and Associated governments affirm and Germany accepts the responsibility of Germany and her allies for causing all the loss and damage to which the Allied and associated governments and their nationals have been subjected as a consequence of the war imposed up them by the aggression of Germany and her allies.

Article 232

The Allied and Associated Governments recognize that the resources of Germany are not adequate, after taking into account permanent diminutions of such resources, which will result from other provisions of the present Treaty, to make complete reparation for all such loss and damage.

The Allied and Associated Governments, however, require and Germany undertakes, that she will make compensation for all damage done to the civilian population of the Allied and Associated powers and to their property.

Re-write Source A in your own words. After reading pages 61–66 answer this question: To what extent did the victorious powers use these two articles as a justification for the terms of the Treaty of Versailles?

Reparations

Although there was general agreement that Germany should pay reparations to the victors, there was considerable debate about the amount to be paid, the nature of the damage deserving compensation and how Germany could raise such large sums of money without rebuilding an export trade which might then harm the Allied industries. Essentially, the major issue behind the Allied demands was the compelling need to cover the costs of financing the war. Britain had covered one-third of its war expenditure through taxation; France just one-sixth. At a time of severe social unrest, no Allied country could easily face the prospect of financing debt repayments by huge tax increases and savage cuts in expenditure. Initially it was hoped that the USA could be persuaded to continue wartime inter-Allied economic co-operation and, above all, cancel the repayment of Allied war debts, but by the end of 1918 it was obvious that this was not going to happen, as Wilson had dissolved all the agencies for inter-Allied co-operation in Washington.

French demands for reparations

KEY FIGURES 

Louis-Lucien Klotz (1868–1930) A French journalist and politician and Minister of Finance, 1917–20.

Louis Loucheur (1872–1931) French Minister of Munitions, 1917–18, and Minister of Industrial Reconstruction until 20 January 1920.

The French Finance Minister, **Louis Klotz**, backed by the press and the Chamber of Deputies, urged a policy of maximum claims, and coined the slogan that 'Germany will pay' (for everything). Behind the scenes, however, **Loucheur**, the Minister for Reconstruction, pursued a more subtle policy and informed the Germans that, such was the need of the French economy for an immediate injection of cash, his government would settle for a more moderate sum which the Germans would be able to raise quickly through the sale of **bonds** on the world's financial markets. The German government, however, suspected that these overtures were merely a means of dividing Germany from the USA, which was seen in Berlin as the country potentially most sympathetic to the German cause. The USA's reparation policy was certainly more moderate than either Britain's or France's as it recommended that a modest fixed sum should be written into the treaty.

British reparation demands

KEY TERMS 

Bonds Certificates issued by a government or large company promising to repay borrowed money at a fixed rate of interest by a specified date.

Imperial War Cabinet A cabinet made up of prime ministers of the self-governing Commonwealth countries.

The British delegation consistently maximized their country's reparation claims on Germany. Some historians explain this in terms of the pressure exerted on the government by the electorate. On the other hand, Lloyd George himself claimed that 'the imposition of a high indemnity … would prevent the Germans spending money on an army'. It was arguable that a high indemnity would also ensure that there would be money left over for Britain and the Dominions after France and Belgium had claimed their share. To safeguard Britain's percentage of reparations, the **Imperial War Cabinet** urged that the cost of war pensions should be included in the reparation bill. By threatening to walk out of the conference, Lloyd George then forced the Council of Four to support his arguments. Later, as reparation debts appeared to paralyze the German economy and prevent a global economic recovery, Lloyd George was to have second thoughts about reparations (see page 85).

Setting up the Reparation Commission

The British pension claims made it even more difficult for the Allied financial experts to agree on an overall figure for reparations. Consequently, at the end of April, it was agreed, much to the anger of the Germans, that the Reparation Commission should be set up to assess in detail by 1 May 1921 what the German economy could afford. In the meantime, the Germans would make an interim payment of 20 **milliard** gold marks and raise a further 60 milliard through the sale of bonds. It was not until December 1919 that Britain and France agreed that Britain should receive 25 per cent of the total amount of reparations to be paid by Germany, while France would have 55 per cent. Belgium was the only power to be awarded full compensation for its losses and priority in payment of the first sums due from Germany, largely because it too had threatened to withdraw from the conference in May at a time when Italy had already walked out and the Japanese were also threatening to do so (see page 65).

German disarmament

The Allies and the USA agreed on the necessity for German disarmament, but there were differences in emphasis. The British and Americans wished to destroy in Germany the tradition of conscription, which they regarded as the cause of militarism. Instead they wanted a small professional army created along the lines of the British or US peacetime armies. **General Foch**, more wisely as it turned out, feared that a professional German army would merely become a tightly organized nucleus of trained men which would be capable of quick expansion when the opportunity arose. Foch was overruled and the **Council of Ten** accepted in March proposals for the creation of **inter-Allied commissions** to monitor the pace of German disarmament, the abolition of the general staff, the creation of a regular army with a maximum strength of 100,000 men, the dissolution of the German air force and the reduction of its navy to a handful of ships.

The territorial settlement

France wished to use every opportunity to weaken Germany by taking territory away from it, while Britain sought to preserve a united, but democratic Germany as a counter to Bolshevik Russia. The USA also hoped to achieve a fair settlement along the lines of the Fourteen Points, but supported ceding German territory to Poland, France and Belgium where the majority of the population was Polish, French or Belgian. In the end the territorial clauses of the treaty were an uneasy compromise:

- Initially Upper Silesia and most of the provinces of West Prussia and Posen were awarded to Poland and northern Schleswig was to be returned to Denmark. Thanks to pressure from Lloyd George there was to be a **plebiscite** in Marienwerder, and Danzig, a city surrounded by a Polish population, was to become a **free city**, under the protection of the League of Nations,
- Along Germany's western borders there was a consensus among the victorious powers that Alsace-Lorraine, which Germany had annexed after the Franco-Prussian war in 1870, should revert to France, **Eupen and Malmedy** ceded to Belgium, and the Grand Duchy of Luxemburg declared neutral.

KEY TERMS 

Milliard One thousand million; now largely superseded by the term billion.

Council of Ten Representatives of Britain, France, Italy, Japan and the US (each had two representatives in it). Until March it was the controlling committee of the Conference.

Inter-Allied commissions Allied committees set up to deal with particular tasks.

Plebiscite A referendum or vote by the electorate on a single issue.

Free city Self-governing city under the protection of the League of Nations.

Eupen and Melmedy After the League consulted the population about their wishes these territories were integrated into Belgium in 1925.

KEY FIGURE 

Ferdinand Foch (1851–1929) Commanded a French army group on the Somme, 1916, then in 1917 became Chief of Staff to Pétain. In April 1918 he was appointed commander-in-chief of the Allied armies on the Western Front. He played a prominent part in the Paris Peace Conference and retired in 1920.

KEY TERM 

Self-determination A state's right to decide its own future.

- The future of the Saarland proved more controversial. It was ethnically German, but Clemenceau insisted on the restoration to France of that part of the Saar which was given to Prussia in 1814. He also aimed to detach the mineral and industrial basin to the north, which had never been French, and place it under an independent non-German administration. Finally, he demanded full French ownership of the Saar coal mines to compensate for the destruction of the pits in northern France by the Germans. Wilson immediately perceived that here was a clash between the national interests of France and the principle of **self-determination** as enshrined in the Fourteen Points. While he was ready to agree to French access to the coal mines until the production of their own mines had been restored, he vetoed outright other demands. To save the conference from breaking down, Lloyd George persuaded Wilson and Clemenceau to accept a compromise whereby the mines would become French for fifteen years, while the actual government of the Saar would be entrusted to the League. After fifteen years the people would have the right to decide in a plebiscite whether they wished to return to German rule. (In 1935 the plebiscite was duly held and the territory reverted to German control.)
- Over the future of the Rhineland there was an equally bitter clash between Britain and France. The British had no ambitions on the Rhine, but to the French, the occupation of the Rhine was a unique opportunity

Figure 2.1 Map showing territorial adjustments to Germany's borders.

to weaken Germany permanently by creating an independent Rhineland state that would look to Paris rather than Berlin. The British feared that this would merely sow the seeds of another war by creating a permanent source of tension between France and Germany. After heated and bitter arguments, Clemenceau agreed that the Rhineland, which was to be divided into three zones, was to be occupied for a period of fifteen years by Allied troops as a guarantee of the execution of the treaty. Each zone was in turn to be evacuated after five, ten and fifteen years and thereafter the Rhine was to remain **demilitarized**. Clemenceau was persuaded to agree to this by the offer of an Anglo-US military treaty guaranteeing France against any future German attack.

KEY TERMS 

Demilitarized Having all military defences removed.

Mandated status Ex-German or Turkish territories entrusted to the Allied powers as mandates to govern in accordance with the interests of the local population.

Germany's colonies

In May, agreement was reached on the division of the German colonies. Germany, as a defeated power, judged to be guilty of starting the war, was no longer to be trusted as a colonial power. In reality of course the victors wanted to keep their colonial conquests. Britain, France and the Dominion of South Africa were allocated most of the former German colonial empire in Africa, while Australia, New Zealand and Japan secured the scattered German possessions in the Pacific. Italy was awarded control of the Juba valley in East Africa, and a few minor territorial adjustments were made to its Libyan frontier with Algeria. Essentially Britain, the Dominions and France had secured what they wanted, despite, on President Wilson's insistence, paying lip service to the League by agreeing to **mandated status** for the former German colonies.

Japan and former German territory in Shandong

A serious clash arose between Japan and the USA over the former German concessions in China. The Japanese were determined to hold on to the ex-German leasehold territory in Shandong, which they had seized in 1914 (see page 38). The Chinese government, however, on the strength of its declaration of war against Germany in 1917, argued that all former German rights should automatically revert to the Chinese state, despite the fact that in 1915 it had agreed to recognize Japanese rights in Shandong. Wilson was anxious to block the growth of Japanese influence in the Pacific and supported China, but Lloyd George and Clemenceau, wanting to protect their own rights in China, backed Japan. A compromise was agreed whereby Japan promised – verbally only – that Chinese control would be restored by 1922. Wilson, already locked in conflict with the Italians over their claims to Fiume (see page 81) and facing Japanese threats to boycott the conference and sign a separate peace with Germany, had no option but to concede. It is arguable that this humiliating defeat did much to turn the US Senate against the Treaty of Versailles.

The Shandong decision outraged China and triggered widespread riots and strikes. In June the Chinese government refused to sign the Treaty of Versailles.

Presentation of the draft terms to Germany

On 7 May the draft peace terms of the treaty were at last presented to the Germans, who were given a mere 15 days to draw up their reply. The German government bitterly criticized the treaty on the basis that it did not conform to the Fourteen Points and demanded significant concessions:

- Immediate membership of the League of Nations from which Germany had been excluded.
- A guarantee that Austria and the ethnic Germans in the Sudetenland, which was a part of the new Czechoslovak state, should have the chance to decide whether they wished to join Germany (see the map on page 70).
- The setting up of a neutral commission to examine the war guilt question.

Allied and US concessions

ACTIVITY 

Re-read the presentation you made on page 60. Now extend it to show to what extent the victorious great powers achieved their aims in the Treaty of Versailles.

Although these demands were not accepted, Lloyd George, fearful that the Germans might reject the treaty, persuaded the French to agree to a plebiscite in Upper Silesia. He failed to limit the Rhineland occupation to five years, but did manage to secure the vague assurance, which later became Article 431 of the treaty, 'that once Germany had given concrete evidence of her willingness to fulfil her obligations', the Allied and associated powers would consider 'an earlier termination of the period of occupation'.

The signature of the Treaty of Versailles and the German reaction

On 16 June the Germans were handed the final version of the treaty incorporating these concessions. Not surprisingly, given the depth of opposition to it among the German people, it triggered a political crisis that split the cabinet and led to the resignation of the Chancellor. Yet in view of its own military weakness and the continuing Allied blockade, the Berlin government had little option but to accept the treaty, although it made it very clear that it was acting under duress. On 28 June 1919 the treaty was signed in the Hall of Mirrors at Versailles, where in 1871 the German Empire had been proclaimed (see page 17).

To what extent does Source B explain why Germany had no option but to accept the peace treaty?

SOURCE B

Gustav Bauer, the German Chancellor, announced Germany's reluctant acceptance of the Treaty of Versailles.

Surrendering to superior force but without retracting its opinion regarding the unheard of injustice of the peace conditions, the government of the German Republic therefore declares its readiness to accept and sign the peace conditions imposed by the Allied and associated governments.

SOURCE C

In the Hall of Mirrors in Versailles, French Prime Minister Georges Clemenceau adds his signature to the Treaty of Versailles on 28 June 1919.

Study Source C. Why did the French choose the Hall of Mirrors as the venue for the peace signature and what impact would this have on the German people?

The resentment of the German people

Although historians such as Margaret MacMillan (2001) and Niall Ferguson (1999) argue that the Treaty of Versailles was less harsh than its critics have claimed, it was nevertheless a deeply traumatic blow to the Germans of all classes and political parties. They particularly resented in what they perceived to be a dictated peace:

- The war guilt clause.
- The burden of reparations, which were considered 'punitive' and savage and would burden the German economy for generations to come.
- The loss of land in east Germany to the Poles was also deeply resented, as the Poles were seen by German nationalists as people of a lower civilization.
- The occupation of the Rhineland, particularly in the French zone, by French colonial troops from West Africa and Indo-China, which was regarded as a deep humiliation.

Although after 1924 the Dawes and Young Plans (see pages 89–91, 96) eased the burden of reparations and in 1930 Britain and France evacuated the Rhineland, Versailles remained a symbol of national humiliation for Germany, which Hitler was to exploit.

How does the information in Sources B, C and D help us to understand the attitude of the Germans to Versailles?

SOURCE D

From a German government proclamation issued on the date of the coming into force of the Treaty of Versailles, on 10 January 1920.

The unfavourable result of the war has surrendered us defenceless to the mercy of our adversaries, and imposes upon us great sacrifices under the name of peace. The hardest, however, which is forced upon us is the surrender of German districts in the east, west and north. Thousands of our fellow Germans must submit to the rule of foreign states without the possibility of asserting their right to self-determination … Together we keep the language which our mother taught us … By all the fibres of our being, by our love and by our whole life we remain united.

Everything that is in our power to preserve your mother tongue, your German individuality, the intimate spiritual connection with your home country will be done…

The peace treaties with Austria, Hungary and Bulgaria

After the ceremony at Versailles the Allied leaders returned home, leaving their officials to draft the treaties with Germany's former allies. The three defeated powers, Austria and Hungary (both treated as the heirs to the former Austro-Hungarian Empire) and Bulgaria, all had to pay large sums of reparations, almost totally disarm and submit to the humiliation of a war guilt clause. The basis of the settlement in south-central Europe and the Balkans was the creation of the new Czecho-Slovak state and Serbo-Croat-Slovene state, or **Yugoslavia**, as it became known.

KEY TERMS 

Yugoslavia Until 1929 Yugoslavia was known as the kingdom of Serbs, Croats and Slovenes.

Rump Austria What was left of Austria after its partition.

The Treaty of Saint-Germain, 10 September 1919

The Treaty of Saint-Germain split up the diverse territories which before the war had been part of the Austro-Hungarian Empire. **Rump Austria** was now reduced to a small German-speaking state of some 6 million people:

- Italy was awarded South Tyrol, despite the existence there of some 230,000 ethnic Germans.
- Bohemia and Moravia were ceded to Czechoslovakia. Any second thoughts the British or Americans had about handing over to the Czechs the 3 million Germans who made up nearly one-third of the population of these provinces were quickly stifled by French opposition. The French wanted a potential ally against Germany to be strengthened by a defensible frontier and the possession of the Skoda munitions works in Pilsen, both of which entailed the forcible integration of large German minorities into Czechoslovakia.
- Slovenia, Bosnia-Herzegovina and Dalmatia were handed over to Yugoslavia.
- Galicia and Bukovina were ceded to Poland and Romania, respectively.

- Only in Carinthia, where the population consisted of German-speaking Slovenes who did not want to join Yugoslavia, did the great powers consent to a plebiscite. This resulted in 1920 in the area remaining Austrian.
- To avoid the dangers of an ***Anschluss*** with Germany, Article 88 (which was identical to Article 80 in the Treaty of Versailles) stated that only the Council of the League of Nations was empowered to sanction a change in Austria's status as an independent state. Effectively this meant that France, as a permanent member of the Council, could veto any proposed change (see the map on page 70).

KEY TERMS 

Anschluss The union of Austria with Germany.

Magyar Ethnic Hungarians.

'Balkan Prussia' Bulgaria was compared to Prussia, which in the eyes of the Allies had an aggressive and militarist reputation.

The Treaty of Trianon, 4 June 1920

Of all the defeated powers in 1919 it is arguable that Hungary suffered the most severely. By the Treaty of Trianon Hungary lost over two-thirds of its territory and 41.6 per cent of its population. It was particularly vulnerable to partition, as essentially only the heartlands of Hungary, the great Central Plain, were **Magyar**. Its fate was sealed, when, in November 1918, Serb, Czech and Romanian troops all occupied the regions they claimed. The negotiation of the treaty was delayed by the communist coup in March 1919 (see page 76) but was resumed after its defeat. The Treaty of Trianon was signed in June 1920:

- Most of the German-speaking area in the west of the former Hungarian state was ceded to Austria.
- The Slovakian and Ruthenian regions in the north went to Czechoslovakia.
- The east went to Romania.
- The south went to Yugoslavia.

The Treaty of Neuilly, 27 November 1919

Essentially Britain and France regarded Bulgaria as the **'Balkan Prussia'** which needed to be restrained, and were determined, despite reservations from Italy and the USA, to reward their allies, Romania, Greece and Serbia (by then part of Yugoslavia), at its expense. Thus, southern Dobruja, with a mere 7000 Romanians out of a total population of 250,000, was ceded to Romania and western Thrace, which had provided Bulgaria access to the Aegean, was given to Greece.

ACTIVITY

Compare Figure 2.2 with Figure 2.1 (page 64) and re-read pages 63–70. Then plan an answer to the following question: How far had the peace treaties fragmented Central Europe and left Germany potentially in a more powerful position? Write out the concluding paragraph of your answer.

Figure 2.2 Central Europe after the peace settlements, 1919–23.

The reaction of Austria, Hungary and Bulgaria to the peace treaties

The immediate reaction to the peace terms in all three countries was a sense of shock and betrayal. One left-wing Austrian newspaper declared that 'never has the substance of a treaty of peace so grossly betrayed the intentions, which were to have guided its construction as is the case with this treaty'. The Austrians were bitterly disappointed by Article 80, which prevented an *Anschluss* with Germany. For the Hungarians, in the words of the historian Margaret Macmillan writing in 2001, 'Trianon became shorthand for Allied cruelty and its memory fuelled an almost universal desire … to undo its provisions'. Until the end of the Second World War the overriding aim of the Hungarian government was to regain the lost territories. In Bulgaria there was initially among the nationalists and the army talk of resistance, but the Prime Minister, Aleksandar Stambolski, accepted the new frontiers and rejected the expansionist policies of the past, even coming to terms with Yugoslavia. He believed that the treaty could in time be changed peacefully, and he also wanted to turn his attention to internal reform.

The settlement with Turkey, 1919–23: the Treaty of Sèvres

The Treaty of Sèvres, which was signed in August 1920, was another Anglo-French compromise. Lloyd George hoped to weaken Turkey, not only by depriving it of Constantinople and of the control of the Straits, but also by forcing it to surrender all territories where there was no ethnic Turkish majority. He now envisaged Greece, which had entered the war on the Allied side in 1917, rather than Italy, filling the vacuum left by the collapse of Turkish power and, in effect, becoming the agent of the British Empire in the eastern Mediterranean. The French, on the other hand, concerned to protect their pre-war investments in Turkey, wished to preserve a viable Turkish state. Above all, they wanted the Turkish government to remain in Constantinople where it would be more vulnerable to French pressure.

The end product of this Anglo-French compromise was a harsh and humiliating treaty. Constantinople remained Turkish, but Thrace and most of the European coastline of the Sea of Marmara and the Dardanelles were to go to Greece. In the Smyrna region the Greeks were also given responsibility for internal administration and defence, while an Armenian state was to be set up with access across Turkish territory to the Black Sea. The Straits were to be controlled by an international commission, and an Allied financial committee was to have the right to inspect Turkey's finances. By a separate agreement zones were also awarded to France and Italy in southern Turkey (see the map on page 73).

The division of Turkey's Arabian territories

In May 1916 Britain and France signed the Sykes–Picot agreement. By this they committed themselves to dividing up Mesopotamia, Syria and the Lebanon into Anglo-French spheres of interest once the war against Turkey had been won. Britain, however, was the only power with a large army in the Middle East, and consequently was able to revise the agreement unilaterally. In 1917 Britain insisted on claiming the whole of Palestine, which was quite contrary to the agreement. By announcing support for the **Zionists'** ambition to establish a national home for the Jews in Palestine through the **Balfour Declaration,** Britain cleverly managed to secure the USA's backing for its aims.

KEY TERMS

Zionists Supporters of Zionism, a movement for re-establishing the Jewish state.

Balfour Declaration A communication to the Zionists by A.J. Balfour, the British Foreign Secretary, declaring British support for establishing a national home for the Jews in Palestine.

In February 1919, in deference to Wilson and the Fourteen Points, Britain and France agreed that they could only exercise power over these territories in the name of the League of Nations. It took several more months of bitter argument before the British agreed to a French mandate in Syria and also French access to the oil wells in Mosul in Iraq. The frontiers between the British mandates of Palestine and Iraq and the French mandate of Syria were then finalized in December (see the map on page 73).

The Turkish reaction

KEY TERM 

Nationalism A patriotic belief by a people in the virtues and power of their nation.

When the Allies imposed the Treaty of Sèvres, they took little account of the profound changes in Turkey brought about by the rise of Mustafa Kemal, the leader of the new Turkish **nationalism**. Kemal had set up a rebel government in Ankara in March 1920 and was determined not to accept the treaty. The long delay until August 1920 ensured that growing Turkish resentment, particularly at the Greek occupation of Smyrna in May 1919 and advance into the Anatolian interior (see page 71), which the Allies had encouraged, made its enforcement increasingly difficult.

Mustafa Kemal

1881	Born in Salonika
1908	As an army officer he originally supported attempts to modernize Turkey
1915	Defeated Allied troops at Gallipoli
1919	Became leader of a nationalist revolution in Turkey
1920	Ejected the Greeks from Smyrna and forced Britain and France to renegotiate the Treaty of Sèvres.
1938	Died

Kemal had supported attempts to modernize Turkey since 1908. He was a brilliant general who defeated the Allies when they landed at Gallipoli in 1915. He was bitterly opposed to the Treaty of Sèvres and forced the Allies to negotiate it in 1923. He was the founder of the Turkish Republic in 1923, and a great modernizer who emancipated women, introduced a Latin alphabet and encouraged Western-style dress. He started to industrialize Turkey and to free it from traditional Islamic loyalties.

ACTIVITY

Copy and complete this chart briefly to summarise the main terms of the peace treaties with Germany's former allies and your assessment of their international significance.

Treaty	Terms	Your assessment

Figure 2.3 The Near and Middle East after the Treaty of Sèvres.

ACTIVITY

To what extent does Figure 2.3 illustrate the dramatic changes in the Near and Middle East and to what extent did these changes fuel Turkish dissatisfaction with the Treaty of Sèvres?

The reaction of the victors to the peace treaties

While the defeated powers deeply resented the peace treaties imposed upon them, the victors too, were critical of many aspects of the treaties. The reason for this was that the treaties were compromises in which no power achieved all that it wanted.

Britain and France

Neither power received all it had hoped for. French public opinion was convinced that France, particularly in the agreements covering the Rhineland, disarmament and eastern Europe (see pages 61–65), had not secured the necessary terms to guarantee its future safety. For this the French blamed the 'naïve' idealism of Britain and the USA. The British on the other hand believed that French stubbornness had prevented the negotiation of a moderate and lasting peace. Over the next five years both countries would attempt to bend the treaty to their wishes.

The USA

By January 1920 the treaty had been **ratified** by all the signatory powers with the important exception of the USA. In Washington, crucial amendments had been put forward by a coalition of **isolationists**, led by

KEY TERMS

Ratified Having received formal approval from the legislature.

Isolationist Remaining aloof from international politics.

KEY FIGURE 

Senator Henry Lodge (1850–1924) Republican Congressman.

KEY TERMS 

'Mutilated victory' A victory which was scarred by the refusal of the Allies to give Italy what had been promised.

Proletarian nation A nation that lacked an empire and raw materials. Like the proletariat (workers), it was poor.

ACTIVITY 

In groups decide which of the victorious Allied powers gained most from the peace treaties. Then explain your decision to the class.

Senator Lodge, rejecting the Shandong settlement with Japan and seriously modifying the Covenant of the League. In essence the isolationists feared that, if the USA joined the League, it could be committed to defend the independence of other League members from aggression, even if this meant going to war. They therefore proposed that Congress should be empowered to veto US participation in any League initiative that clashed with the USA's traditional policy of isolationism and independence. Wilson felt that these amendments would paralyse the League and so refused to accept them. He failed twice to secure the necessary two-thirds majority in the Senate. The consequences of this defeat for Europe were serious. Without US ratification, the Anglo-American military guarantee of France lapsed and the burden of carrying out the Treaty of Versailles fell on Britain and France.

Italy

Despite Italian gains in the South Tyrol, the peace treaties were regarded by many Italian nationalists as a '**mutilated victory**'. The Italians had suffered high casualties and not been awarded what they had been promised by the Treaty of London in 1915. The Italian Prime Minister, Orlando, was desperate to prove to the Italian electorate that Italy was not a '**proletarian nation**' which could be dictated to by the great powers. In the Adriatic, Italy had claimed Istria and Dalmatia and insisted also on its right to annex the port of Fiume in which there was a bare majority of ethnic Italians. However, President Wilson, after compromising over the Saar and Shandong, was stubbornly determined to make a stand on the Fourteen Points in the Adriatic. Orlando and Sonnino, his Foreign Secretary, walked out of the Peace Conference in protest and did not return until 9 May 1919. It was not until November 1920 that Yugoslavia and Italy agreed on a compromise and signed the Treaty of Rapallo. Istria was partitioned between the two powers, Fiume was to become a self-governing free city, while the rest of Dalmatia went to Yugoslavia.

Japan

Although the Japanese gained much of what they had wanted in the Versailles Treaty, it was viewed with mixed feelings in Japan. Their failure to gain a clause in the Covenant of the League of Nations guaranteeing racial equality, which was blocked by Britain and the USA, was seen as a great humiliation by all political parties in Japan and contributed to the suspicion that Britain and the USA were in reality intent on controlling Japanese power in east Asia (see page 206).

Problems in 'successor states' created by the post-war settlements

With the partial exception of Czechoslovakia, the **successor states** were fragile and vulnerable.

Czechoslovakia

Czechoslovakia had an industrial base and a stable democratic government. On the other hand its frontiers were artificial and the state was composed of two historic but very different areas: the Czech lands (Bohemia and Moravia) and Slovakia. The Slovaks rapidly came to resent what they believed to be the domination of the Prague government by the Czechs. There was also a large German minority in the Sudetenland, which in 1930 numbered 22.3 per cent of the population. In the 1930s it increasingly looked to Nazi Germany for protection and ultimately provided Hitler with the excuse to annex the Sudetenland (see page 156).

Poland

In response to Polish attempts to annex Ukraine in 1920, which had in the 16th and 17th centuries been controlled by Poland, Soviet Russia invaded Poland. Only after the Red Army was decisively defeated in the Battle of Warsaw in August 1920 was it possible to determine Poland's eastern frontiers by the Treaty of Riga. Poland annexed a considerable area of Belorussia and western Ukraine (see the map on page 70), all of which lay well to the east of the frontier, which had been proposed in 1919 – the so-called **Curzon line**. The western frontiers with Germany were defined by the plebiscites of 1921 in Upper Silesia, Marienwerder and Allenstein (see page 79), but some 700,000 Germans continued to live, for the most part unwillingly, within the new Polish frontiers.

Armenia, Georgia and Azerbaijan

The Allies and the USA also recognized the independence of Armenia, Georgia and Azerbaijan, which in the power vacuum created by the defeat of Turkey and the Russian Revolution and civil war had managed to establish a fragile independence. However, with the victory of the Bolsheviks and the revival of Turkey under Mustafa Kemal in 1923 (see page 72), these states rapidly lost their independence.

KEY TERMS 

Successor states The states created from former Austro-Hungarian and Russian territory.

Curzon line Frontier proposed by British Foreign Secretary, Lord Curzon (see page 82), for Poland's eastern frontier with the Soviet Union.

The successor states to Austria–Hungary

In their efforts to create homogenous nation states out of the former Austro-Hungarian Empire, the victorious powers faced almost impossible problems as the populations of these states were ethnically very diverse and had been scattered throughout the former Austro-Hungarian Empire. In March 1919 the Communists temporarily seized control of Hungary and were defeated by the intervention of Romanian troops. In Yugoslavia there was tension and often clashes between the Serbs and Croats, while the Treaty of Trianon ensured that 3 million Hungarians suddenly found that they lived in Romania, Yugoslavia or Slovakia.

KEY TERM 

Minorities Treaty Treaty guaranteeing the rights of ethnic minorities.

In Romania the Hungarians were discriminated against despite the **Minorities Treaty**. In Cluj, the former capital of Transylvania, for instance, the Hungarian university was closed down and the professors and students dispersed. In an age of heightened nationalism these minorities were often viewed with suspicion in their new countries and in turn minorities still held passionate loyalties to their old homelands. Integrating the often hostile minorities in the successor states was made more difficult by the way the peace treaties disrupted eastern Europe as an economic and political unit. In the words of the historian Peter Hanak (1992): 'The peace treaties … blocked centuries old commercial routes, and broke off time tested and fruitful economic relations'. This was made worse by inflation and mounting post-war economic and political chaos. In 1922 both Austria and Hungary seemed on the verge of economic collapse and were saved only by the intervention of the League of Nations, which arranged international loans and advised on a programme of financial reform.

Re-read your summary of the Fourteen Points (pages 49–50). Then answer the following question: How far does Source E indicate that Trianon failed to apply successfully Wilson's Fourteen Points to the creation of a modern Hungarian nation state?

SOURCE E

Extract from C.A. Macartney, *Hungary and her Successors: the Treaty of Trianon and its Consequences*, 1937. Macartney was a British historian and an expert on Hungary and the successor states.

…the ethical line was practically nowhere clear cut … long centuries of interpenetration, assimilation, migration and internal colonization had left in many places a belt of mixed and often indeterminate population where each national group merged into the next, while there were innumerable islands of one nationality set in seas of another, ranging in size from the half-million of Magyar-speaking Szekely in Transylvania through many inter-determinate groups of fifty or a hundred thousand down to communities of a single village or less … No frontier could be drawn which did not leave national minorities on at least one side of it.

SUMMARY DIAGRAM

Why was there dissatisfaction with the peace settlements of 1919–20?

The Versailles Settlement, June 1919		
Territorial changes	**Reparations**	**League of Nations**
Independent Poland Plebiscites in Upper Silesia, Schleswig and West Prussia Alsace-Lorraine to France Saar administered by League of Nations Germany loses colonies and foreign investments	Reparation Commission fixes amount of 132 milliard gold marks in May 1921	

The Eastern European, Balkan and Near East peace settlements				
St Germain	**Trianon**	**Neuilly**	**Sèvres**	**Riga**
Czechoslovakia set up Slovenia, Bosnia, Dalmatia to Yugoslavia Istria, Trieste and South Tyrol to Italy Galicia to Poland Austria not to integrate with Germany	Hungary loses 2/3 of its pre-war territory to Austria, Czechoslovakia and Romania	Bulgaria loses territory to Greece, Romania and Yugoslavia	Turks cede Middle East empire; Greeks gain Thrace; Straits controlled by Allies	Russia defeated by Poland, August 1920 Poland's eastern frontiers fixed by Treaty of Riga, March 1921

Reactions of victors and defeated powers			
Victors		**Defeated powers**	
France	Without US–British alliance, Treaty too lenient on Germany	Germany	Traumatic terms and symbol of national humiliation, which through military weakness had to be accepted. Determined to revise Treaty
Britain	Gained war aims before peace negotiations so viewed Treaty as too harsh and source of future problems	Successor states to Austro-Hungarian Empire	Treaties deemed punitive and economically destructive
Italy	Viewed peace settlements as 'mutilated victory' as gains were less than desired		
Japan	Insulted by absence of racial equality clause in League of Nations		

Problems of Successor States
Artificial frontiers Existence of hostile ethnic minorities: racial tension Threat from Bolshevism Inflation Economic links with neighbours cut Political instability

ACTIVITY

Briefly explain why the factors mentioned in the summary diagram created dissatisfaction with the peace treaties.

How and why did international tensions remain high in the period 1920–23?

Crises and tensions, 1920–23

In 1920 Britain and France faced a most complex set of problems in Europe, which all helped keep international tension high during the years 1920–23. They had to:

- ensure that Germany and its allies carried out the peace treaties
- finalize the frontiers of Poland and the other successor states
- deal with the crisis caused by Italian ambitions in the Adriatic
- respond to the threat to the Treaty of Sèvres posed by co-operation between Bolshevik Russia and a resurgent Turkey under Kemal.

All this had to be carried out without the assistance of the USA, which had not ratified the peace treaties and increasingly pursued a policy of neutrality.

International tensions caused by attempts to carry out the Treaty of Versailles, 1920–23

KEY TERM 

Conference of Ambassadors Standing committee set up to supervise the carrying out of the Treaty of Versailles.

Once the Treaty of Versailles had been ratified the victorious powers set up a series of inter-Allied commissions to organize the plebiscites, monitor German disarmament and examine Germany's financial position with a view to payment of its reparations. These reported to the **Conference of Ambassadors** in Paris, which represented the Allied powers, but the real decisions were taken by the Allied prime ministers, who between January 1920 and January 1924 met 24 times to review progress made in carrying out the Treaty of Versailles and the other peace treaties.

ACTIVITY 

Read pages 78–81, then draw a spider diagram to show the extent of Anglo-French disagreements over carrying out the treaty of Versailles and the reasons for this.

Continuing Anglo-French differences over Germany

Both Britain and France had conflicting ideas of how best to ensure that Germany carried out the Treaty of Versailles. Essentially Britain, at the centre of a worldwide empire, wanted to see a balance of power in Europe that would prevent either French or German domination and leave it free to deal with the growing challenges to its power from nationalist movements in India, Egypt and Ireland. Britain was also convinced that only a prosperous and peaceful Germany could pay reparations and play its part in Europe as one of the main engines of the European economy.

For France, the German problem was an overriding priority. French policy swung uneasily between occasionally exploring the possibilities of economic co-operation with Germany, and more usually of applying forceful measures designed permanently to weaken Germany and to force it to fulfil the treaty.

Poland and Germany

For the French it was imperative to ensure that the new Polish state was strong enough to help contain a resurgent Germany. The French therefore worked to ensure that it secured as much territory as possible from Germany. The British on the other hand were convinced that this would only store up problems for the future as it would embitter those Germans who would have to reside in the new Polish state and make Germany more determined to regain the territory it had lost to Poland.

The crisis in Upper Silesia: the plebiscite of March 1921

By the end of 1920 the Marienwerder and Allenstein plebiscites had been held, in both of which the population voted to stay in Germany, and Danzig had become a free city under the administration of the League of Nations in November 1920. Fixing the Upper Silesian frontiers, however, proved to be a much greater problem. Upper Silesia had a population of some 2,280,000 Germans and Poles, who were bitterly divided along ethnic lines, and a concentration of coal mines and industries that were second only in size to the **Ruhr**.

KEY TERM

Ruhr The Ruhr in west Germany had the largest concentration of coal mines and steel mills in Europe.

The plebiscite on 17 March 1921 produced an ambiguous result which did not solve the Anglo-French disagreements over Poland. The British argued that its result justified keeping the key industrial regions of the province German, while the French insisted that they should be awarded to Poland. Fearing that once again British wishes would prevail, the Poles seized control of the industrial area, which was still legally German, and an uprising broke out in May 1921. By threatening to occupy the Ruhr, the French stopped the Germans from intervening and order was eventually restored by British and French troops in July 1921. As a result of insoluble Anglo-French disagreements, the whole question of Silesia's borders was handed over to the League of Nations in August (see page 101).

ACTIVITY

Write a brief explanation of the following terms: plebiscite, hyper-inflation, moratorium, Reparation Commission, the Ruhr.

Germany and the reparation crises, 1920–23

It was, however, the reparation question that caused most international tensions. At the end of April 1921 the Reparation Commission at last fixed a global total for reparations of 132 billion gold marks to be paid over a period of 42 years. When this was rejected by Germany, on the grounds that the sum was too high, an ultimatum was dispatched to Berlin giving the Germans only a week to accept the new payment schedule, after which the Ruhr would be occupied.

To carry out the London ultimatum a new government was formed by Joseph Wirth on 10 May. Assisted by **Walther Rathenau**, his Minister for Reconstruction, he was determined to pursue a policy of negotiation rather than confrontation. The first instalment was paid, and Rathenau made some

KEY FIGURE 

Walther Rathenau (1867–1922) The son of the founder of the German electrical company AEG. In 1914–15 he saved Germany from the impact of the British blockade by setting up the German Raw Materials Department. He was murdered by German nationalists in 1922.

ACTIVITY 

Using the further reading section, find out more details on the Ruhr crisis of 1923–24. Consider why war did not break out between France and Germany over the Ruhr.

KEY TERMS 

Moratorium Temporary suspension of payments.

Productive pledges The possession of mines and factories as pledges or guarantees of German payment of reparations.

Benevolent passivity Favouring one side while not officially supporting them.

Passive resistance Refusal to co-operate, stopping short of actual violence.

Hyperinflation Massive daily increases in the prices of goods and in the amount of money being printed.

progress in persuading the French government to accept the payment of a proportion of reparations in the form of the delivery of industrial goods and coal, but opposition from German industrialists prevented this plan from being implemented. By the end of the year the German government dropped a bombshell by announcing that, as a consequence of escalating inflation, it could not raise sufficient hard currency to meet the next instalment of reparation payments.

The Ruhr crisis and German hyperinflation, 1923–24

With the failure of the Genoa Conference in April (see page 85) to find a solution to the reparation problem a major confrontation between France and Germany now seemed inevitable. In July the German government requested a three-year **moratorium**. At the same time, Britain announced that, as the USA was demanding the repayment of British wartime debts, it must in turn insist on the repayment of money loaned to former Allies, particularly France.

To the French, Britain's demand for these repayments contrasted painfully with the concessions Lloyd George was ready to offer the Germans. On 27 November 1922 the French cabinet decided finally that the occupation of the Ruhr and the seizure of its coal mines and key factories as **productive pledges** were the only means of forcing Germany to pay reparations, and on 11 January 1923 French and Belgian troops moved into the Ruhr. Significantly, Britain did not join in but adopted a policy of '**benevolent passivity**' towards France. In the opinion of the London *Times* 'something as far reaching in its effects as the declaration of war in 1914 or the conclusion of the Armistice' had occurred. Had Germany had the strength, French troops would have been repulsed by force, but Germany was virtually disarmed, and so for nine months the French occupation of the Ruhr was met by **passive resistance** and strikes by the German workers, which were financed by the German government.

German hyperinflation

Passive resistance certainly hindered French operations in the Ruhr and raised international tensions still higher, but it also triggered **hyperinflation** in Germany. To subsidize the strikers and compensate for the lost tax revenues from the Ruhr, the government printed ever larger sums of money. The value of the German mark continued to sink rapidly, and by August it was worthless. From 4.2 marks to the dollar in July 1914 it had risen to 4,200,000,000,000 by 15 November 1923. This completed the impoverishment of the large number of the middle classes who were dependent on fixed incomes, war bonds and pensions.

The end of passive resistance

In September, Germany was on the brink of economic collapse and the new Chancellor, **Gustav Stresemann**, called off passive resistance. The cost of the occupation also seriously weakened the French franc. France's attempts to back **Rhineland separatism** and to create an independent Rhineland currency were unsuccessful. Separatist leaders were assassinated by German nationalist agents from unoccupied Germany or lynched by angry crowds. **Poincaré**, the French Prime Minister, had little option but to accept an American initiative for setting up a commission chaired by the US financier **Charles G. Dawes**. Two committees of experts, one to study Germany's capacity for payment, and the other to advise on how it could best balance the budget and restore its currency, began work in early 1924. Its recommendations are discussed below (see pages 89–91).

International tensions in the Adriatic: the Fiume and Corfu crises

Italian disappointment with the peace treaties led to both the Fiume and Corfu crises. The latter crisis was a major challenge to the authority of the League of Nations. Both crises ended in compromises, but showed the power of nationalism in post-war Italy.

The Fiume crisis

Italy was intent on making the Adriatic an 'Italian sea' by acquiring not only Trieste but also northern Dalmatia, the port of Fiume and the city of Vlore on the Albanian coast (see map, page 70). These claims were rejected by President Wilson, but a compromise seemed possible when Prime Minister Orlando was replaced by Francesco Nitti in June 1919. However, the lynching of nine French troops in Fiume by an Italian mob in July and then the seizure of the city in September by the Italian nationalist poet **D'Annunzio** prevented any settlement and increased the international tension. It was not until November 1920 that Yugoslavia and Italy agreed on a compromise and signed the Treaty of Rapallo: Istria was partitioned between the two powers, Fiume was to become a self-governing free city, while the rest of Dalmatia went to Yugoslavia. In December Italian troops enforced the treaty by clearing D'Annunzio and his supporters out of Fiume.

The Corfu crisis, 1923

In October 1922 the Fascist politician Benito Mussolini (see page 119) became Prime Minister of Italy and gave fresh impetus to Italian nationalism. On 27 August 1923 an Italian general and his staff, who were part of an Allied team demarcating the new Albanian frontiers, were ambushed and killed by Greek bandits near the Albanian frontier. Mussolini immediately seized the chance to issue a deliberately unacceptable ultimatum to Athens. When the Greeks rejected three of its demands, Italian troops occupied Corfu, thereby escalating international tension.

KEY TERM 

Rhineland separatism A movement favouring separation of the Rhineland from Germany.

KEY FIGURES 

Gustav Stresemann (1878–1929) During the war he was an ardent nationalist but in August 1923, as Chancellor, he halted passive resistance in the Ruhr. As Foreign Minister he negotiated the Locarno Treaties and secured Germany a seat on the council of the League of Nations. His great aim was the revision of Versailles (see Source I).

Raymond Poincaré (1860–1934) Prime Minister and former President of France, who adopted a firm line towards Germany.

Charles G. Dawes (1865–1951) US banker and politician. He chaired the committee that proposed what came to be called the Dawes Plan.

Gabriele D'Annunzio (1863–1938) Italian nationalist poet, writer and leader of the coup in Fiume.

The Greeks wanted the League to intervene but bowed to French and Italian pressure to have the incident referred to the Conference of Ambassadors. The Conference, while initially accepting some assistance from the League, ultimately settled the case itself and insisted that Greece should pay 50 million lira in compensation to Italy.

The Chanak crisis, September 1922

The growing crisis in Turkey also contributed to international tension. By December 1921 it was becoming clear that the Treaty of Sèvres was no longer viable. After settling the dispute over the Russo-Turkish frontier in the Caucasus with Russia, Kemal was able to concentrate his forces against the Greeks in Smyrna (see page 71) without fear of Russian intervention from the north. By August 1922, having routed the Greeks, he was poised to enter Constantinople and the **Straits zone**, which were still occupied by Allied troops. Both the Italians and French rapidly withdrew, leaving the British isolated. Poincaré rejected outright **Lord Curzon**'s appeal for diplomatic support, and the British Dominions were also not prepared to provide assistance.

KEY TERMS 

Straits zone The shores along the Straits of Dardanelles and Bosphorus were occupied by Allied troops.

USSR The Union of Soviet Socialist Republics. The new Bolshevik name for Russia and its satellite states.

KEY FIGURE 

Lord Curzon (1859–1925) Viceroy of India and then British Foreign Minister.

On 22 September Kemal sent a detachment of troops to Chanak in the neutral zone between the British and Turkish forces. The cabinet in London sent General Harrington, the British commander, an ultimatum to deliver to Kemal demanding their withdrawal. War between Britain and Kemal's forces was now a very real possibility. The situation was all the more dangerous because Kemal would have been backed by the **USSR**. However, Harrington wisely did not deliver the ultimatum and Kemal was able to avoid direct confrontation with the British forces. Instead both sides negotiated on 11 October the armistice of Mudanya, which gave Kemal virtually all he wanted: the Greeks withdrew from eastern Thrace and Adrianople, and the British recognized Turkish control over Constantinople and the Straits (see the map on page 73). The Treaty of Sèvres was now dead and a new settlement with Turkey was to be negotiated at Lausanne (see page 86).

Aims and impact of international treaties and conferences, 1921–23

The post-war world during the years 1921–23 faced numerous problems, as we have seen above, which increased international tensions:

- The First World War had decisively weakened the power of the European states.
- Yet at this very point when the USA had become the financial centre of the world and potentially its strongest military power, the USA had retreated into what Professor Hildebrand calls 'fortress America' and focused primarily on its regional interests in east Asia, the Caribbean and South America.

ACTIVITY  

After you have read pages 82–86 draw up a table with 3 columns. In the first indicate the conference, in the second its results and in the final column its significance.

- At the same time, Bolshevik Russia, or the USSR, had emerged victorious from the civil war, but was isolated and faced a hostile Western world.
- Japan remained a regional power mainly concerned with increasing its influence in China.
- China itself was in chaos and the government was appointed by whichever **warlord** was temporarily in control of Beijing – between 1916 and 1928 there were 26 prime ministers!
- Britain and France faced the task of implementing the peace treaties in Europe and the Middle East virtually alone. United, both states might just have been successful, but they each pursued rival aims and were deeply distrustful of each other.

KEY TERM

Warlords Military leaders in China who were able to take complete control over Chinese regions thanks to their military strength.

Without the unity of the great powers, attempts to restore peace and prosperity in such a fragmented world were difficult to achieve. Nevertheless, at Washington, Genoa and Lausanne, efforts were made to reduce international tensions. The Washington and Lausanne Conferences achieved real but limited success, while the more ambitious aims of the Genoa Conference ended in failure and ultimately led to the occupation of the Ruhr.

The Washington Conference

The Washington Conference of 1921 was one of the key post-war conferences, and indicated the shape US policy was to take in the 1920s. The USA refused to join the League, but it was willing to play a major role in promoting disarmament and post-war financial stability. At Washington its main achievement was to stop a dangerous arms race developing between Britain, the USA and Japan and to improve US–Japanese relations.

Naval disarmament and the future of the Anglo-Japanese Treaty of 1902

By 1920 the USA was alarmed by the rise of Japanese power in the Pacific. Japan, already possessing the third largest navy in the world, had begun a major naval construction programme. The USA responded by embarking on their own formidable building programme, which, when completed, would make the US navy the largest in the world.

In turn this pushed Britain in early 1921 into announcing its own naval programme, but privately it told Washington that it desired a negotiated settlement as it could not afford a naval race. **President Harding** would only negotiate with Britain if it agreed to terminate the twenty-year-old Anglo-Japanese Alliance, which, theoretically at least, could have involved Britain as Japan's ally in a war against the USA (see page 34–5). As the treaty was due for renewal in July 1921, the British and Japanese agreed under pressure from Washington to replace it with a new four-power treaty, which committed Britain, France, Japan and the USA to respect each other's possessions in the Pacific and to refer any dispute arising out of this

KEY FIGURE 

Warren Harding (1865–1923) US President, 1921–23. Republican and opponent of President Wilson's internationalism.

KEY TERM 

Capital ships The most powerful ships in a navy.

agreement to a conference of the four signatory powers, joined by Italy. The four powers then went on to sign the first Washington Naval Convention in February 1922, which halted the building of any new **capital ships** for ten years and laid down rules for the relative strength of the four navies: a ratio was established of 3 capital ships for Japan and 1.67 each for Italy and France to every 5 for Britain and the USA. In 1929 Britain, Japan and the USA in the London Naval Treaty agreed to extend the main principle of this agreement to smaller fighting ships.

SOURCE F

What is the message of Source F? What additional evidence could you use to evaluate it?

A photograph from the US Navy Historical Center, December 1923. Scrapped guns from the USS *Kansas* and other naval ships are shown with the USS *South Carolina* in the background being dismantled.

The Chinese question

The USA hoped to create a new framework for international trade with China, which would reconcile the treaty port rights of the Western powers (see page 23) with the rapid growth in Chinese nationalism. In November 1921 the countries attending the Washington Conference agreed to 'respect the sovereignty, the independence and territorial and administrative integrity of China', and in February 1922 signed the Nine-Power Treaty, which committed them to upholding the 'open door' in China. Japan also agreed to evacuate all its troops from the Shandong peninsula and to allow China the right to buy the former German railway lease, which Japan had acquired by the Treaty of Versailles (see page 65).

The decisions made at the Washington Conference improved Sino-Japanese relations during the 1920s, but made little progress in stabilising China, which suffered from the growing conflict between the local warlords (see page 178), and was a source of international tension for the next three decades (see Chapter 4).

KEY TERM

Consortium An association of states with a common aim.

The Genoa Conference, April 1922

By calling the Washington Conference in 1921 the USA had shown that it had the power to compel Britain, France and Japan to agree to limiting the size of their navies. It also played a major role in attempts to stabilize the political and economic situation in China. However, it still followed a policy of non-involvement towards the acute international tensions in Europe. Consequently, in the absence of the USA, Lloyd George took the initiative in breaking the Franco-German deadlock over reparations and creating the conditions for a European economic recovery.

He believed that Germany needed a temporary moratorium on reparation payments to give it time to put its economy in order. In the longer term the key to the payment of reparations and a European economic revival would lie in rebuilding the Russian economy through the formation of a European **consortium**, which would include Germany. This would generate an international trade boom, enable Germany to pay reparations and reduce international tensions. Poincaré grudgingly consented to an international conference at Genoa, to which both the USSR and Germany would be invited to discuss these plans, but he vetoed any concession on reparations. The government of the USSR agreed to attend but were highly suspicious of Lloyd George's plans for opening up their economy to foreign capital, which they feared was a subtle attempt to destroy Bolshevism.

The Rapallo Pact

Suspicion of Lloyd George's motives prompted the USSR to secretly negotiate the Rapallo agreement with Germany during the conference, whereby both countries agreed to forgo any financial claims against each other for damages they had suffered at each other's hand in the war. Germany also pledged to consult with Moscow before participating in any international plans for exploiting the Soviet economy. Rapallo led to the collapse of the Genoa Conference and effectively killed Lloyd George's plans for restoring the European economy. Why then did Rathenau sign the Rapallo Pact with the Russians? Poincaré's veto on the discussion of reparations was certainly a major cause, but the German government also feared that France and Britain were attempting to re-establish the pre-war Triple *Entente* with Russia (see page 21).

It is hard not to see Rapallo as a miscalculation by the Germans. While it helped Germany to escape from isolation, it did so at the cost of intensifying French suspicions of its motives, and so increasing international tensions. In

KEY TERMS 

Secret annex Secret addition to a treaty.

Capitulations Exemption of foreign merchants and their agents from Turkish taxation and law.

many ways these suspicions were justified, as a **secret annex** signed in July allowed Germany to train its soldiers in Soviet territory, thereby violating the terms of the Treaty of Versailles. Rapallo did not, of course, stop the USSR from supporting Communist groups in Germany plotting to overthrow the German government.

The Lausanne Conference, November 1922–July 1923

Of all the international conferences between 1920 and 1923, Lausanne was the most successful. Britain and France accepted the military and political realities of Kemal's successes and realized that the Treaty of Sèvres was unenforceable. Turkish control of Anatolia and Thrace up to the River Maritza was recognized and Kemal, anxious not to be dependent on Russia, agreed to the creation of small demilitarized zones on both sides of the Straits and the freedom of navigation through them for Britain, France, Italy and Japan. He also insisted on the abolition of the **capitulations**, which had given foreign states, particularly France, considerable powers over Turkish finances and trading policy. This was a serious blow to the French hopes of re-establishing their pre-war influence over Turkish finances, and arguably they, apart from the Greeks, lost more than any other power as a consequence of the Treaty of Lausanne. Turkey's former Arab provinces remained under the control of Britain and France as League of Nations mandates.

Changing relations between the major powers: Britain, France, Germany, the USA and the USSR, 1920–23

Britain and France

Up to 1922 Britain reluctantly supported France in its efforts to carry out the Treaty of Versailles, but with the collapse of the Genoa Conference their differences over German reparations created major international tensions and brought the *Entente* to the verge of collapse. In the absence of a general inter-Allied debt settlement, the French were determined to refuse any German requests for a moratorium unless they could occupy the Ruhr as a 'productive pledge'. Consequently, in January 1923, French and Belgian troops advanced into the Ruhr, while Britain stood aside, powerless to influence events with its policy of 'benevolent passivity' (see page 80). Effectively the *Entente* was at an end.

ACTIVITY 

What does the historian Peter Krueger mean when he says Germany 'was more an object of policy by the *Entente*' than an independent country? Do you agree with him in reference to the period 1920–23?

Germany

In the early post-war years, to quote the German historian Peter Krueger, writing in 1985, Germany was 'more an object of policy by the *Entente*' rather than an independent country that could make its own decisions. German foreign policy therefore swung between despairing opposition and more constructive attempts to modify Versailles. For Germany, given the US reluctance to involve itself in European politics, there consequently appeared to be two main possibilities for achieving treaty revision: one was to exploit Anglo-French differences in the hope that this would weaken the united front of the *Entente* and lead to concessions to Germany by Britain; the other policy, favoured by the army, influential diplomats and some industrialists, was to come to an understanding with the USSR, which would strengthen Berlin's hand against the *Entente*. The Rapallo Treaty was the consequence of this policy, but a full alliance with the USSR was never practical politics for the German government, as the ultimate aim of the USSR was to create a communist Germany. The only power which could assist Germany was the USA by coming forward with a financial settlement that could break the reparation deadlock. It was thus to Washington that Germany (and Britain) looked during the Ruhr occupation.

The United States

The USA emerged from the Great War as a major international force. Yet it was unwilling to accept a binding commitment to the League of Nations or to guarantee French security. However, that did not mean that it retreated into isolation. As the historian George Herring (2008) said, it pursued a policy of 'involvement without commitment'. It took the initiative in naval disarmament (see pages 83–84) and was ready to help financial reconstruction in both Asia and Europe as long as this did not harm US interests. It insisted on the repayment of Allied war debts and protected its own trade through high tariffs, but was prepared to intervene during the Ruhr crisis with a proposal for setting up a committee of experts to work out a solution to the reparation crisis (see page 81).

The USSR

The new Soviet Russia that emerged from the Russian Revolution and subsequent civil war (see pages 48–49) had survived, to quote the historian Adam Tooze (2014), only by the 'skin of its teeth'. Although ideologically it was a threat to central and western Europe, in reality it was only a shadow of the power it had been in 1914 or was to become in 1945. After its defeat by the Poles in 1920 it attempted to normalize its relations with the Baltic and Scandinavian states, Poland, Germany, Britain and Turkey. It attended the Genoa Conference and signed the Rapallo Pact with Germany, but the USSR never renounced its ultimate aim of world revolution aimed at creating a Communist world in which **capitalism** and imperialism would be destroyed for ever. In September 1920 a Congress of the Peoples of the East was held at Baku and a **Jihad** declared against capitalism and imperialism. Through the **Comintern** it also supported subversive activities in Germany, western Europe and the European colonial empires. During the Ruhr crisis **Trotsky**, as Commissar for the Armed Forces, planned a series of uprisings in Germany, although only one poorly planned operation in Hamburg actually occurred.

KEY TERMS 

Capitalism An economic system in which the production of goods and their distribution depend on the investment of private capital.

Jihad A struggle against the enemies of Islam.

Comintern The Communist international movement set up in 1919 to organize worldwide revolution.

KEY FIGURE 

Leon Trotsky (1879–1940) Organizer of the October Revolution and creator of the Red Army. Murdered by Stalin's agents in 1940.

SUMMARY DIAGRAM

How and why did international tensions remain high in the period 1920–23?

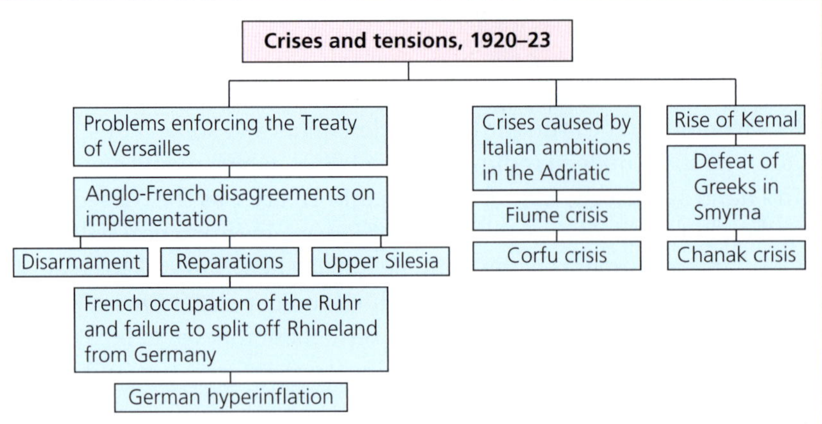

Attempts to solve post-war problems	
Washington Conference 1921	1 Agreed on halting building of capital (major warships) ships for 10 years. Established ratio of capital ships comprising 3 for Japan and 1.67 for Italy and France to every 5 for Britain and the USA. 2 Four-Power Treaty replaced Anglo-Japanese Treaty mutually guaranteeing possessions in Pacific
Genoa Conference 1922	Failure to solve reparation problem and to create a European consortium to rebuild Russian economy caused by the Rapallo pact between Germany and USSR
Lausanne Conference 1923	Successful renegotiation of the Treaty of Sèvres

Role of Great Powers and their changing relations	
Britain	Together with France responsible for enforcing Treaty of Versailles, but increasing differences with France over reparations. Does not occupy Ruhr with France
France	Increasingly diverges from Britain over German policy. In 1923 acts independently of Britain to occupy Ruhr
Germany	Tries to divide Britain and France and seeks US support to revise Treaty of Versailles. Negotiates surprise treaty with USSR to prevent its cooperation with Western forces against Germany (Rapallo)
USSR	Still aiming in the long term for world revolution. In the short term ready to normalize relations with European states, but in 1923 unsuccessfully tries to exploit Ruhr crisis to encourage revolution in Germany
USA	Played no role in carrying out peace treaties but negotiates Washington Naval Convention and Four-Power Treaty, as well as proposing the Dawes Plan

ACTIVITY

Using each factor in the diagram explain briefly why post war tensions remained so high, 1920–23.

3 How successful were attempts to improve international relations from 1924–29?

Economic recovery and the improvement in international relations

The Dawes Plan (see page 81) created a new and more optimistic climate in Europe and led to the French withdrawing from the Ruhr. Germany took **measures to stabilize the mark**, and its industrial production in 1927 reached the level of 1913. The inflow of US financial investment became a crucial prop to the revived German economy. German economic recovery led to an improvement in international relations in the period 1925–29 and opened the way to better relations between France and Germany. However, the recovery, particularly in Germany, was fragile and rested on US investment. If the flow of money stopped, Europe would again face an economic crisis with frightening political consequences.

KEY TERM 

German measures to stabilize the mark In November 1924 the devalued German currency was replaced temporarily by the Rentenmark and then in August 1924 by the new Reichsmark, which was put on the gold standard. Theoretically this meant that paper banknotes could be converted into agreed, fixed quantities of gold.

The aims and impact of the Dawes Plan

The Dawes Plan played a crucial part in ending the bitter conflict over reparations which had nearly escalated into open war during the Ruhr occupation. The aims of the Dawes Plan were to restore economic stability to post-war Europe.

The recommendations of the Dawes Plan

- The overall reparations total of 132 billion gold marks was not changed.
- It did recommend a loan to Germany of 800 million gold marks to be raised mainly in the USA.
- The amount of annual reparations payments was to start gradually and rise at the end of five years to their maximum level.
- These payments were to be guaranteed by the revenues of the German railways and several other key industries.
- A committee of foreign experts sitting in Berlin under the chairmanship of a US official was to ensure that the actual payments were transferred to Britain, France and Belgium in such a way that the German economy was not damaged.
- The plan was provisional and was to be renegotiated over the next ten years.

The reaction to the Dawes Plan

While the British saw the Dawes Plan as a way to ending the escalating conflict between France and Germany, both France and Germany viewed it rather more sceptically.

ACTIVITY

Draw a spider diagram to summarise the Dawes Plan and the attitudes of the British, French and Germans to it.

The British

It was welcomed enthusiastically in April 1924 by the British Treasury as 'the only constructive suggestion for escape from the present position, which if left must inevitably lead to war, open or concealed, between Germany and France'. It also had the advantage of involving the USA in the whole process of extracting reparations from Germany.

The French

There was much that the French disliked about the plan. For instance, it was not clear to them how the Germans could be compelled to pay if they again defaulted and refused to pay, as they had in 1922. However, with the defeat of Poincaré in the elections of June 1924, their willingness to co-operate markedly increased. Essentially, if the French were ever to receive any reparation payments and avoid isolation, they had little option but to go along with the Dawes Plan.

The Germans

The Germans also disliked the plan as it placed their railways and some of their industry under international control and did nothing about scaling down their reparation debts. Stresemann, who after the fall of his cabinet in November 1923 was now Foreign Minister in a new government, realized, however, that Germany had no alternative but to accept the plan if the French were to be persuaded to evacuate the Ruhr sooner rather than later.

The London Conference

KEY TERM 

Permanent Court of International Justice An institution set up at The Hague, the Netherlands, by Article 14 of the Covenant of the League of Nations in 1920.

Agreement to implement the Dawes Plan and to withdraw French and Belgian forces from the Ruhr within twelve months was achieved at the London Conference in August 1924. The new balance of power in Europe was clearly revealed when Britain and the USA devised a formula for effectively blocking France's ability to act alone against Germany in the event of another default in reparation payments:

- If Germany again refused to pay, it was agreed that Britain as a member of the Reparation Commission would have the right to appeal to the **Permanent Court of International Justice** at The Hague.
- A US representative would immediately join the Reparation Commission.

Joint Anglo-American pressure would then be more than enough to restrain France from reoccupying the Ruhr. Deprived of much of their influence on the Reparation Commission, the French had undoubtedly suffered a major diplomatic defeat at the London Conference.

SOURCE G

The British ambassador, in a communication to the Foreign Office on 5 January 1923, describes the great divide between Britain and France over how to treat Germany. At a conference in Paris in early January they argued over whether or not to give Germany a moratorium with or without 'pledges' (gages). The French were convinced that only the seizure of pledges in the form of the occupation of the Ruhr would ensure the payment of reparations.

There was a ditch between us that not only the views of the French government and of the French delegation, but the views of the French people made it impossible they could cross it. The ground of principle constituting that ditch was this simple question: is there to be a moratorium with pledges or without pledges?

SOURCE H

An extract from the concluding speech of the British Prime Minister, Ramsay MacDonald, at the London Conference, August 1924.

We are now offering Europe the first fully negotiated agreement since the War; every party here represented is morally bound to do its best to carry it out because it is not the result of an ultimatum; we have tried to meet each other as far as the public opinion of the various countries would allow us.

This agreement may be regarded as the first Peace Treaty, because we sign it with a feeling that we have turned our backs on the terrible years of war and war mentality.

Study Sources G and H. How far do they explain why the British welcomed the Dawes Plan?

The aims and impact of the Locarno Treaties, 1925

The Dawes Plan did not solve the problem of French security. Without any alliance with Britain, France was still left facing a potentially strong and aggressive Germany. Initially, therefore, the French had little option but to continue to insist on the literal implementation of the Treaty of Versailles. They refused, for instance, to agree to the evacuation of the **Cologne zone**, which was due in January 1925 (see page 64–65), on the grounds that Germany had not yets carried out the military clauses of the treaty 'either in the spirit or in the letter'.

KEY TERM

Cologne Zone Area around Cologne occupied by the British, December 1918–26.

The Locarno negotiations, 1925

To reassure the French of Germany's peaceful intentions, and so secure the evacuation of Cologne, Stresemann, on the unofficial advice of the British ambassador in Berlin, put forward a complex scheme for an international guarantee by the European great powers of the Rhineland and of the status quo in western Europe. **Austen Chamberlain**, the British Foreign Secretary, at first suspected the proposals of being an attempt to divide France and Britain. Then he grasped that it was an opportunity to achieve both French security and the evacuation of Cologne without committing Britain to a military pact with France, which the cabinet would never tolerate. **Aristide Briand**, now back in power, was aware that only within the framework of an international agreement on the lines put forward by Stresemann could he in any way commit Britain to coming to the assistance of France if it were again attacked by Germany.

KEY FIGURES 

Austen Chamberlain (1863–1937) Member of Lloyd George's government, 1919–21, and then British Foreign Secretary, 1924–29. He was the half-brother of Neville Chamberlain.

Aristide Briand (1862–1932) Between 1906 and 1929 Briand headed eleven French governments and was also Foreign Minister from 1925 to 1932. He supported the League of Nations and Franco-German reconciliation. He was awarded the Nobel Peace Prize jointly with Gustav Stresemann (see page 81).

In the ensuing negotiations Briand successfully persuaded Chamberlain and Stresemann to widen the international guarantee to cover the Belgian–

German frontier. He also attempted to extend it to Germany's eastern frontiers, but this was rejected by both Stresemann and Chamberlain. However, Stresemann did undertake to refer disputes with Poland and Czechoslovakia to arbitration, although he refused to recognize their frontiers with Germany as permanent. Chamberlain was quite specific that it was in Britain's interests only to guarantee the status quo in western Europe. He told the House of Commons in November 1925, in words that were to return to haunt the British government (see page 159), that extending the guarantee to the Polish corridor would not be worth 'the bones of a British grenadier'.

The negotiations were completed at the Locarno Conference, 5–16 October 1925, and seven treaties were signed on 1 December. The most important of these were agreements confirming the inviolability of the Franco-German and Belgian-German frontiers (i.e. the borders would not be changed) and the demilitarization of the Rhineland.

The treaties were underwritten by an Anglo-Italian guarantee. If a relatively minor incident on one of the frontiers covered by Locarno occurred, the injured party (for example, France) would first appeal to the Council of the League of Nations (see page 99), and if the complaint was upheld, the guarantors would assist the injured state to secure compensation from the aggressor (for example, Germany). In the event of a serious violation of the treaty the guarantors could act immediately, although they would still eventually refer the issue to the Council of the League.

What does Source I show about the improvement in international relations in 1925?

SOURCE I

The signatories of the Treaties of Locarno: Prime Minister Stanley Baldwin is on the far right; French Foreign Minister Aristide Briand in the front row, centre; behind him, third from left, Stresemann; and Winston Churchill back row, right.

The Locarno Treaties and the improvement in international relations

Throughout western Europe and the USA the Locarno Treaties were greeted with enormous enthusiasm and optimism, which was characterized as the **Locarno Spirit**. It appeared as if real peace had at last come. Had France now achieved the security it had for so long been seeking? Of all the great powers the French gained least from Locarno. It is true that France's eastern frontier was now secure, but under Locarno it could no longer threaten to occupy the Ruhr in order to bring pressure to bear on Berlin in the event of Germany breaking the Treaty of Versailles. The British had managed to give France the illusion of security, but the provision for referring all but major violations of the Locarno agreements to the League before taking action ensured that the British government would in practice be able to determine, through its own representative on the Council, what action, if any, it should take.

KEY TERM

Locarno Spirit The optimistic mood of reconciliation and compromise that swept through Europe after the signing of the Locarno Treaties.

For Britain there were two main advantages to Locarno: it tied France down and prevented it from repeating the Ruhr occupation. Also, by improving relations between Germany and the Western powers and by holding out the prospect of German membership of the League, it discouraged any close co-operation between Moscow and Berlin.

ACTIVITY 

Hold a class debate on the Locarno treaty and its importance. One group will defend it; the other criticize it. Each group should use cards with clear debating points on one side and supporting evidence on the other.

Locarno was deeply unpopular with German nationalists, but for Stresemann it was the key to the gradual process of revising the Treaty of Versailles.

SOURCE J

Extracts from Stresemann's letter of 7 September 1925 to the former heir to the German throne.

There are three great tasks that confront German foreign policy in the more immediate future. In the first place the solution of the reparation question in a sense tolerable for Germany, and the assurance of peace, which is essential for the recovery of our strength. Secondly the protection of the Germans abroad, those 10–12 millions of our kindred who now live under a foreign yoke in foreign lands. The third great task is the readjustment of our eastern frontiers: the recovery of Danzig, the Polish frontier, and a correction of the frontier of Upper Silesia.

Summarise in your own words the message in Source J. How useful is Source J in explaining Stresemann's foreign policy?

By assuring Germany of peace in the west, and by not placing its eastern frontiers with Poland under international guarantee, Locarno left open the eventual possibility of revision of the German–Polish frontier. Stresemann's aims were therefore diametrically opposed to Briand's, but both desired peace and therein lay the real importance of Locarno. It was a symbol of a new age of reconciliation and co-operation. Locarno, as Ramsay MacDonald (1866–1937), the leader of the British Labour Party, observed, brought about a 'miraculous change' of psychology on the continent, and in the short term significantly improved international relations.

Changing relations between Britain, France, Germany, the USA and USSR, 1924–29

The Locarno Pact led to a dramatic improvement in Anglo-French-German relations. Britain, France and Germany agreed that Locarno involved goodwill and concessions, yet the scope and timing of these concessions were a matter of constant and often bitter debate. Both Stresemann and Briand had to convince their countrymen that their Locarno policy was working. Briand had to show that he was not giving too much away, while Stresemann had to satisfy German public opinion that his policy of '**fulfilment**' was resulting in real concessions from the ex-Allies. It can be argued that the survival not only of Stresemann's policy but of the German Republic itself depended on ever more ambitious diplomatic successes.

KEY TERM 

Fulfilment A policy aimed by Germany at extracting concessions from Britain and France by attempting to fulfil the Treaty of Versailles.

Russia, Germany and Britain

The Soviet government, which after the death of Lenin in January 1924 increasingly fell under the control of Stalin (see page 127), viewed the progress made in stabilising western Europe through the Dawes Plan and the Locarno agreements with both dismay and hostility, as it feared that this would strengthen the anti-Bolshevik forces in Europe and delay revolution in Germany. The Russians initially attempted to deflect Stresemann from his Locarno policy, first with the offer of a military alliance against Poland, and then, when that did not work, with the contradictory threat of joining with France to guarantee Poland's western frontiers.

Stresemann, aware of Russia's attempts to stir up revolution in Germany in 1923, was not ready to abandon the Locarno policy, but he was anxious to keep open his links with Moscow and consolidate the Rapallo agreement of 1922 (see page 85), if only as a possible insurance against Anglo-French pressure in the west. Thus, the Russians were able first to negotiate a commercial treaty with Germany in October 1925. Then in April 1926, at a time when the Poles and the French were trying to delay Germany's membership of the League Council, they persuaded Stresemann to sign the German–Soviet Treaty of Friendship (the Berlin Treaty). Essentially, this was a neutrality pact in which both powers agreed to remain neutral if either party was attacked by a third power.

Anglo-Russian relations

Relations between Russia and Britain sharply deteriorated when a Conservative government was elected in October 1924. The outgoing Labour government had just negotiated the Anglo-Soviet General Treaty, which was an agreement on Anglo-Soviet trade and the settlement of pre-war debts. The Conservatives, however, suspicious of attempts by the

USSR to stir up revolution in the UK as revealed by the **Zinoviev letter**, refused to ratify it. Three years later, after ordering a raid on the offices of the official Soviet trading company, Arcos, in an attempt to discover evidence of espionage, the British government severed all official relations with Russia. Only in 1929, with the return of Labour, were ambassadors again exchanged. This outbreak of the first 'Anglo-Soviet cold war', as the American historian Jacobson has called it, strengthened Stalin's determination to cut Russia off from the West. Increasingly, the main thrust of Soviet foreign policy in the late 1920s was to exploit anti-Western feeling in the Middle East, China and India.

Anglo-French concessions to Germany, 1925–27

The atmosphere of ***détente*** created by Locarno quickly led to the evacuation of the Cologne zone in January 1926, and in September 1926 Germany at last joined the League of Nations and received a permanent seat on the Council. Stresemann did, however, manage to extract further concessions from both Britain and France. In January 1927 the remaining Inter-Allied Disarmament Commission (see page 78) was withdrawn from Germany, and in the following August Britain, France and Belgium withdrew a further 10,000 troops from their garrisons in the Rhineland.

The USA and the Kellogg–Briand Pact

In June 1927 Briand wrote an open letter to the American people proposing a **bilateral** treaty outlawing war. He hoped that this would strengthen French ties with the USA and strengthen France in relation to Germany. Initially the US government ignored the proposal, but the American peace movement organized a massive campaign to have war outlawed. In reaction to this **Frank B. Kellogg**, the US Secretary of State, suggested a general pact between as many states as possible, rejecting war 'as an instrument of national policy'. This did not please Briand at all, as it would have opened up the pact to German membership. For that very reason the Germans enthusiastically accepted Kellogg's proposal. In a mirror image to the original French intentions, they hoped that it would improve US–German relations and lead to the US revising the Dawes Plan. They also believed that a **multilateral** peace pact would make it more difficult for the French to build up anti-German alliances in the future. Consequently, in the complex negotiations that led to the signing of the pact on 27 August 1928 the German Foreign Office used all its skills in support of the project while the French raised difficulty after difficulty. Britain was happy to join the pact, believing that it would, by protecting the status quo, help preserve the British Empire.

KEY TERMS

Zinoviev letter A letter from Zinoviev, the head of Comintern, to the leader of the British Communist Party urging him stage strikes and other subversive activities, which was published in the *Daily Mail* a few days before the October general election. It may well have been a fake, but it helped the Conservatives win the election.

Détente A process of lessened tension or growing relaxation between two states.

Bilateral Agreement or action between or by two states.

Multilateral Agreements or action between or by more than two states.

KEY FIGURE

Frank B. Kellogg (1856–1937) US lawyer, statesman, Senator and Secretary of State. For his part in negotiating the Kellogg–Briand Pact he was awarded the Nobel Peace Prize in 1929.

Re-read sections 2 and 3 of this chapter and draw up a list of US involvement in international affairs in the period 1920–29. How far does Source K indicate that the USA did not pursue a policy of isolationism in the 1920s?

SOURCE K

Extract from the Kellogg Peace Pact.

1 *The high contracting powers solemnly declare in the names of their respective peoples that they condemn recourse to war for the solution of international controversies, and renounce it as an instrument of national policy in their relations with one another.*

2 *The high contracting parties agree that the settlement or solution of all disputes or conflicts of whatever nature or of whatever origin they may be, which may arise among them, shall never be sought except by pacific means.*

3 *This treaty … shall remain open … for adherence by all other powers of the world.*

Optimists saw the pact as supplementing the Covenant of the League. It outlawed war, while the League had the necessary machinery for setting up commissions of inquiry and implementing cooling-off periods in the event of a dispute. Pessimists stressed that it was just a general declaration of intention, which did not commit its members, and would certainly not stop war.

The Young Plan and the evacuation of the Rhineland

Two years later Stresemann achieved his greatest success when he managed to secure agreement from Britain and France to agree to a permanent reduction in reparations and an Anglo-French evacuation of the Rhineland five years before the Treaty of Versailles required it. In February 1929, under the chairmanship of the American Owen D. Young, talks on a new reparation settlement opened in Paris. Young gained President Hoover's support to reduce the reparations Germany had to pay from 132 billion to 112 billion over a period of 59 years and to set up a Bank for International Settlements, which Young described 'as the economic arm of the Kellogg Pact'. At the Hague Conference in 1929 the Young Plan was accepted by Britain, France and Germany, and Britain and France also agreed to evacuate the Rhineland in 1930.

The agreement to end the Rhineland occupation helped to make the Young Plan acceptable in Germany, but even so in December the government faced a referendum forced on them by the Nazi and Nationalist parties declaring that its signature would be an act of high treason on the grounds that Germany was still committed to paying reparations. This was easily defeated, and the Young Plan was officially implemented on 20 January 1930. Given continued US loans and German economic growth, it might have been successful and decisively improved international relations, but the Great Depression (see page 120) made it unworkable.

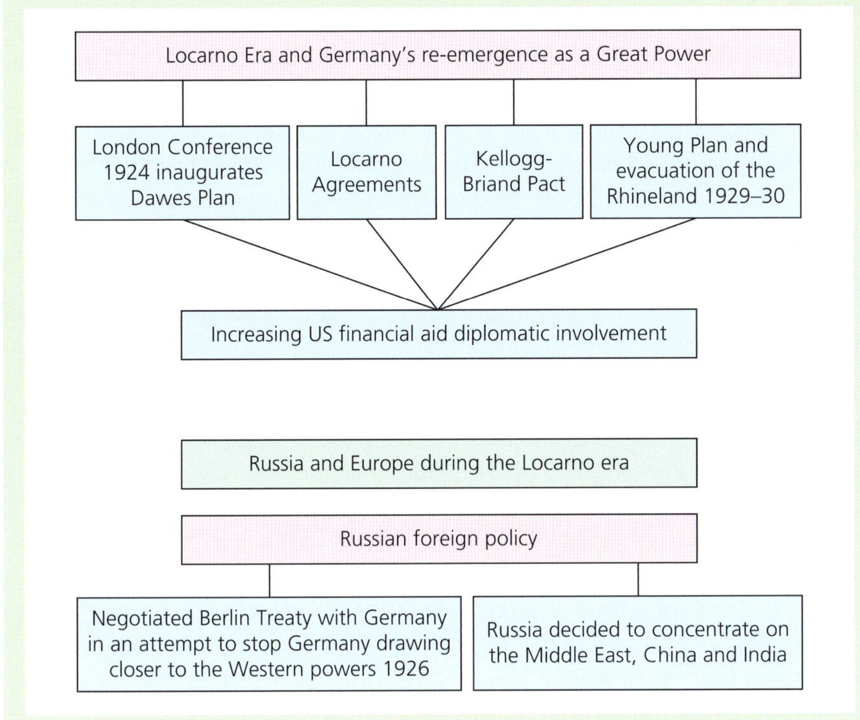

SUMMARY DIAGRAM

How successful were attempts to improve international relations from 1924–29?

4 How successful was the League of Nations during the 1920s?

The League was a part of the international settlements negotiated in 1919–20 and its ultimate success or failure was dependent on the progress made by the great powers in stabilising Europe after the First World War. Not surprisingly, the League's golden age coincided with the temporary stability created by the Locarno era.

Aims, membership and structure of the League

The League was ultimately dependent on its members to enforce its aims. It had no armed forces. In 1920 it was also handicapped in its work by the absence of three great powers: the USA, Germany and the USSR.

Aims

The aims of the League were clearly stated in the Covenant of the League of Nations, which formed the first part of each of the peace treaties. The heart of the Covenant, Articles 8–17, was primarily concerned with the overriding question of the prevention of war. The League's long-term strategy for creating a peaceful world was summed up in the first section of Article 8:

'The members of the League recognize that the maintenance of peace requires the reduction of national armaments to the lowest point consistent with national safety, and the enforcement by common action of international obligations.'

The process for solving disputes between sovereign powers was defined in Articles 12–17. Initially (Article 12) disputes were to be submitted to some form of arbitration or inquiry by the League. While this was happening, there was to be a cooling-off period of three months. By Article 13 members were committed to carrying out the judgements of the Permanent Court of International Justice or the recommendations of the Council. Even if a dispute was not submitted to arbitration, the Council was empowered by Article 15 to set up an inquiry into its origins. The assumption in these articles was that states would be only too willing to eliminate war by making use of the League's arbitration machinery. If, however, a state ignored the League's recommendations, Article 16 made it clear that:

Re-write this source in your own words and then answer this question. Study Sources K and L. How far do these sources differ in their solutions for maintaining the peace?

SOURCE L

Extract from Article 16 of the constitution of the League of Nations.

I *...it shall ... be deemed to have committed an act of war against all other members of the League, which hereby undertake immediately to subject it to the severance of all trade or financial relations...*

II *It shall be the duty of the council in such case to recommend to the several governments concerned what effective military, naval or air force the members of the League shall severally contribute to the armed forces to be used to protect the covenants of the League.*

In Article 17 the League's powers were significantly extended by its right to intervene in disputes between non-members of the League, while in Article 11, member states were encouraged to refer to the assembly or council any international problem which might threaten the peace.

In theory, the League seemed to have formidable powers, but it was not a world government in the making, with powers to coerce independent nations. Its existence was based, as Article 10 made clear, on the recognition of the political and territorial independence of all member states. Article 15, for instance, recognized that if a dispute arose from an internal issue, the

League had no right to intervene. There were, too, several gaps in the League Covenant which allowed a potential aggressor to wage war without sanction. War had to be officially declared before the League could act effectively. It had, for instance, no formula for dealing with acts of guerrilla warfare, which the instigating state could disown. Even in the event of a formal declaration of war, if the International Court or the Council could not agree on a verdict, then League members were free to continue with their war.

Membership

The initial members of the League were the 32 Allied states which had signed the peace treaties and 13 neutral states. Any other state could be admitted to membership by a two-thirds vote of the Assembly. By 1926 all the former enemy states including Germany had joined, but Soviet Russia did not do so until 1934, and the USA never did.

Structure

The League at first consisted of three main organs: the Assembly, the Council and the Permanent Secretariat.

The Assembly

The Assembly was essentially a **deliberative chamber** where each state, regardless of its size, was allotted three representatives. It was a jealously guarded principle that even the smallest state had the right to be heard on international issues.

The Council

The Council in 1920 had four permanent members: Britain, France, Italy and Japan. In 1926 this was increased by one when Germany joined. The smaller states were represented by a changing rota of four temporary members, later increased to seven, who were all selected by the Assembly. As the Council met more frequently than the Assembly and was dominated by the great powers, it gradually developed as an **executive committee** or 'cabinet' of the Assembly and worked out the details and implementation of policies which the Assembly had endorsed in principle. Decisions in both bodies were normally taken by unanimous vote. The votes of states involved in a dispute under discussion by the League were discounted when the Assembly and Council voted on recommendations for its settlement. In this way they could be prevented from vetoing an otherwise unanimous decision.

KEY TERMS

Deliberative chamber An assembly appointed to debate or discuss issues.

Executive committee A committee that can take key decisions.

ACTIVITY

Read pages 97–103. Then create and complete a table with the following 3 columns: League's Aims; structure to carry them out; and its efforts to resolve international disputes, 1920–25.

SOURCE M

Ambassadors from around the world assemble in the Reformation Hall at Geneva's Palais de Nations for the first session of the League of Nations in November 1920. The League was part of the peace settlements of 1919–20.

What can be learnt from Source M about the ambitions of the League of Nations?

KEY TERM

International civil service A permanent administration made up of officials from all the member states.

Permanent Secretariat

The routine administrative work of the League and its agencies was carried out by the Permanent Secretariat which was staffed by a relatively small **international civil service**.

Permanent Court of International Justice

In 1921 a fourth organ was added to the League when the Permanent Court of International Justice was set up at The Hague in the Netherlands with the task of both advising the council on legal matters and judging cases submitted to it by individual states.

Collective security and the League's involvement in the resolution of disputes

Until 1926, when the foreign ministers of Britain, France and Germany began to attend the meetings of the Council and turn it into a body which regularly discussed the main problems of the day, the League of Nations' role in the many post-war crises was subordinated to the Allied leaders and the Conference of Ambassadors, which had been set up to supervise the carrying out of the Treaty of Versailles (see page 78). For the most part it therefore dealt with minor crises only.

In 1920 the inability of the League to act successfully without the backing of the great powers was clearly demonstrated when it failed to protect Armenia from a joint Russo-Turkish attack, as neither Britain, France nor Italy was ready to protect it with force. One of the French delegates caustically observed in the Assembly that he and his colleagues were 'in the ridiculous position of an Assembly which considers what steps should be taken, though it is perfectly aware that it is impossible for them to be carried out'.

Polish-Lithuanian quarrel over Vilna

In October 1920, in response to appeals from the Polish Foreign Minister, the League negotiated an armistice between Poland and Lithuania, whose quarrel over border territories was rapidly escalating into war. The ceasefire did not, however, hold, as shortly afterwards **General Żeligowski**, with a Polish force, which the Warsaw government diplomatically pretended was acting on its own initiative, occupied the city of Vilna and set up the new puppet government of Central Lithuania under his protection. The League first called for a plebiscite and then, when this was rejected, attempted in vain to negotiate a compromise settlement.

KEY FIGURE

Lucjan Żeligowski (1865–1947) A Polish general of Lithuanian origin. He fought in both the First World War and the Polish–Soviet war.

In March 1922 Poland finally annexed Vilna province. A year later, after it was obvious that the League could not impose a solution without the support of the great powers, the Conference of Ambassadors took the matter into its own hands and recognized Polish sovereignty over Vilna. Britain, France and Italy, by failing to use the machinery of the League to stop Polish aggression, had again effectively marginalized it.

The Aaland Islands dispute

In less stubborn disputes, however, where the states involved were willing to accept a verdict, the League did have an important and successful role to play as mediator. The League enjoyed a rare success in the dispute between Finland and Sweden over the Aaland Islands. These had belonged to the Grand Duchy of Finland when it had been part of the Russian Empire. Once Finland had broken away from Russia in 1917, the islanders, who were ethnically Swedish, appealed to Stockholm to take over the islands. When Sweden began to threaten to use force, the British referred the matter to the League. In 1921 the League supported the status quo by leaving the islands under Finnish sovereignty but insisted on itself ensuring the civil rights of the Swedish population there. Neither government liked the verdict, but both accepted it and, what is more important, made it work.

Albania, Upper Silesia and Memel

In the second half of 1921 the League did serve as a useful means of focusing the attention of the great powers on the plight of Albania when it urgently appealed for help against Greek and Yugoslav aggression. As the Conference of Ambassadors had not yet finally fixed its frontiers, the Greeks and Yugoslavs were exploiting the ambiguous situation to occupy as much

Albanian territory as they could. The Council responded by dispatching a commission of inquiry, but it took a telegram from Lloyd George, the British Prime Minister, both to galvanize the Conference of Ambassadors into finalising the frontiers and to push the League Council into threatening economic sanctions against Yugoslavia if it did not recognize them. When this was successful, the League was then entrusted with supervising the Yugoslav withdrawal. Thus, in this crisis the League had played a useful but again secondary role to the Allied powers. The fact that the Conference of Ambassadors then made Italy the protector of Albania's independence indicates where the real power lay.

In August 1921 the League played a key role in solving the bitter Anglo-French dispute over the Upper Silesian plebiscite, which was referred to the League Council (page 79). It again proved useful in the protracted dispute over Memel. When the Lithuanians objected to the decision by the Conference of Ambassadors to internationalize the port of Memel, and seized the port themselves in 1923, the League was the obvious body to sort out the problem. Its decision for Lithuania was accepted by Britain and France.

Attempts by Britain and Sweden to refer the question of the Ruhr occupation of 1923 (see page 80) to the League were blocked by the French, who had no intention of allowing the League to mediate between themselves and the Germans.

Mosul and the Greco-Bulgarian dispute

In 1924 the League was confronted with another crisis involving a greater power and a lesser power. On this occasion it was able to mediate successfully. It provided a face-saving means of retreat for Turkey in its dispute with Britain over the future of Mosul, which according to the Treaty of Lausanne (see page 86), was to be decided by direct Anglo-Turkish negotiations. When these talks broke down and the British issued in October 1924 an ultimatum to Turkey to withdraw its forces within 48 hours, the League intervened and recommended a temporary demarcation line, behind which the Turkish forces withdrew. It then sent a commission of inquiry to consult the local Kurdish population, which, as total independence was not an option, preferred British to Turkish rule. The League's recommendation that Mosul should become a mandate of Iraq for 25 years was then accepted. As Iraq was a British mandate, this effectively put it under British control.

In October 1925, the League's handling of the Greco-Bulgarian conflict, like its solution to the Aaland Islands dispute, was to be a rare example of a complete success. When the Bulgarians appealed to the Council, its request for a ceasefire was heeded immediately by both sides. So too was the verdict of its commission of inquiry, which found in favour of Bulgaria.

It was an impressive example of what the League could do, and in the autumn of 1925 this success, together with the new 'Locarno Spirit', seemed to promise well for the future. Briand was able to claim at the meeting of the Council in October 1925 that 'a nation which appealed to the League when it felt that its existence was threatened, could be sure that the Council would be at its post ready to undertake its work of conciliation'.

The League was not put to the test again until the Manchurian crisis of 1931. Unfortunately Briand's optimism was then shown to be premature (see pages 146–48). The League could function well only if the great powers were in agreement.

Weaknesses of the League

The League was a new experiment in international co-operation, which co-existed uneasily with the traditional system of sovereign states. Its main weaknesses included the following:

- The League was tied into the peace settlement and often appeared to be answerable to the Conference of Ambassadors. It was, for example, responsible for the administration of the Saar and Danzig (see pages 63–64), which inevitably involved it becoming too closely associated with the policy of the Allies.
- It suffered from the absence of the USA and, until 1926 and 1934, Germany and the USSR respectively.
- The Corfu incident, like the Ruhr crisis, underlined the continuing self-interest of the major powers and their ability to ignore the League and to take unilateral action when it pleased them (see pages 80–81). This ensured that it was difficult to achieve unanimity in support of a particular policy.
- Given the economic problems many states faced, they were both unwilling and unable to give the League any support in the event of a crisis which might result in war against an aggressor.
- The League's Covenant provided too many loopholes for war, supported the **status quo** which favoured the great powers and, in the final analysis, lacked the machinery for collective action against an aggressor. In other words it lacked an army.

KEY TERM 

Status quo A Latin term to denote the state of affairs as it exists at the moment.

Yet even if it had had a theoretically perfect constitution, would its history have been any different? Ultimately it was a product of its times and could only do what its members wished.

SOURCE N

Extract from the official British commentary on the Covenant.

[The ultimate and most effective sanction] must be the public opinion of the civilized world … If the nations of the future are in the main selfish, grasping and warlike, no instrument or machinery will restrain them. It is only possible to establish an organization which may make peaceful co-operation easy and hence customary, and to trust in the influence of custom to mould opinion.

How useful is Source N in indicating the basic weakness of the League of Nations?

ACTIVITY 

Read pages 104–6, then create a table with three columns as on page 99. In the first one list the agencies of the League, in the second one their tasks and in the third one assess their success.

Summarise in your own words the message in Source O. Explain what was new about it. How far do Sources O and P indicate that the League's colonial policy was very different from pre-1914 imperialism?

Role and impact of the agencies

In 1945 it was clear that the League had failed in its central task of peace-keeping, but many people felt that its work in improving economic, social and health environments had been successful.

The mandates

Article 22 of the Covenant marked a potentially revolutionary new concept in international affairs:

SOURCE O

Extract from Article 22 of the constitution of the League of Nations.

To those colonies and territories, which as a consequence of the late war have ceased to be under the sovereignty of the states which have formerly governed them, and which are inhabited by peoples not yet able to stand by themselves under the strenuous conditions of the modern world, there should be applied the principle that the well-being and development of such peoples should form a sacred trust of civilization, and that securities for the performance of this trust should be embodied in this Covenant.

When the Allies distributed the former German and Turkish territories among themselves, they were divided into three groups according to how developed they were. The most advanced were in the Middle East, while the most backward were the former German islands in the Pacific. The League's greatest task was to avoid the mandates being treated as colonies by the powers in temporary charge of them. Thus, mandate powers were required to send in annual reports on their territories to the League's Permanent Mandates Commission, which rapidly gained a formidable reputation for its expertise and authority.

The League's attitude towards the mandates was by modern standards paternalistic and condescending, but nevertheless, as the historian F.S. Northedge (1988) has argued, 'it helped transform the entire climate of colonialism', since the imperialist powers were forced by moral pressure to consider the interests of the native populations and to begin to contemplate the possibility that they would one day become independent.

Rights of minorities

The League was also the guarantor of the agreements, signed by the Allies and the successor states created in 1919, which were aimed at ensuring that the various racial minorities left isolated behind the new frontiers enjoyed full civil rights. By 1922 it was responsible for guaranteeing minority rights in Austria, Bulgaria, Czechoslovakia, Hungary, Poland, Rumania and Yugoslavia.

SOURCE P

A German poster of 1922 concerning French rule of the former German colony of Togoland.

Who do you think is the intended audience of Source P? Also, explain why a German paper would have published this cartoon.

How effective was it in carrying out this task? Petitions from minority communities were considered by standing committees and sometimes referred to the Council of the League, but the League had no means of enforcing minority rights except through what the historian P.A. Reynolds calls 'the pressure of persuasion or publicity'. Italy, for example, ignored the League when dealing with its German minority and in 1934 Poland refused the right of the League Council to interfere in minority matters.

The League's welfare, medical and economic work

The League was excluded from dealing with the key financial issues of reparations and war debts, but nevertheless in 1922 its financial committee was entrusted by the Allied leaders with the task of rebuilding first Austria's and then Hungary's economy (see page 76). Its economic committee had the

KEY TERMS 

Protection Stopping foreign goods by levying tariffs or taxes on imports.

Free trade zone An area where countries can trade freely without restrictions.

far greater task of attempting to persuade the powers to abolish **protection** and create a worldwide **free trade zone**. It organized two world economic conferences, held in 1927 and 1933, which both the USSR and the USA attended. But not surprisingly, given the strongly protectionist economic climate of the times, which was caused by the Great Depression, it failed to make any progress towards free trade.

The International Labour Organization

One of the greatest successes of the League was the International Labour Organization (ILO). This had originally been created as an independent organization by the Treaty of Versailles, but it was financed by the League. In some ways it was a League in miniature. It had its own permanent labour office at Geneva, staffed by 1000 officials. Its work was discussed annually by a conference of labour delegates. Right up until 1939 the ILO turned out an impressive stream of reports, recommendations and statistics which provided important information for a wide range of industries all over the world. There were reports and recommendations for regulating the work of:

- workers in the fishing industry
- labour conditions on ships
- minimum wage fixing machinery
- coal miners.

Not all of this was put into effect by the member states, but the recommendations of the League set standards and assisted the trade unions in improving the working conditions of workers. These reports were, for example, appreciated by the USA, which despite not being a member of the League joined the ILO, and even Germany and Japan remained members of the ILO after withdrawing from the League (see pages 145 and 147).

Health Organization

The League's Health Organization provided an invaluable forum for drawing up common policies on such matters as the treatment of diseases, such as leprosy and malaria, and the design of hospitals and health education. The League also set up committees to advise on limiting the production of opium and other addictive drugs, on the outlawing of the sale of women and children for prostitution and on the effective abolition of slavery.

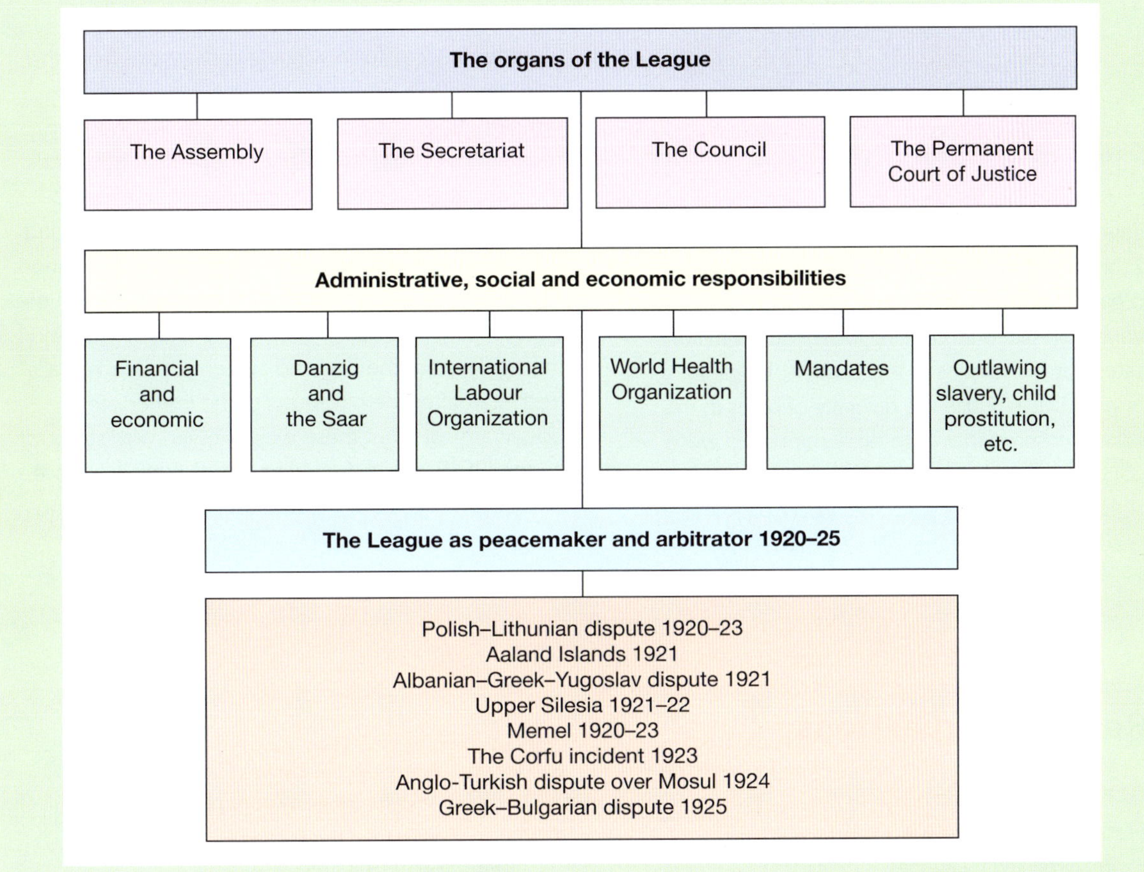

SUMMARY DIAGRAM

How successful was the League of Nations during the 1920s?

ACTIVITY

Add details and evidence to each of the points in the summary diagram to explain briefly each factor.

ACTIVITY

Hold a class debate about whether the League was a success or failure by 1929. One group will argue that it was successful; the other, the opposite. Each group should use cards with clear debating points on one side and supporting evidence on the other.

Chapter summary

In 1919 the Treaties of Versailles, Saint-Germain, Trianon and Neuilly were signed. Each contained the Covenant of the League of Nations. Germany lost its colonies and some 13 per cent of its territory and had to pay reparations and disarm. The Allies and USA were committed to creating independent nation states out of the ruins of the Austro-Hungarian Empire, but in reality the diversity of races in the Balkans ensured that large racial minorities were included against their wishes.

Although Turkey signed the Treaty of Sèvres in 1920, Kemal forced the Allies to make major concessions in the Treaty of Lausanne. The Germans were less successful in winning concessions from the Allies, even though Britain became increasingly sympathetic to their demands for a moratorium on reparations payments. In 1923 the French occupied the Ruhr at great cost to themselves in an effort to break the reparation deadlock. The Germans replied with passive resistance, which triggered hyperinflation. The deadlock was broken by US intervention and the Dawes Plan. The acceptance of the Dawes Plan and the signature of the Locarno agreements marked a fresh start after the bitterness of the immediate post-war years, but these were viewed with suspicion by the USSR, which feared an anti-Bolshevik alliance. The Locarno years witnessed a strengthening of the League and the Kellogg-Briand Pact.

Refresher questions

1 What were the aims of the Allies and USA at the Paris Peace Conference?
2 To what extent were the Fourteen Points implemented by the peace treaties?
3 Why was Turkey and not Germany successful in revising the peace treaties imposed on them?
4 What problems faced the Allies and USA in the years 1920–23?
5 To what extent was the Ruhr occupation the turning point in the history of post-war Europe?
6 To what extent did the Dawes Plan and the Locarno Treaties create a more peaceful Europe?
7 To what extent did the USA pursue an isolationist foreign policy, 1920–29?
8 How effective was the League in solving international disputes, 1920–25?
9 To what extent could the great powers ignore the League and take unilateral action whenever it pleased them, 1920–29?
10 Why was the Kellogg-Briand Pact signed and what was its significance?

Study skills

Paper 1 guidance: sources

Evaluating sources using source content and provenance

Once you are sure what the source is saying about the issue in the question (not just what the source is saying, generally) you need to think what questions you need to ask yourself about its provenance (that is, who wrote it, when it was written, where it was written and why). This means considering first of all what the evidence actually is. Is it a letter; is it a report; is it a record of a conversation; is it a speech; is it a memoir, is it a diary; is it a newspaper article?

The danger is that you will just assume that all diaries are reliable because the person involved in the historical events writes them; or all newspaper articles are unreliable because the journalists want to sell papers; or all records of conversation are useless because the person might not remember the exact words. Try not to generalize about evidence of this type but instead look at the particular source.

After looking to see what the source is, ask yourself some key questions:

- Why was it written? For example, if it is a speech, why was it delivered?
- Who is the intended audience? A diary or a letter will have a different audience from a public report or a newspaper.
- When was it written? Something written in the middle of a historical development, such as enforcing the Treaty of Versailles when it is not clear what will happen, is very different from something written later when the outcome is known.
- How typical is it? For example, if a Briton writes that he wants to treat the Germans fairly, is this a common view held by a member of that nation?
- How useful is this source as evidence, even if you don't think it is 'true' or 'unbiased'? It might be, for instance, that a contemporary source is very critical of the peace treaties of 1919–20 for failing neither to establish a lasting peace nor to weaken Germany sufficiently. This might not be justified but is the source still useful as evidence for a widely held view in France that the Versailles settlement was too lenient on Germany, while in Britain it was considered too harsh?

Activity

Look at the following four sources and fill in the table below.

'The Treaty of Versailles failed because of its harshness towards Germany.' How far do the sources support this view?

Source	What is it?	When was it written? Is this important?	Why was it written?	Was the author in a position to know?	Might the author be prejudiced or inaccurate?
A	Extract from the Treaty of Versailles	1919 Yes	To stress German guilt to justify reparations	Those diplomats who drafted the treaty were influenced by the mood of the time	The treaty was drawn up by the Allied and Associated powers
B					
C					
D					

Which do you think the most useful source here is? Explain your answer.

SOURCE A

The claim that Germany was guilty of starting the war is strongly asserted in Article 231 of the Treaty of Versailles.

The Allied and associated governments affirm and Germany accepts the responsibility of Germany and her allies for causing all the loss and damage to which the Allied and associated governments and their nationals have been subjected as a consequence of the war imposed upon them by the aggression of Germany and her allies.

SOURCE B

Gustav Bauer, the German Chancellor, announces Germany's reluctant acceptance of the Treaty of Versailles. A memorandum addressed to Hitler as Chancellor, in 1934.

Surrendering to superior force but without retracting its opinion regarding the unheard of injustice of the peace conditions, the government of the German Republic therefore declares its readiness to accept and sign the peace conditions imposed by the Allied and associated governments.

SOURCE C

Extract from a book published in 1933 by Harold Nicholson, a British diplomat, who was a member of the British delegation at the Paris Peace Conference of 1919.

Many paragraphs of the treaty, and especially in the economic section, were in fact inserted as 'maximum statements' such as would provide some area of concession to Germany at the eventual congress. This congress never materialized: the last weeks flew past us in a hysterical nightmare; and these 'maximum statements' remained unmodified and were eventually imposed by ultimatum. Had it been known from the outset that no negotiations would ever take place with the enemy, it is certain that many of the less reasonable clauses of the treaty would never have been inserted.

SOURCE D

French Prime Minister Clemenceau in a speech to the French parliament on 29 December 1918, stating his belief in the effectiveness of an alliance system to deter aggressors.

There was a system, which seems condemned today and to which I do not hesitate to say that I remain to some extent faithful: nations tried to organize their defence. It was very prosaic. They tried to have strong frontiers … this system seems condemned today by the very high authorities. Yet I believe that if this balance, which had been spontaneously produced during the war, had existed earlier: if, for example, England, America and Italy had agreed in saying that whoever attacked one of them had attacked the whole world, this war would have never taken place.

Comparing and contrasting two sources

In the previous Chapter (page 54) you were given advice on how to compare two sources and a table that you could use to help you approach such a question.

The example below shows a completed table using Source D and J from pages 68 and 93.

SOURCE D

From a proclamation issued by German government on the date of the coming into force of the Treaty of Versailles on 10 January 1920

The unfavourable result of the war has surrendered us defenceless to the mercy of our adversaries, and imposes upon us great sacrifices under the name of peace. The hardest, however, which is forced upon us, is the surrender of German districts in the east, west and north. Thousands of our fellow Germans must submit to the rule of foreign states without the possibility of asserting their right to self-determination… . Together we keep the language which our mother taught us… .By all the fibres of our being, by our love and by our whole life we remain united.

Everything that is in our power to preserve your mother tongue, your German individuality, the intimate spiritual connection with your home country will be done …

SOURCE J

Extracts from Stresemann's letter of 7 September 1925 to the former heir to the German throne from E. Sutton, ed., *Gustav Stresemann: His Diaries, Letters and Papers*, Vol. 3, Macmillan, New York, 1937, p.505

There are three great tasks that confront German foreign policy in the more immediate future. In the first place the solution of the reparation question in a sense tolerable for Germany, and the assurance of peace, which is essential for the recovery of our strength. Secondly the protection of the Germans abroad, those 10–12 millions of our kindred who now live under a foreign yoke in foreign lands. The third great task is the readjustment of our Eastern frontiers: the recovery of Danzig, the Polish frontier, and a correction of the frontier of Upper Silesia.

Sources	Points on which sources agree	Points of each source that show this	Reasons as to why sources might agree (Provenance)	Points on which sources disagree or contain different information	Parts of each source which show this	Reasons as to why the sources might disagree (Provenance)
D	Weakness of Germany Germans in the surrenderd territories Negotiate to improve matters	'Surrendered us defenceless' 'Thousands of Germans … must submit to the rule of foreign states' '…to negotiate …'	A German government proclamation	Concentrates on the fate of Germans in the lost territories	The emphasis is on protection of German culture in the lost territories	Written immediately after the Treaty of Versailles came into force Aimed primarily at the Germans in the lost territories
J	Weakness of Germany Germans in the surrenderd territories Show skill in dealing with problesm	'… get the strangler from our neck.' Protections of Germans abroad '...showing finesse ...'	Letter by Stresemann, the German foreign minister, to former Crown Prince	Solution of reparation question first priority Aims to revise frontiers ultimately Dismisses cooperation with Bolshevism	Stresemann stresses the three great tasks which confront Germany He puts the problem of the Germans in the conquered territories into the context of the other problems	Written later and just before the Locarno Conference with the purpose of explaining his policy of negotiation with Britain and France

The key to a good answer would be a point by point comparison of the two sources. You could begin your answer by showing that both sources are in overall agreement about Germany's weakness in relation to Britain and France, the victors in the First World War. Both also mention the problem of the Germans in the lost or surrendered territories and will seek to better their lot whenever possible through negotiations or 'finesse'. However, you could go on and mention that in Source D this is main object of the proclamation. It is issued on the date the Treaty of Versailles came into force and directed primarily towards the Germans in the surrendered territories. Source J on the other hand, is five years later and is a private letter to the former Crown Prince of Germany. You will need to show that it differs from Source D in that it outlines three tasks, of which only once concerns directly the Germans in the conquered areas, and although the third aim of the 'readjustment' of the frontiers would also help them. Stresemann is explaining to the Crown Prince in effect why he will agree to Locarno and why skilful German diplomacy or 'finesse' will begin to loosen France's grip on Germany.

Once you have made a point-by-point comparison which includes a consideration of the provenance of each source and use of some contextual knowledge, you would then make an overall judgement about the similarity and difference of the views in the two sources.

Paper 2 guidance: essay questions

Writing an introduction

Having planned your answer to the question, as described in the previous chapter (pages 55–56), you are now in a position to write your crucial opening paragraph. This should set out your main line of argument and briefly refer to the issues you are going to cover in the main body of the essay. The essays will require you to reach a judgement about the issue in the question and it is a good idea to state in this vital opening paragraph what overall line of judgement you are going to make.

It might also be helpful, depending on the wording of the question, to define in this paragraph any key terms mentioned in the question.

Consider the following question:

> **How far did the Locarno agreements mark the beginning of a new era of conciliation in Europe?**

In the opening paragraph of an answer to this question you should do the following:

- Identify the issues or themes that you will consider – these might be the impact of the Ruhr crisis and Dawes Plan and the need to give France security so the way was cleared for better Franco-German relations, seen in Germany joining the League. You might also consider the terms of Locarno, particularly Germany's western border.
- State your view as to whether it did mark a new period of conciliation.

This type of approach will help you to keep focused on the demands of the question rather than writing a general essay about Europe in 1925. It might also be helpful to occasionally refer back to the opening paragraph, so that the examiner can more easily follow your arguments.

This approach will also ensure you avoid writing about the background to the topic, for example explaining in general terms the contents of the Versailles Treaty since 1919, which has no relevance to the question set. Another mistake is to fail to write a crucial first paragraph and rush straight into the question. Readers appreciate knowing the direction the essay is going to take, rather than embarking on a mystery tour where the line of argument becomes apparent only in the conclusion.

The following is a sample of a good introductory paragraph:

Despite the acceptance of the Dawes Plan, the situation in Europe was still tense in early 1925. The French refused to agree to the evacuation of the Cologne Zone in the Rhineland and hence there was the danger that Franco-German relations could deteriorate again. However, the Locarno Treaty was to solve this problem by guaranteeing the Franco–Belgian–west German frontiers. This guarantee was the single biggest contribution to the new era of European conciliation.

Avoiding irrelevance

You should take care not to write irrelevant material as not only will it gain no marks, but it also wastes your time. In order to avoid this:

- look carefully at the wording of the question
- avoid simply writing all you know about the topic; remember you need to select information relevant to the actual question, use the information to support an argument and reach an overall judgement about the issue in the question
- revise *all* of a topic so that you are not tempted to pad out a response in which you do not have enough material directly relevant to the actual question.

Consider the following question:

> **'The League of Nations was on balance a success during the 1920s.' How far do you agree?**

The following is a sample of an irrelevant answer to the question above:

Although the paragraph contains valuable facts such as details of its members, its constitution and agencies, at best it offers only some limited background to the question, which requires you to analyze both the evidence for the positive role of the League and the arguments against its effectiveness. This introductory paragraph is purely factual and makes no effort to focus on the question set. It does not indicate that there are two sides to the argument, which will be focused on in your answer.

The Covenant of the League of Nations formed the first part of the peace treaties. Initially it had 32 Allied states as members. Germany did not join until 1926. It was made up of the Assembly, the Council, the Permanent Court of International Justice and a small permanent secretariat. By Article 16 it had the powers to ask its members to resort to military action in the case of aggression by a member state. The League was also responsible for the International Labour Organization and the Health Organization, as well as setting up various committees for advising on drugs, the abolition of slavery and prostitution.

QUESTION PRACTICE

The focus of this section has been on avoiding irrelevance and writing a focused vital opening paragraph. Using the information from the chapter, write an opening paragraph to two of the essays below, ensuring that you keep fully focused on the question. It might also be helpful to consolidate the skill developed in the last chapter by planning the answer before you start writing the paragraph.

1 'Anglo-French disagreements on Germany were the real causes of the Allied failure to enforce effectively the terms of the peace treaties.' How far do you agree?

2 How successful were the Dawes Plan and the Locarno Pact in resolving tension between Germany, Britain and France?

3 To what extent was the Treaty of Sèvres a failure?

4 'The French had no option but to occupy the Ruhr in 1923.' How far do you agree?

Paper 2 guidance: the short questions

It is very important to write analytically in both the essay questions and also the shorter questions which ask for explanation. The short question is not asking you to describe events or developments but is asking you to explain causes or consequences. You should also distinguish between the relative importance of causes to show that you have thought about which might be more convincing.

Look at these two extracts from answers. One describes and one explains.

Explain the importance of the Washington Conference of 1921.

Answer A

The USA had not joined the League of Nations nor had it any alliance with the Entente powers. By 1920 it was concerned by the rise of Japanese naval power in the Pacific, and responded by building more warships, which, when completed, would make the US navy the largest in the world. In 1921 Britain, France, the USA and Japan met at Washington. They agreed to a new four-power treaty. By this Britain, France, Japan and the USA would respect each other's possessions in the Pacific and, if any dispute arose, the four powers would call another conference to solve it. The four powers plus Italy then went on to sign, in February 1922, the first Washington Naval Convention, which halted the building of any new battleships for ten years and laid down rules for the relative strength of the four navies: a ratio was established of 3 capital ships for Japan and 1.67 each for Italy and France to every 5 for Britain and the USA. In the London Naval Treaty of 1929, Britain, Japan and the USA agreed to extend the main principle of this agreement to smaller fighting ships.

This answer is factually correct but it merely narrates events rather than analysing them.

The second extract not only avoids telling the story but shows why the Washington Conference was important.

Answer B

The Washington Conference of 1921 was one of the key post-war conferences, and indicated the shape US policy was to take in the 1920s. The USA would not join the League, but it was willing to play a major role in promoting disarmament and post-war stability. At Washington its main achievement was to stop a dangerous arms race developing between Britain, the USA and Japan and to improve US–Japanese relations. In early 1921, the powers with interests and territorial possessions in the Pacific faced two problems, which could have escalated into war: naval rivalry and deteriorating US–Japanese relations. One issue that particularly worried both London and Washington was what would Britain do in the event of a Japanese–US naval war? By the 1902 treaty, Britain would be neutral unless another country intervened on the side of the USA. Then Britain would have to help Japan.

To solve these problems, the US President Harding took the initiative to call a conference of the main naval powers in Washington. As a result of this initiative it was agreed that Britain, the USA, France and Japan would halt the building of capital ships for ten years, scrap a number of existing battleships and stop the construction of bases in Guam, Singapore and Hong Kong. This was regarded as a significant achievement as it was believed that arms races ended in war – as they had done in 1914. This made Japan the strongest naval power in the west Pacific and made it easier to persuade it to replace the Anglo-Japanese Treaty of 1902 by a vaguer agreement that the four powers would respect each other's territory in the Pacific.

Essentially, under US leadership, the great imperial powers now recognized Japan as a major power as well. The Washington Conference therefore cleared the way for better relations between the USA and Japan. A less successful result of the Washington Conference was the Nine-Power Treaty concerning China. Its independence was respected, and the powers promised not to interfere in internal Chinese politics. Independently Japan also agreed to hand back to China the territory it had seized from Germany in Shandong in 1914. However, no machinery was set up to enforce these promises and China continued to remain in a state of chaos.

EXPLAIN QUESTIONS

Using the information from the chapter, write an opening paragraph to two of the short questions below, ensuring that you keep fully focused on the question.

1 Explain why the French occupied the Ruhr.

2 Explain why the Genoa Conference of 1922 was a failure.

3 Explain why reparations caused increasing ill-will between France and Germany, 1920–24.

CHAPTER 3

The League of Nations and international relations in the 1930s

This chapter analyzes how the Great Depression unleashed forces that destroyed the peace settlement of 1919 and led to the rise of Hitler and more militant policies in Italy and Japan, which ultimately led to the outbreak of the Second World War. It analyzes these problems by considering the following questions:

- ★ How did the rise of extremism affect international relations?
- ★ Why did the League of Nations fail to keep the peace in the 1930s?
- ★ Why, and with what effects, did Britain and France pursue a policy of appeasement?
- ★ Why did war break out in 1939?

KEY DATES

1929–33		Great Depression
1931–33		Manchurian crisis
1933	**30 January**	Hitler appointed Chancellor of Germany
1935	**March**	Hitler reintroduces conscription
	October	Abyssinia invaded by Italy
1936	**March**	Rhineland remilitarized
	July	Spanish Civil War starts
	October	Rome-Berlin Axis
1938	**12 March**	German occupation of Austria (*Anschluss*)
	September	Four-Power Conference at Munich
1939	**15 March**	Germany occupies Bohemia and Moravia
	31 March	Anglo-French guarantee of Poland
	23 August	Nazi-Soviet Pact
	1 September	Germany invades Poland
	3 September	Britain and France declare war on Germany

How did the rise of extremism affect international relations?

The inter-war period saw the rise of extreme political ideas and regimes. In 1917 the Russian Revolution brought a Communist regime to power which intensified its hold on the Russian people by increasing use of violent repression. Its stated aim was to encourage world revolution and in 1919 it set up a body to spread communism – the Comintern. Although in practice the regime concentrated on 'Socialism in One Country', the threat of the spread of communism was an important element in international affairs and on the rise of dictatorships in other European countries.

In 1922 Benito Mussolini took office as the head of a paramilitary organization, the Italian fascist party, whose aim was to resist communism and socialism while delivering national revival under a dictatorship rather than a parliamentary state. By 1925 Mussolini's authority had been established and a state based on an extreme right-wing ideology was set up. This had come about because of economic distress in post-war Italy.

Benito Mussolini

1833	Born in Romagna in Italy
1904–14	Socialist agitator and journalist
1915–18	Supported the war against Germany
1919	Founded the Italian Fascist Party
1922–43	Gained power in Italy and gradually established a Fascist dictatorship
1943–45	After the Allied invasion of Italy he was kept in power in northern Italy by the Nazis
1945	Captured and shot dead by Italian partisans

Mussolini was the son of a blacksmith. Originally a socialist, he was expelled from the party when he supported Italy's entry into the First World War. He created the **Fascist Party** in 1919 and successfully exploited the post-war economic crisis, the fear of Bolshevism and the disappointment with the peace treaties to gain power in 1922.

By 1929, he had consolidated his position and established a one-party government. Mussolini was determined to re-establish the Roman Empire and turn the Mediterranean into an 'Italian lake'. In October 1935, Italian forces invaded Abyssinia, and in May 1936 Mussolini declared it part of the Italian Empire. Hitler had been a great admirer of Mussolini and in many ways regarded him as a role model. Mussolini's fatal mistake was to enter the Second World War as an ally of Hitler in June 1940 on the assumption that Germany would win. After a series of defeats in Greece and North Africa, Germany had to send troops to stop Italy from being knocked out of the war. From that point on, Italy effectively became a Germany satellite.

KEY TERMS

Fascist Party The Fascist Party was formed in Italy by Mussolini in 1919. Its programme combined social reforms and a tax on war profits with an intensely nationalist foreign policy.

National Socialism German National Socialism had many similarities with Fascism, but its driving force was race, and in particular anti-Semitism.

However, the most significant development was the rise of **National Socialism** and the establishment of the National Socialist (Nazi) state under Adolf Hitler in 1933. This was a direct result of a mixture of post-war grievances being intensified by the impact of one of the world's most severe economic depressions.

The Great Depression, triggered by the Wall Street Crash, marked a turning point in inter-war history. Not only did it weaken the economic and social stability of the world's major powers, but it also dealt a devastating blow to the progress made since 1924 towards creating a new framework for peaceful international co-operation. Along with the two world wars, it could be seen as 'the third global catastrophe of the century' (as historian Robert Boyce called it in 1989).

The impact of the Great Depression on political ideologies

It is hard to exaggerate the international impact of the Great Depression. After 1924, Europe's economic recovery had been, to a large extent, dependent on short-term US loans, of which $4 billion went to Germany. After the Wall Street stock exchange crashed in 1929, US investors abruptly terminated these loans and no more were forthcoming. This was a devastating blow to the European and global economies. Between 1929 and 1932, the volume of world trade fell by 70 per cent. Unemployment rose to 13 million in the USA, to 6 million in Germany and to 3 million in Britain. Japan was particularly hard hit: some 50 per cent of its mining and heavy industrial capacity was forced to close, and the collapse of the US market virtually destroyed its large and lucrative export trade in silk.

The Depression alone did not bring about political extremism. In Japan nationalism had been growing since the First World War and had its origins in resentment at foreign influence since 1854. In Germany the loss of the First World War and resentment at the Treaty of Versailles had already caused the rise of nationalist parties, while economic hardship saw the growth of communism. However, the effects of the Depression intensified loss of faith in the democratic system. As hardship increased – with unemployment, hunger and despair for the future – the attractions of extreme groups who promised a completely new system rather than just the usual domestic policies increased. Neither communism nor Nazism had much electoral support by 1928 but after the Crash of 1929 both parties attracted more voters as the moderate politicians seemed unable to cope with the crisis. The Nazis offered a national revival based on the unity of the German race, ending the hated restrictions of Versailles and promoting Germany as a great power. The Communists offered a social revolution which would give workers power and end the effects of the hated world capitalist system. By 1932 very large numbers of Germans were supporting anti-democratic parties and the prospect of one-party dictatorships. This was in a very large part the result of the prolonged economic depression which showed, at least in the public's view, few signs of getting better by early 1933 when Hitler finally took office as Chancellor.

ACTIVITY 

Re-read pages 119–21 and also look at pages 207–8. Prepare a presentation on the global impact of the Great Depression. Then write a paragraph explaining why it has been called 'the third global catastrophe' of the twentieth century.

The Depression also had a major effect on international affairs. It saw the rise of nationalist policies; Japan backed a military expansion in the Chinese province of Manchuria to gain raw materials and markets in 1931. The USA became more isolationist and imposed tariff restrictions to protect its economy. Powers like Britain and France became more concerned with their economies than in spending money on defence or supporting international order through the League of Nations. In Germany Hitler's regime had clearly stated aims for expansion and overturning the restrictions of the Treaty of Versailles. Thus the Depression changed the whole way that international relations were conducted.

SOURCE A

German soldiers serving food from their soup kitchen to unemployed and destitute civilians in 1931. The Nazi Party successfully exploited the Depression to gain political support.

How useful is Source A in helping the historian understand the impact of the Great Depression on Germany?

The impact of the rise of dictatorships on the relations between the great powers, 1933–35

There had been a gradual rise in dictatorial regimes in Europe after 1920 and also an increase in nationalism. The foreign policy of Italy had been aggressive and expansionist in the 1920s, though Italy had also participated in international agreements. However, the rise to power of Hitler led to Germany adopting an even more uncompromising foreign policy, leading eventually to war in 1939.

Nazi foreign policy and rearmament, 1933–35

Hitler's intense nationalism and desire to overturn Versailles could not be delivered in the early stages of his foreign policy because of the weaknesses of the German armed forces. The French had the strongest army in Europe and could invade Germany at any time if they so wished. At sea, Germany could not begin to match the power of the British navy (see Source B). Hitler had no foreign allies – Mussolini was suspicious of Hitler's rise even though he was a fellow dictator and feared that German-speaking inhabitants of northern Italy would be a target for German expansion. Hitler was obliged to show that he was in fact a moderate statesman so that, even though he deeply resented Polish control of German-speaking areas, he made a pact to avoid any possible confrontation in the east. The pact seriously weakened France's security system in eastern Europe (see page 79), as it had relied on its alliance with Poland to put pressure on Germany's eastern frontiers.

SOURCE B

A warning from B.W. von Bülow, a senior German diplomat, in a letter to Hitler in August 1934.

…we should never overlook the fact that no kind of rearmament in the next few years could give us military security. Even apart from our isolation, we shall for a long time yet be hopelessly inferior to France in the military sphere. A particularly dangerous period will be 1934–35 on account of the re-organization of the ***Reichswehr****. Our only security lies in a skilful foreign policy and in avoiding provocation … if we armed intensively France and Britain also would then intervene, the more so as they could not permit an unlimited unilateral rearmament. It would be wishful thinking to expect them to wait until we are strong enough to be a serious danger to them.*

Read Source B. Why was von Bülow so cautious in his advice and to what extent did Hitler follow it?

KEY TERMS 

Reichswehr The German army, 1919–35.

Nazi Party (NSDAP) The National Socialist German Workers Party. In 1921 Hitler became chairman. The party was banned after the Munich *putsch* in 1923, but refounded in February 1925. On 14 July 1933 it was declared the only legal party in Germany.

Putsch Take-over of power.

Adolf Hitler

1889	Born
1914–18	Served in the German army
1921	Chairman of the NSDAP (**Nazi Party**)
1923	Played a key role in the Munich ***Putsch*** for which he was imprisoned for a year
1925–29	Rebuilt the Nazi Party
1933 January	Became Chancellor of the German Reich
1936	Launched the Four-Year Plan to prepare the German economy for war
1939 September	Germany invaded Poland and unleashed Second World War
1945 April	Shot himself in his bunker in Berlin

Hitler, the son of an Austrian customs official, left school without any qualifications in 1905. Convinced of his artistic gifts, he tried unsuccessfully to gain a place at the Academy of Fine Arts in Vienna. Up to 1914 he lived the life of an increasingly penniless artist in Vienna and Munich. He showed great interest in the current social Darwinistic, nationalist and racist thinking of the time, which was to form the basis of his future foreign policy.

In August 1914 Hitler volunteered for the German army and fought for the next four years with considerable personal bravery, winning the Iron Cross (First Class). In 1919 he joined the German Workers' Party, which was subsequently renamed the NSDAP, and became its chair in July 1921. After his failure to seize power in Germany in the Munich *Putsch* of November 1923, he was imprisoned and wrote ***Mein Kampf***. On his release, he rebuilt the Nazi Party.

The Depression made the NSDAP the largest party in the Reichstag. Hitler came to power in 1933 because the Conservative–Nationalist elites were convinced (wrongly) that they could control him. By August 1934, Hitler had destroyed all opposition and was able to combine the post of Chancellor and President and call himself 'Führer of the German Reich'.

By 1937 Hitler had laid the foundations for 'rearmament in depth' and had dismantled the Versailles system. From 1938 onwards his foreign, domestic and racial policies became increasingly radical. He annexed Austria and Czechoslovakia, and invaded Poland, which caused Britain and France to declare war. In June 1941 he made the major error of attacking the USSR and then, in December, of declaring war on the USA while leaving Britain undefeated in the west. Hitler committed suicide on 30 April 1945 when the Soviet Union's Red Army had reached Berlin.

KEY TERMS 

Mein Kampf Literally 'My Struggle': Hitler's major political work in which he outlined his beliefs and political intentions.

Buffer state Small state positioned between two much larger ones.

Luftwaffe The German air force.

Conscription Compulsory military service.

The attempted Nazi coup in Austria, July 1934

Hitler was aware of Germany's vulnerability, but over Austria he adopted a more provocative line. In June 1934 he met Mussolini in Venice, and tried to convince him that Austria should become a German satellite. When Mussolini rejected this, as he was determined to keep Austria as a **buffer state** between Italy and Germany, Hitler gave the Austrian Nazis strong unofficial encouragement to stage in July what turned out to be a disastrously unsuccessful uprising in Vienna. Mussolini immediately mobilized troops on the Brenner frontier and forced Hitler to disown the coup. The incident brought about a sharp deterioration in German-Italian relations and appeared to rule out any prospect of an alliance. Hitler was not strong enough to offer support for the Austrian Nazis at this stage.

German rearmament, 1933–35

Without a build-up of arms and ending the Treaty of Versailles' restrictions, Germany would not be able to play a major role in European affairs. The Depression (see Source A) had not only helped to bring Hitler to power with this plan but it also helped to explain why the other European powers took so little action to defend the Versailles Treaty. German rearmament brought about a considerable change in international relations. Ultimately Hitler's intention was to mobilize the whole German economy and society for war:

- In July 1933 the decision was taken to create an independent ***Luftwaffe***.
- In December plans were announced for a peacetime army of 300,000 men.
- In March 1935 **conscription** was reintroduced, despite the fears of his advisers that this would lead to French military intervention.

- A naval programme was also drawn up which would produce a moderate-sized German fleet of 8 battleships, 3 aircraft carriers, 8 cruisers, 48 destroyers and 72 submarines by 1949.

In reaction to the introduction of German conscription, the British, French and Italian heads of government met in April at Stresa in Italy to condemn German rearmament and resolve to maintain the peace settlements. Hitler responded by attempting to reassure the powers of his peaceful intentions. He proposed a series of **non-aggression pacts** with Germany's neighbours, and promised to observe Locarno (see pages 91–93) and to accept an overall limitation on armaments. He also offered Britain an agreement limiting the German fleet to 35 per cent of the total strength of the Royal Navy. Britain accepted this offer in June without consulting the other Stresa powers and effectively destroyed the unity of the Stresa Front.

KEY TERMS 

Non-aggression pact An agreement between two or more countries not to resort to force.

Social cohesion The social unity of a country.

The reaction of the great powers to Nazi Germany, 1933–35

For the great powers, 1933–35 was a period in which they had to come to terms with the reality of Nazi Germany. In 1933, even though Germany was only just beginning to rearm, its strength was potentially far greater than in 1914, as it was enhanced by a ring of weak states which had been created in 1919 out of the ruins of the Austrian and Russian Empires around its eastern and southern frontiers (see pages 68–69).

France and Germany

By 1934 France had lost the diplomatic leadership of Europe which it had exercised in the immediate post-war years. The French economy had been weakened by the Depression and its **social cohesion** threatened by a wave of rioting sparked in February 1934 by the exposure of a series of financial scandals. French society was deeply divided as the right wanted to negotiate with Hitler and Mussolini, while the left wanted to fight fascism and looked to Russia as an ally.

Even if France had still possessed the will to intervene militarily in Germany, the Locarno Treaties prevented it from reoccupying the Rhineland. Neither could it rely on Poland after the German-Polish Non-Aggression Pact of January 1934. France's response to the new Nazi Germany was therefore hesitant and sometimes contradictory. The French sought to contain Germany, as they had done since 1919, through a network of alliances and pacts but, like the British, they also tried to negotiate with Hitler.

Although ultimately Britain remained France's major European partner, it was not ready to commit itself to an alliance with France. The French therefore attempted to strengthen their links with the eastern European states and negotiate agreements with Italy and Russia.

Franco-Italian negotiations and the Rome agreement

In its attempts to negotiate an Italian alliance, France was greatly assisted by the unsuccessful Nazi coup in Vienna, which more than anything convinced Mussolini that a military agreement with France was essential. In January 1935 both countries signed the Rome agreement by which they undertook not to meddle in the affairs of their Balkan neighbours and to act together in the event of German rearmament or another threat to Austrian independence. In June, direct Franco-Italian military **staff talks** started to discuss joint military action in the event of a German attack on Austria, Italy or France.

KEY TERMS

Staff talks Talks between officers of the planning and administrative departments of national armies.

Treaty of Mutual Assistance A treaty between two or more states whereby each state would assist the other in the event of war.

Franco-Russian negotiations

Parallel with these negotiations, talks were proceeding between the French and the Russians. The French intended to enmesh Soviet Russia in an elaborate treaty of regional assistance or, in other words, an eastern European version of the Locarno Treaty, which would be signed not only by Russia but also by Germany, Poland, Czechoslovakia and the Baltic states. This was to be strengthened by a separate Franco-Russian agreement which would associate Russia with the Locarno agreements in western Europe and France with the proposed eastern pact.

But the whole plan came to nothing as both Germany and Poland refused to join. The Poles were more suspicious of the Russians than of the Germans. France had therefore little option but to negotiate with Soviet Russia alone. By May, the Franco-Soviet **Treaty of Mutual Assistance** was signed, but Paris refused to follow up the treaty with detailed military staff talks between the two armies. This was mainly because French public opinion on the right was deeply suspicious of the USSR.

Franco-German negotiations

France, conscious of economic weakness at home and its deep social divisions, together with a considerable amount of feeling against another costly war, was willing to negotiate with Hitler. Its aim was to draw the Germans into negotiating an agreement guaranteeing the Versailles system. Hitler was ready, when it suited him, to lower the political temperature through cordial diplomatic exchanges, but he was not ready to tolerate the restrictions with which French – and British – diplomacy was attempting to entangle him.

Great Britain and Germany

Britain was also suffering from economic problems and the huge costs of defending a worldwide empire. It was therefore prepared to negotiate than actively oppose German rearmament. In 1933 it faced a growing threat not only from Germany in Europe, but also from Japan in the Far East. Consequently, the main aim of British policy towards Germany was to blunt Hitler's aggression by continuing to modify the Treaty of Versailles peacefully while simultaneously drawing Germany back into the League where it could be tied down in multilateral agreements on security. Sir John Simon, the Foreign Secretary, summed up this policy in a letter to King George V in February 1935:

What is the message of Source C? How successful was Britain in achieving a reconciliation with Germany in 1935?

SOURCE C

The British Foreign Minister wrote to King George V on 14 January 1935.

It is becoming more and more clear that the early months of the present year may offer the opportunity for a definite improvement in European relations … The coming year is likely to be a vital year in the sense that if European improvement is not secured, and some element of German reconciliation effected, the world may enter into a most dangerous future … The practical choice is between a Germany which continues to rearm without any regulation or agreement and a Germany which, through getting a recognition of its rights and some modification of the peace treaties, enters into the comity [community] of nations and contributes, in this and other ways, to European stability. As between these two courses, there can be no doubt which is wiser.

Italy

ACTIVITY 

Draw a spider diagram showing the reaction of the great powers to Nazi Germany, 1933–35.

Mussolini, who had extensive territorial aims in the Balkans and north Africa, at first attempted to maintain a special position as mediator between Germany on the one hand and Britain and France on the other. He hoped that this would result in concessions from both sides. However, the unsuccessful Nazi *putsch* in Vienna in July 1934 and the German announcement of conscription in March 1935 led Italy to align itself firmly with Britain and France at the Stresa Conference in an attempt to preserve what was left of the Versailles settlement.

Mussolini's hopes that this alignment with Britain and France would result in British and French support for the Italian colonization of Abyssinia (Ethiopia) were not realized. As we shall see later, Italy's invasion of Abyssinia in October 1935 was opposed by the League, Britain and France, and ultimately resulted in Italy looking to Berlin for support and the emergence of the Rome-Berlin Axis (see Source E).

Soviet Russia

Stalin, like the other European leaders, reacted cautiously to the Nazi take-over of power. His distrust of the West was at least as great as his fear of Nazi Germany. Consequently, even though he negotiated a defensive agreement with the French (see above) and sought collective security by joining the League of Nations in September 1934, he also attempted to maintain good relations with Germany despite such setbacks as the German-Polish Non-Aggression Pact (see page 122).

The Soviet negotiations with the French in the spring of 1935 were also accompanied by a series of secret talks with the Germans, which mirrored the French tactics of trying for a settlement with Hitler in the summer of 1935 (see page 125). Soviet-Nazi talks continued intermittently right up to

Joseph Stalin

1879	Born
1903	Joined the Bolshevik Party
1917	Assisted Lenin in the Russian Revolution
1922	Secretary of the Communist Party
1929	Effectively dictator of the USSR and introduced a policy of 'Socialism in One Country'
1936–38	Conducted the great purge of his enemies
1939 23 August	Signed the Nazi-Soviet Pact
17 September	Ordered Soviet occupation of eastern Poland
30 November	Ordered invasion of Finland
1941–45	Supreme Director of the Soviet war effort
1953	Died

Stalin, whose family name was Djugashvili, was born in Georgia as the son of a cobbler. He originally intended to become a priest but was expelled from the seminary for being a revolutionary in 1899. He was twice sent to Siberia but each time managed to escape. At various times he was in exile in Paris and Vienna, and in 1912 became the Bolshevik Party's expert on racial minorities. He edited *Pravda* in 1917 and became Commissar for Nationalities in the first Soviet government. In 1922 he became Secretary of the Bolshevik Party.

By 1929 he had defeated his rivals for control of the Bolshevik Party, and was in a position to launch the first of the Five-Year Plans involving the collectivization of agriculture and the massive expansion of heavy industry. He defended himself from the criticism which followed the ruthless implementation of these policies through purges, show trials and 'the terror'. In May 1941 he became Chairman of the Council of Ministers, and during the Second World War took over supreme control of the Soviet war effort. The Soviet victory in 1945 was celebrated as his supreme achievement, and enabled the USSR to control most of eastern Europe. After 1945, until his death in 1953, Stalin's position in the USSR was unchallenged.

February 1936. Only with the ratification of the Franco-Soviet Treaty of Mutual Assistance by the French parliament were they broken off, but were renewed in the summer of 1939 (see page 160).

The USA

The USA was committed to a foreign policy which would not involve it in a European war. Thus the rise of Hitler and his early moves to rearm by 1935 produced little official reaction in the USA.

In 1933 there was considerable sympathy in the USA for the economic hardships that Germany was suffering as a result of the Depression, while both Britain and France were viewed with some suspicion on account of their huge colonial empires. However, with the coming to power of Hitler

KEY FIGURES 

Franklin Roosevelt (1882–1945) Democratic Governor of New York in 1928 and then in 1932 President of the USA, a post he held until his death in 1945. He countered the Great Depression with a massive programme of public works.

Francisco Franco (1892–1975) Spanish general, leader of the Spanish Nationalists and then ruler of Spain, 1939–75.

and the beginning of the persecution of the Jews, public opinion in the USA began to become more hostile to Germany, even though US foreign policy still remained firmly isolationist. The main concern of the government was the Far East, not Germany. Even there, there was no indication of active intervention. The USA was alarmed by the Japanese occupation of Manchuria (see page 148), but did no more than make diplomatic protests. Indeed, the Temporary Neutrality Act of 1935, by empowering **President Roosevelt** to ban the supply of arms to all belligerents – whether aggressors or victims of aggression – in the event of the outbreak of war, strengthened the US policy of non-involvement.

Summary

The reaction to the rise of Hitler and his initial policies, which showed that he would not be bound by the disarmament restrictions of the Treaty of Versailles, demonstrated that the other powers were unlikely to make a united stand to protect the treaty. Hitler was thus encouraged to take further steps towards his immediate goals of overturning it, and moving towards his longer-term aims of creating 'living space' by conquests in eastern Europe (see page 132). This lack of opposition can be explained by fear of public opposition to war; by economic problems; by concerns about the problems and costs of defence in other areas, especially the Far East, and by unease about the fairness of the peace settlement. Only a minority of statesmen understood the true extent of the long-term aims of Hitler and his extreme personality, and most assumed that he could be negotiated with in a normal, rational, diplomatic manner.

Foreign responses to the civil war in Spain, 1936–39

The extreme political ideas of the inter-war period were evident in Spain which had also suffered from economic hardships. These led to the outbreak of a civil war in 1936 which came to have a major impact on international relations.

KEY TERM 

Anarchist A supporter of anarchism, a political theory advocating small, self-governing societies.

In 1931 the Spanish monarchy ended and a republic was set up. This was deeply divided between the forces of the left – **anarchists** and communists – and the forces of the right – traditional monarchists and conservatives and the new Fascist Party, the *Falange*. The left-wing groups were bitterly opposed to the power of the Catholic Church, and the forces of conservatism rallied to its support. Strikes and political violence increased. The army was politically conservative, and in 1936 it launched a take-over which aimed to overturn the left-wing Republican government. The war which followed lasted until 1939.

The civil war in Spain was essentially a domestic matter which rapidly became an international issue threatening to involve the major powers in a European conflict. The Nationalists, as the rebels called themselves, were led by **General Franco**, and looked to Germany and Italy for help, while the Republicans approached Britain, France and Soviet Russia. Foreign aid was given to both sides.

Figure 3.1 A map showing the geographical division of Spain between the Nationalists and the Republicans by the end of July 1936.

German and Italian intervention

Hitler quickly agreed to provide a fleet of transport aircraft to fly Franco's soldiers in Spanish Morocco across to Spain. He then followed this up with the dispatch of some 6000 troops. Hitler certainly wanted to stop Spain becoming communist but he also wanted to distract the Western powers so that he could continue to rearm without fear of intervention. He was too aware of the advantages of having a friendly government in Madrid which would not only supply Germany with Spanish mineral resources but also in wartime possibly provide bases for German submarines.

Mussolini also agreed to assist Franco for the same mixture of ideological and strategic reasons: he hoped to defeat the left in Spain, gain a new ally in Franco, who might grant Italy a naval base on one of the Balearic islands, and 'strengthen' the Italian character by exposure to war. As the Italian invasion of Abyssinia had been opposed, admittedly ineffectually, by Britain, France and the League of Nations (see pages 148–50), he also anxious to draw closer to Germany.

The non-intervention policy of Britain and France

With both Germany and Italy openly helping Franco, there was a real danger of a European war should France and Britain be drawn in on the Republican side. When the French Prime Minister, **Léon Blum** (whose power rested on a left-wing coalition), was first asked for help by the Republic, he was tempted to give it – if only to deny potential allies of Germany a victory in Spain. However, two factors forced him to have second thoughts.

First, the actual dispatch of French military aid to the Republicans would have polarized French society, which was already deeply divided between

KEY FIGURE 

Léon Blum (1872–1950)
France's first socialist prime minister. Led the Popular Front Government, 1936–36. Imprisoned by the Vichy regime in 1940.

ACTIVITY

Create a table with 3 columns. In the first one list the foreign states which intervened in the Spanish civil war; in the second state in what ways they intervened; and in the third assess the consequences of their intervention.

right and left, and run the risk of plunging France into a civil war of its own. Second, the British government came out strongly against intervention. The British ambassador in Paris even threatened neutrality should French assistance to the Republicans lead to war with Germany. Despite the strategic dangers for Britain's position in the Mediterranean in the event of a Nationalist victory, the cabinet viewed the civil war as essentially a side issue which must not be allowed to prevent its continued search for a lasting settlement with Germany. In addition, there were powerful voices within the Conservative Party who actively sympathized with Franco.

To prevent the war spreading, Britain and France proposed a non-intervention agreement. This was signed by the other European powers, but Germany and Italy ignored it and continued to assist Franco.

Soviet intervention

The Republican government therefore had little option but to approach Soviet Russia for help. In September 1936 Stalin sent hundreds of military advisers and large quantities of military equipment, while the Comintern was made responsible for recruiting brigades of international volunteers. Stalin, like Hitler, saw the civil war as a way of dividing his enemies.

A conflict between the Western powers and Germany would certainly have suited Stalin's policy, but he was also anxious to prevent a Nationalist victory in Spain since this would strengthen the forces of international fascism and make a German attack on the Soviet Union more likely. However, by early 1937, when he realized that the Republicans could not win, he reduced the flow of arms to a level that was just sufficient to prolong the conflict. In this he was successful, as it was not until March 1939 that Franco at last occupied Madrid.

Table 3.1 Military equipment supplied to Spain by the USSR, Germany and Italy during the civil war.

	Republicans	Nationalists	
Equipment type	**USSR**	**Germany**	**Italy**
Aircraft of all types	648	621	632
Tanks and armoured vehicles	407	250	150
Artillery units	1,186	700	1,930
Machine guns	20,486	31,000	3,436
Rifles	497,813	157,309	240,747
Ammunition (rounds)	862,000,000	250,000,000	324,900,000
Submarines	0	0	4

The consequences of the civil war

It was undoubtedly Germany who benefited most from the conflict since it diverted the attention of the powers during the crucial period of April 1936–February 1938 away from the Nazi rearmament programme. For the democracies the civil war could not have come at a worse time. It polarized public opinion between right and left, threatened France with encirclement and cemented the Italian-German *rapprochement*. In October 1936 Germany and Italy, after a visit by the Italian Foreign Minister, signed the October Protocols, which were in effect an Italian-German *entente* and eventually led the way to the Pact of Steel in May 1939 (see page 161).

The defeat of the Republic was a blow for the cause of democracy and might have caused a serious encirclement for France had not Franco's Spain been too exhausted by war to want to take any part in a conflict in support of Germany and Italy.

The war divided opinion in Europe and brought about a feeling among some people that fascism was on the move and needed to be stopped. It also showed the destructive power of modern war, as in the well-publicized bombing by German aircraft of the Republican town of Guernica, immortalized by a painting by Picasso (see Source D) and increased fear of war. The war also revealed to Hitler and Mussolini the weaknesses of Britain and France. It showed, too, that Stalin's communists were more intent on fighting their internal opponents than the forces of fascism and so generally encouraged Hitler to risk greater expansion.

SOURCE D

Picasso's *Guernica* was a large oil painting painted in response to the bombing of Guernica in northern Spain by Nazi and Italian bombers.

What is the purpose of Source D? How might this affect its reliability?

SOURCE E

Extract from Mussolini's speech in Milan, 1 November 1936.

The meeting at Berlin resulted in an agreement between the two countries on certain questions, some of which are particularly interesting in these days. But these agreements, which have been included in special statements and duly signed – this vertical line between Rome and Berlin – is not a partition, but rather an axis round which all the European States animated by the will to collaboration and peace can also collaborate. Germany although surrounded and solicited, did not adhere to sanctions … And may I remind you that even before the Berlin meeting [in October 1936] Germany had practically recognized the Empire of Rome.

Summarise in your own words the message in Source E. To what extent does it explain the changes in Italian foreign policy between 1934 and 1936? (Re-read pages 123–26 and see also 148–51.)

ACTIVITY 

Read pages 132–42 carefully. Hold a class debate about Hitler's foreign policy aims. One group will argue that he had definite aims, the other group will be more sceptical and claim that he was an opportunist. Each group should use cards with clear debating points on one side and supporting evidence on the other.

Aims and impact of Hitler's expansionist policies, 1936–39

The immediate aim of Hitler's expansionism was the revision of the Treaty of Versailles. He sent troops into the Rhineland to end the forced demilitarization imposed by the treaty. He would have supported a coup by the Nazis in Austria but was prevented by Italian opposition and by the fact that German armed forces were still limited as rearmament had only started the year before. Nevertheless, he achieved a union with Austria in 1938 because Italy no longer opposed this. Thus far the reaction of France and Britain was limited because it would have been hard to enthuse their populations for a war to prevent German people being together in a state which had, despite its extreme ideas, a great deal of popular support for its economic achievements and the ending of internal political conflict.

Revision of the peace treaties now focused on Germany gaining the German-speaking areas of Czechoslovakia and Poland. The so-called Sudetenland of Czechoslovakia contained largely German speakers but the area had never been part of Germany as such. Hitler's demands were met by a policy of appeasement (see page 155) by Britain, followed by France, of avoiding war by offering to make what appeared to be reasonable concessions. Though both countries were uneasy, the policy commanded public support until Germany invaded the rest of Czechoslovakia in 1939. This crossed the line from revision of a peace treaty to naked aggression and conquest of other nations. The aims of Germany were now seen to be wider than merely regaining lost land and seemed to be closer to the wilder ideas of creating 'living space' for the German race that had hitherto been regarded as mere rhetoric. Thus the German invasion of Poland was met by declarations of war by France and Britain. The war against Poland had the character of a violent racial conquest and indicated that ideological motives would dominate future German foreign policy.

Hitler's long-term aims

In *Mein Kampf* (see page 123), Hitler was quite specific about the main thrust of Nazi foreign policy. Germany was to turn its 'gaze towards the land in the east', which above all meant Russia. This country was to be turned into a huge German colony whose resources would eventually enable Germany to challenge the British Empire and the USA. Historians debate whether this was still his intention in 1933. A.J.P. Taylor (1961) argued that he was just aiming to make Germany 'the greatest power in Europe from her natural weight by exploiting every opportunity that presented itself'. Hans Mommsen, a German historian, also doubts whether Hitler had a consistent foreign policy of 'unchanging … priorities' and points out that it was usually determined by economic pressures and demands for action from within the Nazi Party itself. The history of Nazi foreign policy generates such controversy because Hitler's actions were so often ambiguous and contradictory. Despite this, there is a general consensus among historians that Hitler did intend to wage a series of wars which would ultimately culminate in a struggle for global and racial hegemony. As the historian Alan Bullock (1971) has argued, the key to understanding Hitler's foreign policy is that he combined 'consistency of aim with complete **opportunism** in method and tactics'.

KEY TERMS

Opportunism Seizing the opportunity when it occurs.

Stresa Powers The powers who attended the Stresa Conference in 1935.

Remilitarization of the Rhineland, 1936

The remilitarization of the Rhineland marked an important stage in Hitler's plans for rebuilding German power. The construction of strong fortifications there would enable him to stop any French attempts to invade Germany. Hitler had originally planned to remilitarize the Rhineland in 1937, but the favourable diplomatic situation created by the Abyssinian crisis (see pages 148–50) persuaded him to act in March 1936. He justified this arguing that the Franco-Soviet Pact (see page 127) was contrary to the Locarno agreement and a direct threat to German security.

SOURCE F

German soldiers cross the Cologne Bridge during Germany's remilitarization of the Rhineland in 1936, in direct violation of the Treaty of Versailles. Anglo-French failure to intervene was a turning point in international affairs.

What message does Source F give about the aims of Hitler's foreign policy?

Crucial to the success of his plan was the attitude of Italy. Mussolini, isolated from the other **Stresa Powers** because of his Abyssinian policy (see page 148), had little option but to reassure Germany that he would not co-operate with the British and French to enforce Locarno if German troops entered the Rhineland.

German troops marched into the Rhineland on 7 March 1936. In order to reassure France that they did not intend to violate the Franco-German frontier they were, initially at any rate, few in number and lightly equipped. So why did the French army not immediately intervene? The French general staff, which since the late 1920s had been planning for a defensive war against Germany based on the fortifications of the **Maginot line** on France's eastern frontier, refused to invade the Rhineland unless they had full backing from the British. The most the British government was ready to do was to promise France that, in the event of an unprovoked German attack on French territory, it would send two divisions of troops across the Channel. Essentially, British public opinion was convinced that Hitler was merely walking into 'his own back garden'.

KEY TERM 

Maginot line A line of concrete fortifications, which France constructed along its borders with Germany. It was named after André Maginot, the French Minister of Defence.

The crucial element here, it seemed, was that Germany was not occupying new territory. It was putting forces into German territory and allowing for a legitimate defence of frontiers that was the right of any state yet was denied to Germany by the Treaty of Versailles. Given that Britain and France had accepted German rearmament and that Britain had even signed a naval treaty, it would have seemed illogical to have taken military action to stop this remilitarization. Also, in an age of air power, arguably the shifting of border defences an extra 50 miles (80 km) or so had little real military significance. In itself the remilitarization would have made an unconvincing case for war. However, the consequences were to make war more likely.

The remilitarization of the Rhineland was a triumph for Hitler, as it marked a decisive shift in power from Paris to Berlin. It was also a considerable gamble. German rearmament had not got very far by 1936 and any decisive French resistance would have driven the German forces out and possibly toppled the Hitler regime. At a stroke Hitler had violated both the Treaty of Versailles and the Locarno Pact without any effective response from Britain and France.

SOURCE G

What can we learn from Source G about the international consequences of the German re-militarization of the Rhineland?

Extract from an internal French Foreign Office memorandum of 12 March 1936 on the consequences of the German action.

A German success would likewise not fail to encourage elements which, in Yugoslavia, look towards Berlin … In Romania this will be a victory of the elements of the right which have been stirred up by Hitlerite propaganda. All that will remain for Czechoslovakia is to come to terms with Germany. Austria does not conceal her anxiety. 'Next time it will be our turn' … Turkey, who has increasingly close economic relations with Germany, but who politically remains in the Franco-British axis, can be induced to modify her line. The Scandinavian countries … are alarmed.

Rearmament, 1936–39

After the remilitarization of the Rhineland the pace of German rearmament accelerated. Hitler appointed **Hermann Göring** to implement the Four-Year Plan which was to prepare Germany for war by 1940. Through raising taxes, government loans and cutting consumer expenditure, military expenditure nearly quadrupled between 1937 and 1939. An ambitious programme for the production of **synthetic materials** was also started to beat the impact of a future British blockade. By August 1939 the *Luftwaffe* had 4000 front-line aircraft and the strength of the army had risen to 2,758,000 men. In January 1939 Hitler also announced plans for the construction of a major battle fleet to challenge Britain.

Despite the initial target of 1940 set by the Four-Year Plan, the German rearmament programme was planned to be ready by the mid-1940s. In the meantime, as the historian Richard Overy observes, 'Hitler pursued a policy of putting as much as possible in the "shop window" to give the impression that Germany was armed in greater depth than was in fact the case'.

KEY FIGURE

Hermann Göring (1893–1946) Nazi leader and First World War air ace. In charge of the *Luftwaffe* and the Four-Year Plan. Committed suicide in October 1946.

KEY TERM

Synthetic materials Objects imitating a natural product but made chemically.

Hitler considers his options, April 1936–February 1938

By the autumn of 1937 Hitler had virtually dismantled the Europe created by the Locarno and Versailles Treaties. Owing to the following factors, he had also greatly strengthened Germany's position in Europe, even though he had given up the idea of an alliance with Britain:

- The Spanish Civil War and the outbreak of the Sino-Japanese war (see page 210) had distracted his potential enemies.
- Italy was drawing ever closer to Germany, as the October Protocols showed (see page 131).
- In November Germany was further strengthened when Hitler signed the Anti-Comintern Pact with Japan. This was of more symbolic than practical importance, as it was aimed at the Comintern rather than the USSR, but it nevertheless showed that Nazi Germany was no longer isolated. Potentially Italy, Japan and Germany were in a position to put the democracies under great pressure.

Hitler was thus in a favourable position to consider options for a new and more aggressive phase of foreign policy. On 5 November 1937 he was therefore able to outline to his commanders-in-chief and foreign and war ministers a possible scenario involving civil war in France or even a Franco-Italian war, which would enable him to annex Austria and dismember Czechoslovakia without fear of international intervention. He achieved these aims in 1938–39, even though the circumstances that he had predicted never in fact came about. Both the *Anschluss* and the eventual destruction of Czechoslovakia do indeed show Hitler's ability to adapt his tactics to the prevailing circumstances while steadily pursuing his overall aims.

SOURCE H

Extract from Hitler's address of 5 November 1937.

The aim of German policy was to make secure and to preserve the racial community and to enlarge it. It was therefore a question of space [Lebensraum] … The question for Germany was: Where could she achieve the greatest gain at the lowest cost? German policy had to reckon with two hate-inspired antagonists, Britain and France, to whom a German colossus in the centre of Europe was a thorn in the flesh … Germany's problem could only be solved by the use of force … If the resort to force with its attendant risks is accepted … there then remains still to be answered the questions 'When?' and 'How?'

Summarise in your own words the message of Source H. How useful is Source H in understanding Hitler's foreign policy in 1938–39?

The *Anschluss*

The annexation of Austria had long been a key aim of Nazi foreign policy, but Hitler did not plan the actual events that enabled him to achieve it. The crisis was ultimately triggered when **Schuschnigg**, the Austrian Chancellor, alarmed by the activities of the Austrian Nazis, requested an interview with Hitler. Hitler welcomed the chance to achieve an easy diplomatic success by imposing on Schuschnigg an agreement which would not only have subordinated Austrian foreign policy to Berlin but also have given the Austrian Nazi Party complete freedom. However, Schuschnigg then decided unexpectedly to regain some room for manoeuvre by asking his countrymen to vote in a referendum, which he planned to hold on Sunday 14 March, for a 'free and German, independent and social, Christian and united Austria'.

KEY FIGURE 

Kurt von Schuschnigg (1897–1977) Chancellor of Austria 1934–38. He was imprisoned by the Nazis after the *Anschluss*.

The German army occupies Austria

The immediate danger for the German government was that if Schuschnigg's appeal was endorsed by a large majority, he would be able to renounce his agreement with Hitler. Confronted by this challenge, Hitler rapidly dropped his policy of gradual absorption of Austria and not only forced Schuschnigg to cancel the referendum but on 12 March ordered the German army to occupy Austria. Then Hitler decided, apparently on the spur of the moment after a highly successful visit to the Austrian city of Linz where he had attended secondary school as a boy, to incorporate Austria into the Reich rather than install a satellite Nazi government in Vienna.

The reaction of Italy, Britain and France

Besides violating the Treaty of Versailles, which specifically forbade the union of Germany and Austria (see page 69), Hitler had for the first time invaded an independent state, even though the Austrian army did not oppose him, and put himself in a position from which to threaten Czechoslovakia. Why then did this not bring about a repetition of the Stresa Front that was briefly formed in 1934 against German aggression (see page 124)? Although British Prime Minister Chamberlain was in contact with the Italian government, and in April had concluded an agreement aimed at lowering the tension in the Mediterranean, essentially Mussolini had decided as long ago as 1936 that Austria was a German sphere of interest. Not surprisingly therefore, on 11 March 1938, he backed Hitler's decision to invade Austria. Both Britain and France protested to Berlin but neither had any intention of going to war over Austria. Indeed, the French were paralysed by an internal political crisis caused by the resignation of **Camille Chautemps**' ministry, and between 10 and 13 March did not even have a government.

KEY FIGURE 

Camille Chautemps (1885–1963) Served in several French governments and was Prime Minister three times

Figure 3.2 Central Europe showing German expansion from 1935 to August 1939. It was an impressive achievement, which increased Hitler's popularity in the Reich.

The Sudeten crisis

The annexation of Austria with the minimum of international protest greatly increased the vulnerability of Czechoslovakia to Nazi pressure, as it was now surrounded on three sides by German territory. Hitler had long regarded Czechoslovakia, with its alliances with both France and Russia, as a strategic threat to Germany which would eventually have to be eliminated. It is, however, arguable that in April 1938 Hitler was not sure how he was to carry out this aim. He certainly played with the idea of launching a sudden attack on Czechoslovakia if a major crisis were to be triggered, for instance by the assassination of the German ambassador in Prague. An easier and safer way to bring about the disintegration of Czechoslovakia was to enflame the nationalism of the **Sudeten Germans**. Czechoslovakia was a fragile state undermined by an ethnically divided population. Its unity was

KEY TERM 

Sudeten Germans Ethnic Germans who had been settled in the Sudetenland since the thirteenth century.

KEY FIGURE 

Konrad Henlein (1898–1945) Leader of the Sudeten German Nazis and later Nazi *Gauleiter* of the Sudetenland.

particularly threatened by the 3 million Sudeten Germans and the 2 million Slovaks. Hitler therefore specifically instructed **Konrad Henlein**, the Sudeten German leader, to keep making demands for concessions which the Prague government could not possibly grant if it wanted to preserve the unity of Czechoslovakia.

In the aftermath of the *Anschluss* both Britain and France were acutely aware of the growing threat to Czechoslovakia. Britain was unwilling to guarantee Czechoslovakia and yet realized that it might well not be able to stand aloof from the consequences of a German attack on it. Chamberlain told the Commons on 24 March that if fighting occurred:

What according to Source I was the likely impact of a German attack on Czechoslovakia?

SOURCE I

Extract of Chamberlain's speech to the House of Commons, 24 March 1938.

It would be well within the bounds of possibility that other countries, besides those which were parties to the original dispute, would almost immediately become involved. This is especially true in the case of two countries like Great Britain and France, with long associations of friendship, with interests closely interwoven, devoted to the same ideals of democratic liberty and determined to uphold them.

The French, unlike the British, were pledged by two treaties signed in 1924 and 1925 to consult and assist Czechoslovakia in the event of a threat to their common interests. In reality the French were in no position to help the Czechs. The Chief of the French Air Staff, who was in charge of operational planning, made no secret of his fears that the French air force would be wiped out within 15 days after the outbreak of war with Germany. The French government was therefore ready to follow the British lead in seeking a way of defusing the Sudeten crisis before it could result in war.

The May crisis

The urgency of this was underlined by the war scare of the weekend of 20–21 May 1938, when the Czech government suddenly partially mobilized its army in response to false rumours that a German attack was imminent. Hitler, warned by both Britain and France of the dangerous consequences of any military action, rapidly proclaimed the absence of any mobilization plans. Yet far from making Hitler more reasonable, this incident appears to have had the opposite effect, as he immediately stepped up military preparations for an invasion and set 1 October as a deadline for 'smashing Czechoslovakia'. A.J.P. Taylor (1961) sees this as bluff and argues that 'Hitler did not need to act. Others would do his work for him.' There were certainly, as we have seen, powerful forces working for the disintegration of the Czech state, but most historians do not dismiss Hitler's plans so lightly. It is more likely that he was just keeping his options open, as Bullock argues, to the 'very last possible moment'.

Meanwhile, France and Britain were redoubling their efforts to find a peaceful solution. The Anglo-French peace strategy aimed to put pressure on both the Czechs and the Sudeten Germans to make concessions, while continuing to warn Hitler of the dangers of a general war. In early September, **Beneš**, the Czech Prime Minister, responded to this pressure by granting almost all Henlein's demands. As this threatened the justification for Hitler's campaign against Czechoslovakia, Hitler immediately instructed Henlein to provoke a series of incidents which would enable him to break off the talks with Beneš.

KEY FIGURES 

Edvard Beneš (1884–1948) A leader of the Czechoslovak independence movement before 1918, then Minister of Foreign Affairs and President 1935–48 and 1945–48.

Édouard Daladier (1884–1970) A radical French politician and Prime Minister, 1938–41.

Chamberlain intervenes

On 12 September 1938 Hitler's campaign moved into a new phase when, in a speech at the Nuremberg Rally, he violently attacked the Czechs and assured the Sudetens of his support. Both Britain and France desperately attempted to avoid war. **Daladier**, the French Prime Minister, suggested that he and Chamberlain should meet Hitler, but Chamberlain seized the initiative and flew to see Hitler on 15 September at Berchtesgaden. There he agreed, subject to consultation with the French, that Czechoslovakia should cede to Germany all areas which contained a German population of 50 per cent or over. This would be supervised by an international commission. Hitler also demanded that Czechoslovakia should renounce its pact with Soviet Russia.

When Chamberlain again met Hitler at Bad Godesberg on 22 September, after winning French backing for his plan, Hitler demanded that the German occupation of the Sudetenland should be speeded up so that it would be completed by 28 September. Nor was it to be supervised by any international commission. Why Hitler should suddenly have changed his mind has puzzled historians. Taylor argued that Hitler was anxious to avoid accepting Chamberlain's plan in the hope that the Hungarians and Poles would formulate their own demands for Czechoslovakian territory and that he would then be able to move in and occupy the whole state under the pretext of being 'a peacemaker creating a new order'. On the other hand it is possible that Hitler had no such elaborate plan in mind and merely wanted to eliminate Czechoslovakia once and for all through war. At this stage Chamberlain's peace initiative seemed to have failed. France and Britain reluctantly began to mobilize, although both powers still continued to seek a negotiated settlement.

Neville Chamberlain

1869	Born
1915–18	Lord Mayor of Birmingham
1918	Entered parliament
1923–29	Minister of Health
1931–37	Chancellor of the Exchequer
1937–40	Prime Minister
1940	Died

Chamberlain was an energetic politician, who had been a very successful Minister of Health and Chancellor of the Exchequer. When he became Prime Minister he was determined to solve the German problem and avoid plunging Europe into war. He took control of British foreign policy and marginalized the Foreign Office. He believed that he would be able to come to an agreement by a direct man-to-man discussion with Hitler. He was convinced that German grievances could be met through a policy of appeasement. Even though he reluctantly realized that war was probable after Hitler's seizure of Bohemia in March 1939, he never completely abandoned appeasement.

The Munich agreement

In retrospect it is often argued that the French and British should have gone to war and called Hitler's bluff. Chamberlain's critics particularly stress that Russia was ready to come to the aid of Czechoslovakia, but at the time offers of Russian help seemed to the British, French and even the Czechs to be unconvincing. As neither Poland nor Romania would allow Russian troops through their territory, how could they help Czechoslovakia? It is thus not surprising that Chamberlain and Daladier warmly welcomed Mussolini's last-minute proposal on 28 September for a Four-Power Conference in Munich.

The next day, under pressure from his generals and from Mussolini, who both dreaded a premature war, Hitler reluctantly agreed to delay the occupation of the Sudetenland until 10 October and to allow an international commission to map the boundary line. He also consented, together with Britain, France and Italy, to guarantee what remained of the independence of Czechoslovakia and signed a declaration which affirmed the desire of Britain and Germany 'never to go to war with one another again'. This was supplemented by a similar declaration signed by Ribbentrop, Hitler's Foreign Minister, in Paris in December.

It is too simple to call Munich a triumph for Hitler. He had, it is true, secured the Sudetenland, but arguably he had been cheated of his real aim, the destruction of Czechoslovakia, which apparently was now about to be protected by an international guarantee. Germany seemed to be in danger of being enmeshed in just the sort of international agreement Hitler had always hoped to avoid. However, it is difficult to argue that Munich was a great victory for Chamberlain. Arguably he did buy more time for rearmament, but to the outside world Munich seemed to be a major defeat for Britain and France. The British ambassador in Tokyo reported that 'the Japanese reaction … is that we are prepared to put up with almost any indignity rather than fight. The result is that, all in all, our prestige is at a low ebb in the East…'

The destruction of Czechoslovakia

The argument that Hitler merely responded to events is hard to sustain when his foreign policy from October 1938 to March 1939 is analysed. His main priority remained the destruction of Czechoslovakia. On 21 October 1938, the German army was ordered to draw up fresh plans for military action. Simultaneously Hitler dangled the bait of territorial gains at the expense of the Czechs in front of the Hungarians, Poles and Romanians in order to enlist their support. German agents were also sent into Slovakia to fuel agitation against Prague. In practice Britain and France were already beginning to recognize Czechoslovakia as a German sphere of influence. The German representatives were allowed to dominate the international commission that was to map out the new frontiers after the secession of the Sudetenland and neither power protested when Germany refused to participate in finalizing the terms of the joint guarantee of Czechoslovakia in February 1939.

On 6 March 1939 the Germans were given the opportunity finally to dismember Czechoslovakia. When the Czechs suddenly moved troops into Slovakia to crush local demands for independence, which the Nazis of course had helped to stir up, Hitler persuaded the Slovaks to appeal to Berlin for assistance. On 14 March 1939 the Czech President, Emil Hácha, was ordered to travel to Berlin where he was ruthlessly bullied into resigning the fate of his country into 'the hands of the Führer'. The next day German troops occupied Prague, and Slovakia was turned into a German protectorate. This action was to precipitate a major diplomatic revolution in Europe: Britain broke decisively with its traditional foreign policy of avoiding a continental commitment, and together with France guaranteed Poland against a German attack (see pages 159–61).

Munich became a byword for surrender and cowardice. Critics pointed to the following:

- The Czechs were not consulted and were simply told to hand over part of their country.
- Nazi persecution was inflicted on Jews and socialists in the occupied areas.

ACTIVITY

List five reasons for the destruction of Czechoslovakia. Then choose the reason you think the most important and explain why.

ACTIVITY

Draw up a list of the successes Hitler achieved in his foreign policy, 1936–March 1939. Then write two paragraphs explaining the reasons for these successes.

- The safeguards in the agreement were ignored.
- It gave clear signals to Hitler that the democracies were weak.
- Any chance of co-operation with the USSR was lost and Stalin was led to the conclusion that he had to ally with Hitler instead.
- The League of Nations was ignored.
- The 35 army divisions and strong defences of Czechoslovakia were lost.
- France and Britain overestimated German ability to wage successful war in 1938 – the German army was not strongly mechanized and Hitler's own generals had reservations about its operational ability. However, by 1939 Germany was stronger and better prepared for war.

Defenders have pointed out the following:

- In 1938 Britain and France did not have public support for war.
- British defences, particularly in the form of air power, had greatly increased by 1939 and the Munich Conference gave the time needed to rearm more intensively.
- The British Empire and the USA would not have supported a war which would have denied German speakers the right to be part of Germany in 1938.
- Hitler wanted war and was deprived of it by British diplomacy.
- Britain was in a much stronger position morally and in military terms to go to war in 1939 than in 1938.

The German reaction to the British guarantee

In October 1938, and then again in January and March 1939, Hitler unsuccessfully sounded out the Poles about the return of Danzig, the construction of a road and rail link through the corridor and about joining the Anti-Comintern Pact. In return the Poles were offered the eventual prospect of acquiring land in Ukraine. Essentially Hitler wanted to turn Poland into a reliable satellite, but given the fate of Czechoslovakia it was precisely this status that the Poles finally rejected in March 1939. The Anglo-French guarantee of Poland, far from deterring Hitler, convinced him that Poland would have to be eliminated, even if this meant war with Britain and France. On 23 May Hitler told his generals:

Summarise in your own words the message in Source J. Compare Sources H and J as evidence for Hitler's foreign policy aims.

SOURCE J

Extract from Hitler's speech to his generals, 23 May 1939.

Poland will always be on the side of our adversaries … Danzig is not the objective. It is a matter of expanding our living space in the east … We cannot expect a repetition of Czechoslovakia. There will be fighting. The task is to isolate Poland … Basic principle: conflict with Poland, beginning with the attack on Poland, will be successful only if the West keeps out. If that is impossible, then it is better to attack the West and finish off Poland at the same time. It will be a task of dexterous diplomacy to isolate Poland…

SUMMARY DIAGRAM

How did the rise of extremism affect international relations?

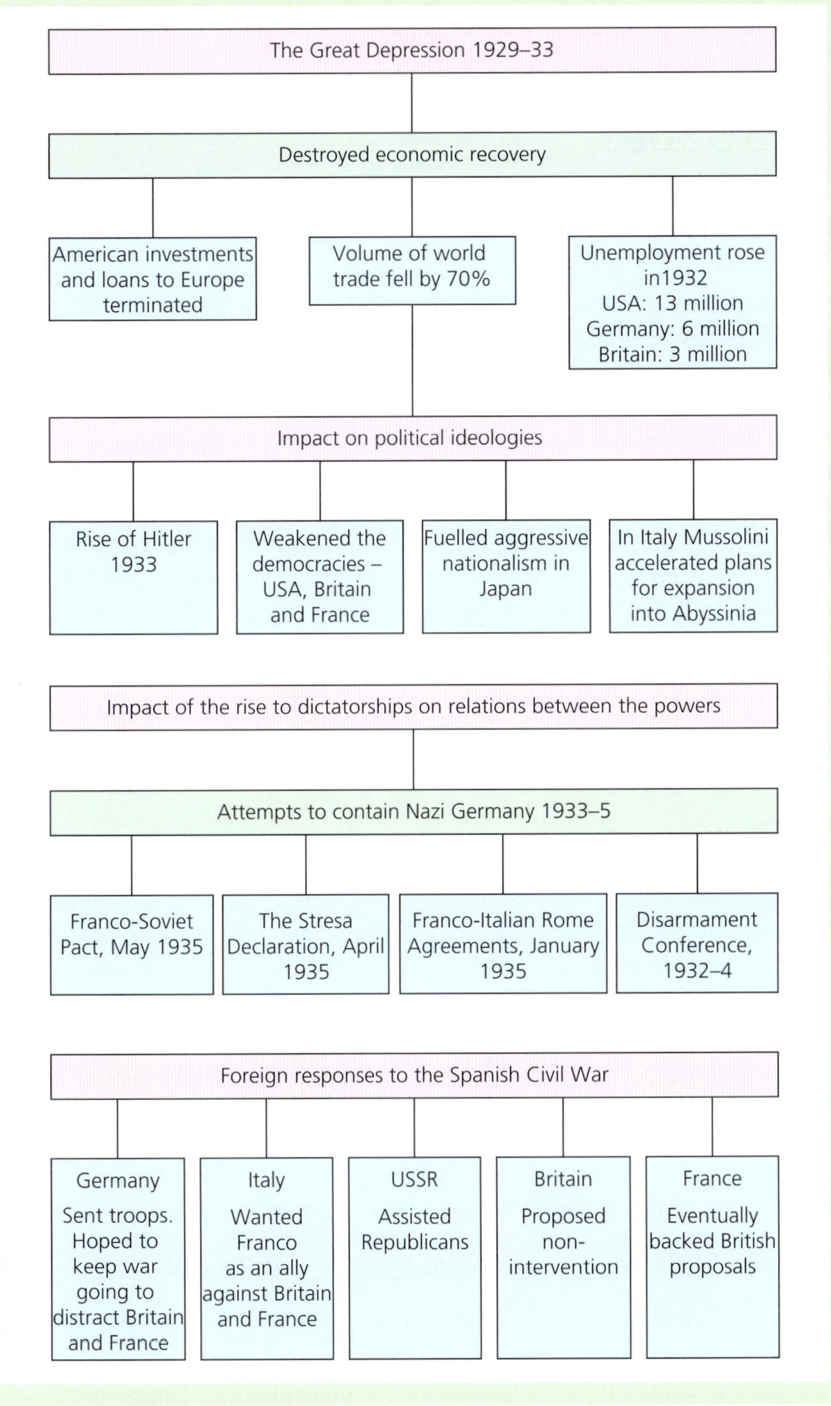

2 Why did the League of Nations fail to keep the peace in the 1930s?

The League of Nations did make efforts to solve disputes and to promote an atmosphere of international co-operation in the 1920s. Given that this had not been attempted on such a scale before, the achievements were promising. Though there were regimes which were nationalistic in outlook, they were prepared to take part in League activities and discussions. However, in the 1930s, the rise of nationalism and more extreme policies by powers discontented with the post-war peace settlements made the task of the League even more difficult. The intense economic depression brought a change of regime in Germany and resulted in Hitler leaving the League, rejecting the restrictions of the Treaty of Versailles and expanding German territory. Economic pressures resulted in Japanese expansion into China from 1931. In Italy the growing radicalism of Mussolini's fascist regime brought about a colonial war of conquest in Abyssinia. There was no effective international action to prevent these threats to peace and the League was bypassed by France and Britain in attempts to deal directly with Germany and Italy. By the time of the outbreak of war in 1939 the League had become irrelevant.

The failure of disarmament

One of the major tasks of the League was to work out an acceptable world disarmament programme. Disarmament, however, could not be divorced from the question of security, for if a state did not feel secure, it would hardly disarm. In an attempt to solve this problem the League in 1924 drafted an ambitious **collective security** agreement, the Geneva Protocol, but this was rejected by Britain, which feared that, as a consequence of its huge empire, it would be committed to policing the world. However, four years later in the optimistic mood created by the Locarno agreements and the Kellogg-Briand Pact (see pages 91–92 and 95–96), the League set up a Preparatory Commission, of which both the USA and USSR were members.

KEY TERM 

Collective security Security gained through joining an alliance or signing an agreement where the security of each state is guaranteed by the others.

ACTIVITY 

Re-read pages 118–21 and 144–45. Draw a spider diagram to show why disarmament had failed by 1934.

The World Disarmament Conference, 1932–34

In 1930 the Preparatory Commission, after protracted discussions on different models of disarmament, produced its final draft for an international convention. The League Council called the long-awaited World Disarmament Conference in February 1932 at Geneva. It could not have been convened at a more unfortunate time: the Manchurian crisis (pages 146–48) had weakened the League, the rise of National Socialism in Germany made France and Poland less likely to compromise over German demands for equality in armaments, while the impact of the Depression on the USA was reviving the isolationist tendencies of the early 1920s. In July 1932 Germany demanded 'equal rights' with the other powers as far as armaments went and withdrew from the conference in protest, but in December it was persuaded to return when agreement was reached that Germany would 'have equality of rights in a system that would provide security for all nations'.

For France the problem with this formula, particularly after Hitler came to power in Germany in January 1933, was how would 'security for all nations' be provided when neither Britain nor the USA were ready to guarantee French security or to strengthen the League of Nation's ability to intervene in international disputes. Attempts to satisfy both France and Germany failed. Germany rejected a Franco-British proposal whereby a general disarmament plan for all the powers would only come into force after eight years, as that would have prevented Germany from immediately rearming. In October Hitler decided to pull Germany out of the conference, and to rearm as quickly as possible. This effectively ensured the failure of disarmament. On 11 June 1934 the conference adjourned, never to meet again.

SOURCE K

'Mars the God of War tied down': a 1932 cartoon referring to the World Disarmament Conference of 1932.

Who do you think is the intended audience for Source K? To what extent is this source 'wishful thinking'?

Reasons for and actions taken in response to the crises in Manchuria and Abyssinia

Together, the League's failure to intervene decisively in the Manchurian and Abyssinian crises destroyed its credibility as a peace-keeping organization. The League's prestige might just have survived its mishandling of the Manchurian crisis, but its failure to stop Italian aggression in Abyssinia effectively destroyed it. In the words of the historian of the League of Nations, F.S. Northedge (1988), 'the blow suffered by the League was instant and fatal'.

The Manchurian crisis

The failure of the Japanese government to deal with the impact of the Depression on the economy convinced the Japanese officer corps that it would have to act decisively and occupy the whole of Manchuria. This would then enable Japan to control the region's valuable coal and iron resources at a time when economic nationalism was already making it difficult for it to purchase these vital raw materials elsewhere. Consequently, Japanese officers in Manchuria decided to devise an incident which would provide the pretext for intervention. On 18 September 1931 a bomb exploded on the railway line just outside Mukden where both Chinese and Japanese troops were stationed. This was immediately blamed on the Chinese and provided the Japanese forces with the desired excuse to occupy not only Mukden but the whole of southern Manchuria.

The response of the League of Nations

KEY FIGURE

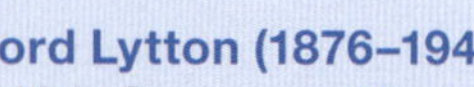

Lord Lytton (1876–1947) British Governor of Bengal, 1922–27. In 1931 he chaired the Lytton Commission in Manchuria.

China immediately appealed to the League of Nations, but the Council responded cautiously. It first asked Japan to withdraw its troops back into the railway zone and, when this was ignored, sent a commission of inquiry under the chairmanship of **Lord Lytton**. The Japanese were able to complete the occupation of Manchuria and turned it into the satellite state of Manchukuo while the Lytton Commission was conducting a leisurely fact-finding operation in the spring of 1932.

Refusal of Britain and the USA to use force

KEY TERM 

Gold standard A system by which the value of a currency is defined in terms of gold. The value of the pound was linked to gold. On 20 September 1931 the pound was forced off the gold standard and its value fell from $4.86 to $3.49.

It is easy to criticize the League for not acting more decisively, but without the commitment of the great powers it was not in a position to take effective action. Neither of the two most important naval powers, Britain and the USA, were ready to use force against Japan. From the Japanese point of view, the timing of the Mukden incident could not have been better. On 15 September a minor mutiny at the naval base at Invergordon in Scotland, which was caused by a cut in the sailors' wages, threatened temporarily to paralyse the Royal Navy; and five days later Britain was forced off the **gold standard.** The USA, shell-shocked by the Depression, was unwilling to do more than denounce Japanese aggression. President Hoover, for instance, argued that economic sanctions would be like 'sticking pins in tigers' and would run the risk of leading to war.

It is sometimes argued that the British government and powerful financial interests in the City of London secretly supported Japan. It is true that Britain did have some sympathy with Japanese action in Manchuria. Like Japan it had commercial interests in China (see page 23), which it felt were threatened by the chaos and civil war there. Britain also appreciated Japan's potential role in providing a barrier against the spread of Bolshevism from the USSR into northern China. Nevertheless, the real reason why Britain was not ready to urge more decisive action against Japan was that neither the government nor the people desired to fight a war on an issue that was not central to British interests. In February 1933 Sir John Simon, the Foreign Minister, told the House of Commons:

SOURCE L

Extract from Sir John Simon's speech to the House of Commons, February 1933.

I think I am myself enough of a pacifist to take the view that, however we handle the matter, I do not intend my own country to get into trouble about it … There is one great difference between 1914 and now and it is this: in no circumstances will this government authorize this country to be party to this struggle.

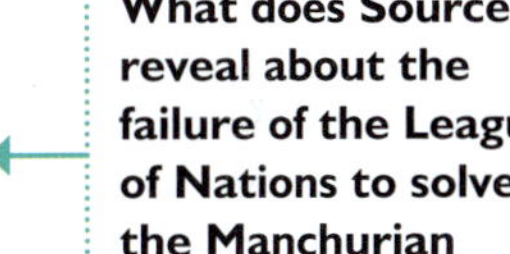

The report of the Lytton Commission

It was not until September 1932 that the League received the Lytton Commission's report. Although it conceded that the treaty rights, which Japan had enjoyed in Manchuria since 1905 (see pages 36–37), had made Sino-Japanese friction unavoidable, it nevertheless observed that 'without a declaration of war a large area of what was indisputably Chinese territory had been forcibly seized and occupied by the armed forces of Japan and has in consequence of this operation been separated from and declared independent of the rest of China'. It proposed that Japanese troops should withdraw back into the railway zone, and then both China and Japan should negotiate not only a treaty guaranteeing Japan's rights in Manchuria but also a non-aggression pact and a trade agreement.

Essentially the report was mistakenly based on the assumption that the Japanese had no territorial designs in China and were ready to compromise over Manchuria. When it was adopted unanimously, with the single exception of Japan, by the League Assembly on 24 February 1933, Japan withdrew from the League in protest. It was obvious that only armed intervention by the great powers would now be able to force Japan out of Manchuria, and that option was not politically realistic in 1933.

The consequences of the occupation

The Japanese occupation of Manchuria changed the balance of power in the Pacific. Japan had broken free from the restraints that had been imposed on it at the Washington Conference in 1922 by Britain and the USA (see page 83) and had guaranteed its access to valuable coal and iron ore resources. Above all, Japan was now in a favourable strategic position to plan a large-scale military invasion of China.

The Abyssinian crisis

In Abyssinia the League was to face its greatest challenge since its creation. The Italian fascist dictator Mussolini had for a long time wanted to build up a large empire in North Africa which would have the added advantage of distracting his people from the impact of the Depression on the Italian economy. By 1932 he had begun to plan in earnest the annexation of Abyssinia. Not only would Abyssinia provide land for Italian settlers, but it would also connect Eritrea with Italian Somaliland and thus put most of the Horn of Africa under Italian control (see map on page 150). In December 1934 a clash occurred between Italian and Abyssinian troops at the small oasis of Wal-Wal, some 50 miles (80 km) on the Abyssinian side of the border with Italian Somaliland, and in the following October the long-expected invasion of Abyssinia began.

What information does Source M provide about the ability of the Abyssinian army to defend Abyssinia?

SOURCE M

Abyssinian troops marching near to the northern frontier.

The failure of Anglo-French attempts to compromise

Mussolini was convinced that neither Britain nor France would raise serious objections. In January 1935 **Laval**, the French Foreign Minister, had verbally promised him a free hand, while the British Foreign Office was desperate to avert the crisis either by offering Mussolini territorial compensation elsewhere or by helping to negotiate an arrangement, comparable to Britain's own position in Egypt, which would give Italy effective control of Abyssinia without **formally annexing** it (see page 6).

KEY FIGURE 

Pierre Laval (1883–1945) French socialist and Prime Minister, 1931–32. He was Chief Minister in Vichy France and was executed in 1945.

SOURCE N

Sir Robert Vansittart, a senior British diplomat, forcefully pointed out in a Foreign Office memorandum on 8 June that:

The position is as plain as a pikestaff [obvious]. Italy will have to be bought off – let us use and face ugly words – in some form or other, or Abyssinia will eventually perish. That might in itself matter less, if it did not mean that the League would also perish (and that Italy would simultaneously perform another **volte-face** *into the arms of Germany).*

Compare the views in Sources L and N on the role of the League in Manchuria and Abyssinia. To what extent do they help to explain its failure?

Why then could such a compromise not be negotiated? The scale and brutality of the Italian invasion confronted both the British and French governments with a considerable dilemma. The British government was facing an election in November 1935 and was under intense pressure from the electorate to support the League. In an unofficial 'peace ballot' in June 1935 organized by the League of Nations Union, which was formed in 1918 to win public support for the League, 10 million out of 11 million replies backed the use of economic sanctions by the League in a case of aggression. In France, public opinion was more divided, with the left supporting the League and the right supporting Italy. However, both powers feared the diplomatic consequences of alienating Italy over Abyssinia. In particular, Britain's persistent refusal to join France in guaranteeing the status quo in central and eastern Europe inevitably increased the importance for the French of their friendly relations with Italy.

KEY TERMS 

Formal annexation Taking over full control of a territory by another power.

Volte-face An about turn; a sudden and complete change of policy.

On 18 October the League Council condemned the Italian invasion of Abyssinia, and under Article 16 of the League's constitution voted for a gradually escalating programme of sanctions. In the meantime, both Britain and France continued to search for a compromise settlement. In December Laval and the British Foreign Minister, Sir Samuel Hoare, produced a plan which involved placing some two-thirds of Abyssinia under Italian control. There was a strong possibility that it would have been acceptable to Mussolini, but it was leaked to the French press, and an explosion of rage among the British public forced Hoare's resignation and the dropping of the plan.

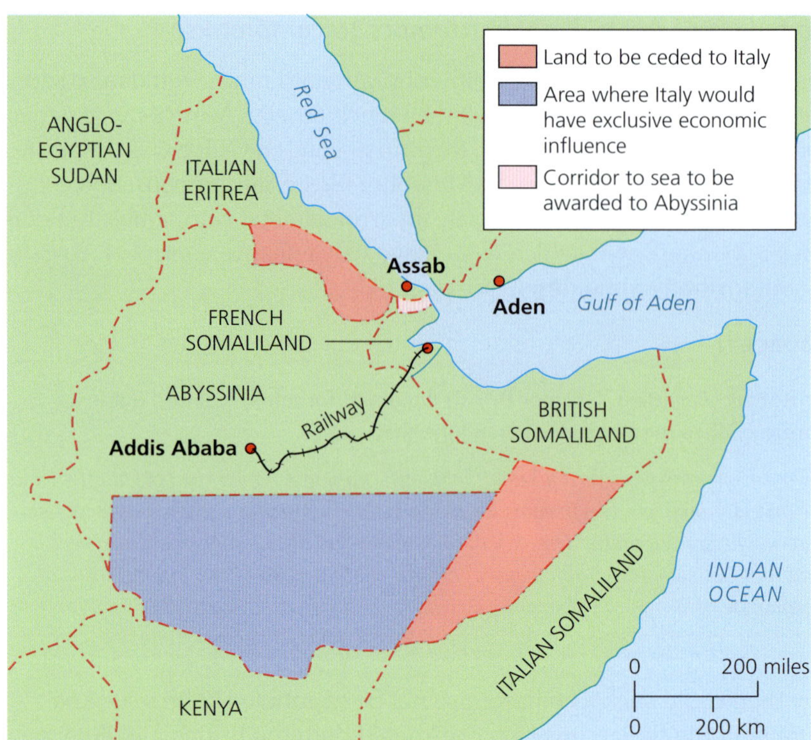

Figure 3.3 The Hoare-Laval Plan for the partition of Abyssinia. In the face of opposition from the League of Nations Union it was dropped.

ACTIVITY

In groups decide why the League failed to solve the Abyssinian and Manchurian crises. Then individually write two paragraphs indicating how the two crises differed.

The failure of diplomacy did not then ensure vigorous action against Mussolini. The League put no embargo on oil exports to Italy, and Britain refused to close the Suez Canal to Italian shipping on the grounds that this might lead to war with Italy. Mussolini was thus able to step up his campaign and by May 1936 had overrun Abyssinia.

The consequences of the Abyssinian war

The Abyssinian crisis was a crucial turning point in the 1930s. Not only did it irreparably weaken the League and provide Hitler with an ideal opportunity for the illegal remilitarization of the Rhineland (see pages 133–34), but it also effectively destroyed the Franco-Italian friendship and ultimately replaced it with the Rome-Berlin 'Axis' (see page 126). This eventually enabled Hitler in 1938 to absorb Austria without Italian opposition. The 'Axis' was also to threaten vital British and French lines of communication in the Mediterranean with the possibility of hostile naval action and thus seriously weaken their potential response to future German – or indeed Japanese – aggression.

Changing attitudes of the major powers towards the League of Nations

On 4 July 1936 the League terminated sanctions against Italy. It had failed to halt Italian aggression in a situation where its two most powerful members, Britain and France, could easily have brought pressure on Italy through sanctions and naval blockade. The consequence of this failure was an increasing lack of confidence in the League's capacity to protect the smaller countries and solve conflicts. In September 1936 the League Council invited member states to draw up proposals for reforming the League, but was reform possible and what was the attitude of the major powers?

- Germany, Italy and Japan had all withdrawn from the League. Germany totally ignored the League when it annexed Austria, the Sudetenland and Bohemia and attacked Poland in 1939. Italy, by drawing closer to Germany through the Axis agreements and the Pact of Steel, also rejected the League. Japan, despite appeals from the League Council, continued to wage all-out war against China.
- The USA was still isolationist and increasingly believed that the League should confine itself only to health, humanitarian and economic issues.
- Britain and France initially hoped in 1936 that they could persuade Germany to rejoin a reformed League of Nations to work out a security system to replace the Locarno Treaties. After the German rejection of this, and in response to its increasingly aggressive foreign policy in central Europe, both powers had little option but to ignore the League and prepare for war against Nazi Germany.
- The only major power to give the League its support was the USSR. It saw the League as a means of rallying the smaller countries against Germany, and insisted that it had not 'broken down'. During the Sudeten crisis of September 1938 the Russians were ready to help Czechoslovakia as long as they secured the agreement of the League Council.

The last session of the League's Council met in May 1939. It did not discuss the gathering crisis between Nazi Germany and Poland that was to lead to war. Instead it dealt with purely technical matters such as the standardization of signalling at railway level crossings. Ironically its last significant action was to expel its most loyal member, the USSR, from the League after it had invaded Finland in November 1939. In May 1946 the League was officially replaced by the United Nations.

ACTIVITY 

Re-read Chapter 2, pages 97–107 and Chapter 3, pages 120–21 and 144–52. Consider the statements below and find evidence to support and to challenge each one:

1. 'The League was a failure from start to finish.'
2. 'The League failed to keep the peace but its agencies were a success.'
3. 'It was the consequences of the Great Depression that destroyed the League.'

With which of these statements do you most agree and why?

SUMMARY DIAGRAM

Why did the League of Nations fail to keep the peace in the 1930s?

The failure of disarmament, 1933–35

- Germany withdraws from Disarmament Conference 1933 and begins to rearm
- Japan renounces treaties controlling naval construction, 1935

The Manchurian Crisis

Causes

- Threats to Japanese interests in Manchuria through Chinese Civil War
- The Depression
- Weak Japanese government
- Pressure from the army

↓

The Mukden incident, 18 September 1931

↓

Japanese occupation of Manchuria

↓

China appealed to League of Nations

↓

Lytton Commission sent

↓

Recommended withdrawal of Japanese troops and then a negotiated settlement

↓

Japan quit League of Nations when the Assembly adopted the recommendations, February 1933

The Abyssinian Crisis

October 1935: Italian troops invaded Abyssinia

↓

Britain and France sought a compromise to keep Italy as a potential ally against Nazi Germany

↓

Hoare-Laval Pact

↓

Leaked to French press and dropped

↓

League pursued an ineffective policy of sanctions against Italy

↓

Mussolini became increasingly dependent on German help

↓

Hitler exploited the crisis to remilitarize the Rhineland

↓

Rome-Berlin Axis

Changing attitudes of major powers towards League of Nations, 1937–9	
Germany and Italy	Ignored League and carried out independent and aggressive foreign policies
Britain and France	Unable to persuade Germany to rejoin League, had no option but to ignore the League and prepare for war against Germany without consulting it
Japan	Despite appeals from League continued to wage war in China
USA	Believed League should confine work to health, economic and humanitarian issues
USSR	Increasingly saw League as means of building an alliance against Germany. Argued it had not 'broken down'

ACTIVITY

For each of the factors shown on the summary diagram explain how they brought about the failure of disarmament.

Why, and with what effects, did Britain and France pursue a policy of appeasement?

The policy which Britain and France followed towards Germany from 1933 to 1939 has become known as appeasement. This has now become a 'bad' word – meaning the giving in to the demands of a bully. However, at the time 'appeasement' was seen as a positive policy. It was used by Winston Churchill when he spoke in the 1920s of the need 'for the appeasement of European hatreds'. In the 1930s it came to mean being ready to listen and respond to legitimate demands to maintain peace. Until 1937 it meant doing nothing to endanger peace but after Chamberlain became prime minister in 1937 it meant taking active steps to reduce tensions to keep peace – of being, in modern terms, 'proactive' even when Britain's direct interests were not involved. That policy became controversial when Britain pressured Czechoslovakia to accept German demands to keep peace.

The impact of economic and military considerations for foreign policy

It was not until 1935–36 that the scale of German rearmament became clear (see pages 121–24 and 133–35). Inevitably the pace of German military expansion created concern in both France and Britain, and caused both powers to start major rearmament programmes, the economic and military implications of which influenced their foreign policy.

Unlike in 1914, there was no calm assumption that the next war would be soon over. All three countries, learning from the First World War, expected a long struggle. Even though the tank and aeroplane had restored mobility to the battlefield, most military experts still thought in terms of First World War tactics. The French built the Maginot line, which was an enormous series of concrete fortifications along their frontier with Germany, while the Germans built the Westwall fortifications along the east bank of the Rhine.

An important lesson from the First World War was that the armed forces needed so much equipment that the economy and the workforce had to be totally mobilized in order to supply them. The nation which could most efficiently supply and finance its armed forces in a long, protracted struggle would in all probability win the war.

What impact did this arms race have on the diplomatic situation? The heavy financial burdens of rearmament made the appeasement of Germany an attractive proposition for both Britain and France, since rearmament caused considerable economic and social problems. In France, for instance, the franc

KEY TERM

Devalue Reduce the value of.

had to be **devalued** three times between 1936 and 1938 to help pay for rearmament. In November 1938 a general strike was called in Paris in protest against wage cuts and the decline in living standards caused by diverting resources to rearmament. The pace of French rearmament was slowed by the weakness of their economy, but even so military expenditure had increased six times between 1936 and 1939. In Britain, too, rearmament caused considerable financial strain, which Prime Minister Neville Chamberlain feared might 'break our backs'.

The impact of the arms race on the diplomatic situation

The German rearmament programme would not be completed until the mid-1940s. This would not, however, stop Hitler from waging a limited war against Czechoslovakia or Poland if he believed that Britain and France would stand aside.

ACTIVITY 

In groups prepare a presentation on how rearmament influenced German, British and French foreign policy. Re-read Section 1 of this chapter and also look at pages 158–59.

The British and French programmes, on the other hand, were planned to be ready by 1939–40. Neither Britain nor France wanted war, and both were ready to seek agreement with Nazi Germany to prevent it, but if there was no option but war, then 1939–40 was the best possible date for it to occur. Beyond that point both countries would find it increasingly difficult to maintain the high level of spending that their armament programmes demanded.

The changing nature of relations with the USSR and impact on foreign policy

In reaction to the rise to power of Hitler and the rearming of Germany, the USSR under Stalin joined the League of Nations and signed a defensive pact with France (see page 125). Both Britain and France, however, continued to view the USSR with suspicion and considered it to be an unreliable ally:

- The Red Army had been seriously weakened by Stalin's purge of the Soviet officer corps, which eliminated some 65 per cent of its senior officers.
- The USSR was feared and distrusted by the small countries on its western frontier with Europe who viewed it as potentially as great a threat to their independence as Germany.
- The USSR faced a threat from Japan along its southern border with China, which Britain and France reckoned would make it reluctant to risk war with Germany.
- British and French fear of Bolshevism was reciprocated in the USSR by a hatred and fear of capitalism and imperialism.

In light of this assessment, Britain and France during the Munich crisis preferred to deal with Hitler directly rather than exploring the statement by Litvinov, the Soviet Foreign Minister, in March 1938 that if, necessary 'means would be found' of assisting Czechoslovakia even though it had no common frontier with the USSR. Significantly the Czechs themselves never at any time during the Munich crisis asked for help from the USSR.

It was only in the spring of 1939, after Hitler had broken the Munich agreement by destroying what was left of Czechoslovakia and forced Lithuania to hand back the former German city of Memel, that Britain and France attempted to build up a 'peace front' against Nazi Germany in eastern Europe by guaranteeing first Poland and then two weeks later Greece and Romania (see page 159). These guarantees, as Winston Churchill argued, had no value 'except within the framework of a general agreement with Russia', but this, as we shall see, was difficult to achieve.

Actions taken to appease Hitler, 1936–38

Essentially appeasement was a realistic policy for the rulers of the large and vulnerable British Empire. It was based on the assumption that a willingness to compromise would avert conflict and protect the essential interests of the Empire. It was in this spirit that Britain signed the Anglo-German naval agreement of 1935 and tolerated the remilitarization of the Rhineland (see pages 133–34). Appeasement did, however, fail to achieve any lasting settlement with Hitler, and appeared in retrospect to its critics to be a cowardly policy of surrender.

ACTIVITY 

After re-reading Chapter 2, pages 132–33 and then pages 154–56, hold a class debate on appeasement. One group will condemn it, the other support it. Each group will use cards with clear debating points on one side and supporting evidence on the other.

Chamberlain and appeasement

In the autumn of 1937 Chamberlain launched a major initiative aimed at achieving a settlement with Hitler. He hoped to divert German expansion in eastern Europe by offering Germany colonies in Africa. In late November an Anglo-French summit was held in London where this policy was more fully explored. Chamberlain won over the French to this policy and by March 1938 he was ready to negotiate a package of colonial concessions with Berlin, but the gathering pace of German expansion signalled first by the *Anschluss* and then by the destruction of Czechoslovakia made this approach irrelevant.

SOURCE O

Extract from Neville Chamberlain's letter to Mrs Morton Prince, an American citizen, 16 January 1938.

...as a realist I must do what I can to make this country safe ... [The British people] are perfectly aware that until we are fully rearmed our position will be one of great anxiety. They realize that we are in no position to enter light-heartedly upon a war with such a formidable power as Germany, much less if Germany were aided by Italian attacks on our Mediterranean possessions and communications. They know that France, though her army is strong, is desperately weak in some vital spots...

To what extent does Source O explain Chamberlain's policy towards Nazi Germany in 1938–39?

Appeasement and the *Anschluss*

ACTIVITY

Write a brief explanation of the following terms: Appeasement, *Anschluss*, total mobilization, arms race and Sudeten problem.

The initial reaction of the British government to the *Anschluss* was to hope that the storm would blow over and that talks could resume with Berlin on a package of possible colonial concessions, details of which had already been handed to the German government on 3 March. These concessions were, after all, aimed at distracting Berlin from pursuing its ambitions in central Europe. Whether Chamberlain really believed that Hitler could be bought off is hard to say. Privately he wrote that 'it was now clear' that force was the only argument that Germany understood, but publicly he was not yet ready to draw the logical conclusion from this and confront Hitler. Was he gaining time for his country to rearm or was he seriously giving peace one more chance?

Czechoslovakia and the Munich crisis

After the *Anschluss* was completed, Chamberlain was determined to defuse the Sudeten problem before it could lead to war, and so prepare the ground for a general settlement with Germany. After the 'May crisis' (see page 138), when it momentarily seemed that Hitler was about to attack Czechoslovakia, France and Britain appealed to both the Czechs and the Sudeten Germans to compromise, and warned Hitler repeatedly not to risk a European war.

In response to Hitler's inflammatory speech at the Nuremberg rally on 12 September 1938 (see page 139), Chamberlain seized the initiative and flew to Germany to negotiate directly with Hitler. He told Hitler at the meeting at Berchtesgarden that 'on principle' he had 'nothing against the separation of the Sudeten Germans from the rest of Czechoslovakia provided that the practical difficulties could be overcome'. It was, however, as we have seen (see page 140), only on the third meeting at Munich that Hitler reluctantly agreed to a compromise over Czechoslovakia and to sign a declaration which affirmed the desire of Britain and Germany 'never to go to war with one another again'.

When Chamberlain returned from Munich he was greeted with enormous crowds at Heston airport in London, and the great majority of the country welcomed the Munich agreement with relief that the British Empire – and indeed Europe – had been spared another great war. Privately Chamberlain realized that the agreement was a gamble. At best it might secure 'peace in our time' as he told the crowds outside **Downing Street**. If it failed it would have at least bought more time for rearmament.

KEY TERM

Downing Street The London residence of the British Prime Minister.

The events of the next six months were to show that appeasement as an effective policy for avoiding war with Nazi Germany had failed.

SUMMARY DIAGRAM

Why, and with what effects, did Britain and France pursue a policy of appeasement?

Impact of economic and military considerations for foreign policy

Legacy of First World War

Total war: nations totally mobilized

War of attrition and long duration

Military planners still thought in terms of the defensive: Maginot line and Westwall

The arms race between Britain and France and Germany

Germany
- Four-Year Plan concentrating on synthetic materials 1936
- Military rearmament plans to be ready by mid-1940s

Britain
- 1936: launched a four-year armaments plan, key part of which was construction of a bomber strike force
- Rearmament planned to peak 1939/40

France
- France's armed forces larger than Britain's in 1936. Rearmament proceeded slowly, but even so between1936 and 1939 expenditure increased six times
- Armament production would peak in 1939–40

Actions taken to appease Hitler, 1933–7

- Anglo-German naval agreement 1935
- Failure to react to remilitarization of the Rhineland
- Chamberlain's 'proactive' policy of appeasement

Changing nature of relations with the USSR and impact on international diplomacy: USSR on the defensive

- Threats from Japan on southern borders
- Red Army weakened by Stalin's purges
- Anti-Comintern Pact
- Viewed with suspicion by Britain and France

Anschluss and the destruction of Czechoslovakia

Eruption of Austrian and Czech crises 1938

Anschluss
- Faced with threat of referendum on Austro-German Agreement, Germany annexed Austria, 12 March
- Chamberlain accepted *Anschluss* and hoped talks with Germany on a comprehensive settlement would go ahead

Sudeten crisis
- Hitler intended to exploit Sudeten demands for independence to 'smash' Czechoslovakia
- Fearing war, Chamberlain negotiated Munich Agreement with Hitler: Sudetenland ceded to Germany; rest of Czechoslovakia guaranteed by Britain, France, Italy and Germany (29 September)

German occupation of Prague, March 1939 marked total failure of appeasement policy

Why did war break out in 1939?

In September 1939 war in Europe broke out over the revision of the Treaty of Versailles. Poland had refused German demands for a return of former German territory in the so-called Polish corridor – Posen, West Prussia and the city of Danzig. Germany accused Poland of hostile acts against the German population and invaded on 1 September 1939. This was a culmination of German actions against Versailles which began with rearmament in defiance of the agreement signed in 1919 and the remilitarization of the Rhineland. The union with Austria in 1938 was in express defiance of Versailles and Hitler was able to negotiate the transfer of German-speaking areas of Czechoslovakia in 1938 to the Reich, changing the territorial boundaries established in the post-war peace treaty.

The lack of resistance by the signatories of the peace treaties encouraged Hitler to think that there was limited will to prevent German expansion. He was also encouraged by a pact with Italy and a non-aggression treaty with the USSR. With the USA still isolationist, the chances of expansion leading to war were worth taking for Germany. The war for Britain was seen as essential to prevent total German control of mainland Europe which would have endangered British security and also to prevent the total breakdown of international relations based on legal norms rather than aggression. Domestic pressure in favour of standing against obvious German aggression was strong and the earlier policy of appeasement had clearly failed. France could hardly stand aside and see German power expand into eastern Europe and do nothing once Britain had decided to act. However, neither France not Britain had any plan or any intention of sending forces to help Poland and both had largely defensive strategies and capabilities, so the war that began soon became known as 'the phoney war'; not until Hitler invaded France in 1940 did it begin in earnest.

British rearmament in response to Germany's expansionism

As a consequence of German rearmament and Hitler's increasingly aggressive foreign policy, in 1936 Britain drew up a Four-Year Plan for rearmament in which priority was given to the navy and air force. In a future war with Germany the navy would play a key role in blockading Germany and in ensuring that it could not import vital raw materials for its war industries. An important part of the programme was also the construction of a bomber strike force. Using British bases, bombers could attack German cities and factories.

Despite his support for appeasement, the programme was accelerated when Chamberlain became prime minister in 1937 and increased funds were also made available for the army. Between 1936 and 1939 expenditure on armaments increased from £185.9 million to £719 million. On 22 February 1939 the government authorized aircraft production 'to the limit' regardless of cost. British (and French) rearmament preparations were planned to reach their peak in the period 1939–40. Thereafter the sheer cost of rearmament would begin to cause a political and economic crises. Consequently, as we have already noticed (see page 154), viewed from Paris and London it was better for war to come in 1939–40 rather than a few years later.

Table 3.2 Numbers of aircraft produced in Britain, France and Germany.

	Britain	France	Germany
1935	1,140	785	3,183
1936	1,877	890	5,112
1937	2,153	743	5,606
1938	2,827	1,382	5,235
1939	7,940	3,163	8,295
1940	15,049	2,133	10,247

The British guarantee to Poland and the failure of appeasement

In the 1920s there was no commitment to defending Poland, yet on 31 March 1939 Britain broke decisively with its traditional foreign policy of avoiding a continental commitment, and, together with France, guaranteed Poland against a German attack. In many ways it appeared a foolhardy gesture as both Britain and France lacked the military power to defend Poland. What caused this U-turn was the speed and brutality of the German occupation of the Czech province of Bohemia (see page 141), which clearly indicated that Hitler could no longer be trusted to respect treaties and guarantees. It is also important to stress that, in the spring of 1939, the French economy, and with it French self-confidence, had made a strong recovery. Thus a tougher policy towards Hitler increasingly appeared to the French government to be a realistic option.

Britain was initially stampeded into this revolutionary new policy by panic-stricken and inaccurate rumours on 17 March that Hitler was about to occupy Romania and seize the oil wells there. Access to these would greatly strengthen the German war industry and enable it to survive any future British naval blockade. At first Britain aimed to contain Germany by negotiating a four-power pact with France, Russia and Poland, but given the intense suspicion with which Russia was viewed by Poland and the other eastern European states this was not a practical policy. Yet when Hitler went on to force Lithuania to hand back the former German city of Memel to the Reich on 23 March, it became even more vital to deter Hitler by any means possible. Thus, Chamberlain and Daladier had little option but to announce on 31 March 1939 an immediate Anglo-French guarantee of Poland against

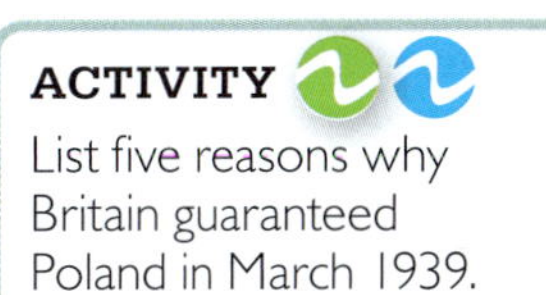
ACTIVITY

List five reasons why Britain guaranteed Poland in March 1939.

external attack. The Polish guarantee was, however, seen as merely the first step towards constructing a comprehensive security system in eastern Europe. Chamberlain hoped to buttress it with a series of interlocking security pacts with other eastern European and Baltic states.

When, on 7 April, Mussolini invaded Albania a similar wave of panic among the eastern Mediterranean states led Britain and France to guarantee both Greece and Romania. In May, Britain considerably strengthened its position in the eastern Mediterranean by negotiating a preliminary agreement with Turkey for mutual assistance 'in the event of an act of aggression leading to war in the Mediterranean area'. By July both Bulgaria and Yugoslavia were beginning to gravitate towards the Anglo-French '**peace bloc**'.

KEY TERM 

Peace bloc A group of states committed to opposing aggressor powers.

The reasons for the Nazi-Soviet Pact

Once war against Poland seemed inevitable, it made good sense for Hitler to gain the support or at least the neutrality of the USSR. As soon as victory was assured over Poland and the Western democracies, Soviet Russia could in due course be dealt with. Britain and France also needed a pact with Russia to build up their 'peace front'. Stalin was now in the enviable position of being able to play off Hitler against Chamberlain and Daladier.

Protracted negotiations between Russia, Britain and France began in April 1939, but both sides deeply mistrusted each other. Stalin's demand that Russia should have the right militarily to intervene in the affairs of the small states on its western borders if they were threatened with internal subversion by the Nazis, as Austria and Czechoslovakia had been in 1938, was rejected outright by the British. They feared that the Russians would use the threat of Nazi indirect aggression as an excuse to seize the territories for themselves. Stalin, on the other hand, was equally suspicious that the democracies were attempting to manoeuvre the Russians into a position where they would have to do most of the fighting against Germany. The British delegate, William Strang (1893–1978), reported during the negotiations:

SOURCE P

Summarise in your own words the message in Source P. To what extent does this source reveal why Stalin's policy towards Nazi Germany changed between 1935 and 1939? (Re-read pages 125–27 and 130.)

Extract from a report by the British ambassador in Moscow, Sir William Seeds, to the Foreign Office 20 March 1939 on Stalin's speeches to the Congress of the Soviet Communist Party.

M. Stalin and various other speakers at the Congress emphasize Soviet readiness to defend the frontiers of the Soviet Union … should they be attacked, the line taken by all of them is that the chief care of those responsible for Soviet foreign policy must be to prevent the Soviet Union from being dragged into the struggle now taking place between the fascist states and the so-called democracies … Those innocents at home who believe that Soviet Russia is only awaiting an invitation to join the Western democracies should be advised to ponder M. Stalin's advice to his party: 'To be cautious and not allow Soviet Russia to be drawn into conflicts by warmongers who are accustomed to have others pull the chestnuts out of the fire.'

The Nazi-Soviet Pact

The Russians thus had ample time to explore the possibility of a pact with Germany, who became genuinely interested in negotiations once the decision was taken on 23 May to prepare for war against Poland. Right through to the middle of August, Moscow continued to keep both options open, but by then the slow pace of the military discussions with Britain and France seems finally to have convinced Stalin that an agreement with Hitler would be preferable. With only days to go before the start of the military campaign against Poland, Hitler was ready to accept Stalin's terms and the Nazi-Soviet Pact was signed on 23 August.

ACTIVITY 

Make a list of reasons why the Second World War broke out. For each reason give a score out of 6 (1 = not important; 6 = very important). Which do you think is the most important reason and why?

Not only did the pact commit both powers to benevolent neutrality towards each other, but in a secret protocol it outlined the German and Russian spheres of interest in eastern Europe: the Baltic states and Bessarabia in Romania fell within the Russian sphere, while Poland was to be divided between the two. Above all, by neutralising Soviet Russia, the pact made an attack on Poland a much less risky policy for Hitler, even if Britain and France did try to come to its rescue. The pact made a German attack on Poland almost inevitable. Hitler counted on France and Britain doing little to attack in the west while Poland would fall easily with a joint invasion from Germany and the USSR.

The outbreak of war

On 22 August 1939, on the eve of the signature of the Nazi-Soviet Pact, Hitler boasted that:

SOURCE Q

Extract from speech made by Hitler to his military commanders on 22 August 1939.

To be sure a new situation has arisen. I experienced those poor worms, Daladier and Chamberlain, in Munich. They will be too cowardly to attack. They won't go beyond a blockade. Against that we have **autarky** *and the Russian raw materials. Poland will be depopulated and settled with Germans. My pact with the Poles was merely conceived of as a gaining of time ... After Stalin's death – he is a very sick man – we will break the Soviet Union. Then there will begin the dawn of German rule of the earth.*

Summarise in your own words the message in Source Q. How far does this source support the view that appeasement was responsible for war in 1939?

KEY TERM

Autarky Economic self-sufficiency.

The omens did indeed look good for Hitler. Although he had failed to convert the Anti-Comintern Pact (see page 135) into a military alliance against Britain and France, he had in May concluded the Pact of Steel with Italy by which Mussolini rashly agreed to support Germany militarily. Privately Mussolini had been assured that Hitler had no intention of going to war for at least three years!

Neither did it appear that appeasement in Britain and France was quite dead. In June, **Lord Halifax**, the British Foreign Secretary, stressed that while Britain would defend Poland against any threat to its independence, this did

KEY FIGURE

Lord Halifax (1881–1959) Viceroy of India, 1926–31, and British Foreign Minister, 1938–40.

not necessarily mean that its existing frontiers could not be altered or the status of Danzig changed.

Overall Hitler had good grounds to be confident. On 23 August he ordered the army to prepare to attack Poland. Before Britain had a chance to consider a last-minute offer to send a negotiator to Berlin, German troops attacked on 29 August. Why was there no repeat of the Munich Conference to prevent war?

- The Polish government would not accept the loss of their western territories to Germany.
- There was no time to talk before Hitler invaded. Once German troops were in Poland the only way for negotiations to take place would have been if they halted or withdrew and that was not possible, for Hitler had to maintain his image as a strong man and would have been difficult in military terms.
- The opinion of the British public had changed. Even when Chamberlain hesitated before declaring war he came under pressure from his own party and from parliament not to repeat what was widely seen as the humiliation of Munich.

ACTIVITY

Discussion point: To what extent did the outbreak of the Second World War in September 1939 mark a failure in Hitler's foreign policy?

War breaks out

Even when, on 1 September 1939, Germany at last invaded Poland, frantic efforts to avert war still continued. Mussolini urged a Four-Power European Conference, and only when it was absolutely clear that Hitler would not

What is the message that Source R is communicating to the German people?

SOURCE R

German troops demolish a Polish frontier barrier during the invasion of Poland which began in September 1939. Poland was rapidly defeated and partitioned between Germany and Russia.

withdraw his troops from Poland did Britain and France declare war on Germany on 3 September. Italy, despite the Pact of Steel, remained neutral, until France was defeated in June 1940, as Mussolini was initially unsure of a speedy German victory and wanted to hedge his bets. German troops completed the occupation of Poland within six weeks and Soviet forces rapidly moved into the areas allocated to them by the Nazi-Soviet Pact.

SUMMARY DIAGRAM

Why did war break out in 1939?

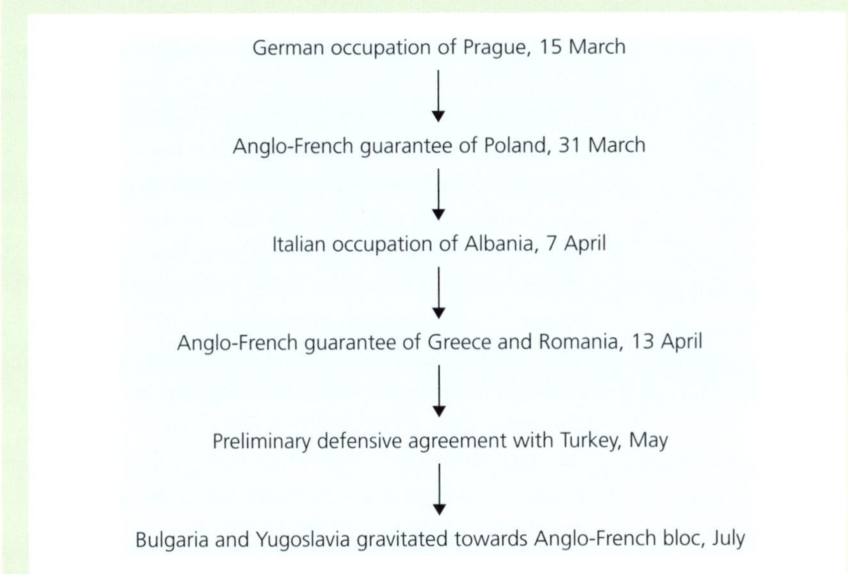

ACTIVITY

Add details and evidence to each of the points to support each factor mentioned in the summary diagram.

What were the causes of the Second World War?

From 1945 to the early 1960s it was accepted that Hitler was the main if not sole cause of the Second World War. In 1961 this view was challenged principally by historians both in Britain and Germany, who argued that Hitler's foreign policy aims were similar to his predecessors' both before 1914 and in the 1920s. These views caused furious debates, which ultimately resulted in a deeper understanding of the causes of the Second World War. Some historians have argued that the Treaty of Versailles, which humiliated but did not permanently weaken Germany, could well be seen as the 'seedbed' of the Second World War. Arguably, the chain of crises that started with the German remilitarization of the Rhineland and ended in the German attack on Poland owed its origins to the Versailles settlement. Others have placed emphasis on the Great Depression. This, at the very least, made the outbreak of the Second World War more likely. It weakened the democracies, helped bring Hitler to power in Germany and strengthened militant nationalism in Japan. While the role of Hitler with his well-documented aims for territorial expansion cannot be overlooked, it does obscure the fact that the British and French governments went to war to maintain their position as great powers rather than to wage a crusade against the evil force of Nazism.

Chapter summary

In 1930 Britain and France, thanks to their victories in 1919, still dominated Europe. By 1937 all this had changed. The Great Depression had weakened the Western democracies, brought Hitler to power in Germany in 1933, and strengthened the power of the army in Japan, which had occupied Manchuria in 1931.

In reaction to German rearmament, France, Britain and Italy formed the Stresa Front in 1935, but this was destroyed by the Abyssinian crisis, which Hitler exploited to remilitarize the Rhineland in March 1936. In July 1936 Italy and Germany intervened on behalf of the Nationalists in the Spanish Civil War, and in November the October Protocols and the Anti-Comintern Pact were signed. It was now the democracies and not Germany that were on the defensive. Thanks to its failure to solve the Manchurian and Abyssinian crises the League of Nations had become an irrelevance. In 1937 Chamberlain launched his appeasement campaign. At Munich he persuaded Hitler to compromise over Czechoslovakia, but in March 1939 Germany occupied Bohemia. This led to the Anglo-French guarantee of Poland and Romania. An attempt to negotiate an alliance with the USSR failed when Stalin signed the Nazi-Soviet Pact. On 1 September Germany invaded Poland.

Refresher questions

1. What was the impact of the Great Depression on international affairs?
2. How did France, Britain and Italy respond to the rise of Hitler, 1933–35?
3. Why did France and Britain propose to the European powers an agreement not to intervene in the Spanish Civil War, and why did this fail?
4. Why did Italy in the spring of 1935 align itself with Britain and France, but in October 1936 sign the October Protocols with Hitler?
5. Why did the League of Nations fail to halt aggression in Manchuria and Abyssinia?
6. How many of his foreign policy aims had Hitler achieved by October 1939?
7. Why did appeasement fail?
8. How did Germany, France and Britain prepare for war, 1936–39?
9. What was the main aim of British policy towards Germany?
10. Why did the USSR sign the Nazi-Soviet Pact in August 1939?

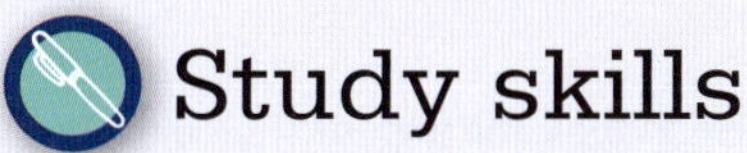

Study skills

Paper 1 guidance: sources

Evaluating sources using contextual knowledge

In answering a source-based question on a set of sources you should aim to establish what the sources say about the issue in the question and group them. You should consider how useful the evidence is by considering provenance but you also need to test the evidence using your own knowledge of the issue.

To take an example from the chapter:

SOURCE A

Extract from an internal French Foreign Office document on the consequences of the German action in remilitarizing the Rhineland, 12 March 1936.

A German success in the Rhineland would likewise not fail to encourage elements which, in Yugoslavia, look towards Berlin. In Romania this will be a victory of the elements of the right which have been stirred up by Hitlerite propaganda. All that will remain for Czechoslovakia is to come to terms with Germany. Austria does not conceal her anxiety. 'Next time it will be our turn.' Turkey, who has increasingly close economic relations with Germany, but who politically remains in the Franco-British axis, can be induced to modify her line. The Scandinavian countries are alarmed.

How useful is this source for the view that the remilitarization of the Rhineland was a major diplomatic defeat for Britain and France?

On 7 March lightly armed German troops marched into the Rhineland, which had been demilitarized by the Treaty of Versailles in 1919. This was therefore a major challenge to the treaty and to the attempt by Britain and France to limit German power on the continent of Europe. The demilitarization of the Rhineland had ensured that, in the event of war with Germany, French troops would be able to cross the Rhine quickly and occupy the great industrial centre of the Ruhr. This source is particularly useful in explaining the potential scale of the diplomatic and strategic defeat suffered by Britain and France. It argues that the remilitarization of the Rhineland, unless reversed, would shift the whole balance of power in Europe away from London and Paris to Berlin. The source points out that in Yugoslavia, Romania and Turkey pro-German forces would now be encouraged to look towards Berlin instead of 'the Franco-British axis'. Even the Scandinavia countries were alarmed about the remilitarization of the Rhineland.

An even greater consequence of the German action was the impact it would have on Austria and Czechoslovakia. The document argues that Czechoslovakia would have to 'come to terms' with Germany, which would mean that it would have to cede the Sudetenland to Germany, while Austria saw quite clearly that 'next time, it will be our turn'. By this the document meant annexation or at least satellite status.

This document is, of course, French. The British government took a more relaxed view of the remilitarization and was unwilling to use force or the threat of force to drive the German troops out, as much of the British public believed that Hitler was merely walking into his own 'back garden'. However, Hitler's policy over the next three years shows how perceptive and useful a source this document is for explaining why the remilitarization of the Rhineland was such a major diplomatic defeat for Britain and France. Although, Romania, Yugoslavia and Turkey did draw closer to Britain and France in 1939, this was only so because Germany had already annexed Austria and the Sudetenland in 1938 and in March 1939 destroyed Czechoslovakia. Emboldened by the chain of successes starting with the remilitarization of the Rhineland, Hitler attacked Poland in September and so triggered the outbreak of the Second World War. The source is useful for showing how the remilitarization of the Rhineland would have such a disastrous 'domino effect'.

Activity

What contextual knowledge would help you judge this source as evidence for this particular issue?

Look at this analysis. Find where the answer has shown what the source is saying about the key issue and highlight. Find any comment on the provenance of the source and highlight in another colour. Find where the answer has used knowledge to assess the source as evidence; highlight in a third colour.

In your next answer, highlight these elements and see if you have written about content, provenance and added any knowledge.

SOURCE B

Extract from Hitler's address of 5 November 1937 to assembled generals, politicians and industrialists, as recorded by Colonel Hossbach who was present.

The aim of German policy was to make secure and to preserve the racial community and to enlarge it. It was therefore a question of space. The German racial community comprised over 85 million people and, because of their number and the narrow limits of habitable space in Europe, constituted a tightly packed racial core such as was not to be met in any other country and such as implied the right to a greater living space than in the case of other peoples. Political conditions pose the greatest danger to the preservation of the German race at its present peak. Germany's future was therefore wholly conditional upon the solving of the need for space, and such a solution could be sought, of course, only for a foreseeable period of about one to three generations. Germany's problem could only be solved by the use of force.

How useful is this source as evidence for the view that Hitler had a long-term plan of conquest based on ideological aims?

This source shows that Hitler's policies of securing 'the racial community' and creating Lebensraum, or living room, would ultimately use force. He refers to the need for living space for the racial community and the threat to the 'preservation of the German race', showing his concern for racial purity and expansion. He says that 'Germany's problems can only be solved by force', indicating a belief that war was planned.

Hitler was addressing a high-powered meeting of generals, Nazi politicians and industrialists. By November 1937 Hitler had managed to build up his armed forces and had ended the restrictions of Versailles, so it is likely he was thinking how to use them. He had spoken of the need for more space for the Aryan people, so the source may well explain his plans. However, he may just have been trying to get support for his plans from industry and the army.

The actions he took after the meeting, however, confirm that he was trying to expand the Reich to include all Germans in the 'Aryan community'. Austria was annexed in 1938 and he forced the French and British to accept the ceding of the German-speaking Sudentenland to Germany. In 1938, after annexing Bohemia, he claimed the German areas of Poland. This was in accord with his beliefs in the 'racial community' expressed in 1937. None of these involved force, merely the threat of force, but with the invasion of Poland in 1939 he did fulfil his plan that force should be used. He did not just take over western Poland but established control over central Poland and German settlers were encouraged to move there to find 'living space'. Thus the source is useful evidence for this intention, even though Hitler might not have had a precise timetable.

Try to make sure that when you answer part (b) questions you incorporate all three elements – interpretation; evaluation by provenance and evaluation by knowledge. Try to offer a distinct view of the usefulness of each source.

Now try to interpret and evaluate all the sources in the question below.

How far do Sources C to F support the view that in August Hitler invaded Poland because he thought there would be little opposition?

SOURCE C

A speech by Hitler to his military commanders, 23 May 1939.

Poland will always be on the side of our adversaries … Danzig is not the objective. It is a matter of expanding our living space in the east … We cannot expect a repetition of Czechoslovakia. There will be fighting. The task is to isolate Poland … Basic principle: conflict with Poland, beginning with the attack on Poland, will be successful only if the West keeps out. If that is impossible, then it is better to attack the West and finish off Poland at the same time. It will be a task of dexterous diplomacy to isolate Poland…

SOURCE D

Extract from a speech made by Hitler to his military commanders on 22 August 1939.

To be sure a new situation has arisen. I experienced those poor worms, Daladier and Chamberlain, in Munich. They will be too cowardly to attack. They won't go beyond a blockade. Against that we have autarky and the Russian raw materials. Poland will be depopulated and settled with Germans. My pact with the Poles was merely conceived of as a gaining of time … After Stalin's death – he is a very sick man – we will break the Soviet Union. Then there will begin the dawn of German rule of the earth.

SOURCE E

Extract from Neville Chamberlain's letter to a friend, Mrs Morton Prince, an American citizen, 16 January 1938.

…as a realist I must do what I can to make this country safe … [The British people] are perfectly aware that until we are fully rearmed our position will be one of great anxiety. They realize that we are in no position to enter light-heartedly upon a war with such a formidable power as Germany, much less if Germany were aided by Italian attacks on our Mediterranean possessions and communications. They know that France, though her army is strong, is desperately weak in some vital spots…

SOURCE F

Extract from a report of 20 March 1939 to the British Foreign Office by the British ambassador in Moscow.

Those innocents who believe that Soviet Russia is only awaiting an invitation to join the Western democracies should ponder M. Stalin's advice to his party: 'To be cautious and not allow Soviet Russia to be drawn into conflicts by warmongers who are accustomed to have others to pull the chestnuts out of the fire…'

Comparing and contrasting two sources

It is important not just to describe each source but to explain how they agree and disagree and what might explain that by looking at the provenance of the different passages. Now Look again at Sources C and D on page 168, which you have used in the above question, and then at the question which follows them. Then read the two answers. Which is the better answer and why?

What accounts for the different view by Hitler of the coming conflict with Poland?

Answer 1

Source C is a message by Hitler to his generals on 23 May. He is telling them that Danzig is not important and that the real objective is gain living space in the East. There will be war with Poland, but will be only successful if the West keeps out. Source D is again from Hitler and is a speech to his military commanders. He is now saying that that the leaders of France and Britain are 'poor worms', who won't attack. He therefore outlines his policy and even foresees the ultimate conquest of the USSR.

Answer 2

The two sources (C and D) both concern the coming conflict with Poland, but differ in the ways Hitler feels this can be achieved. In May Hitler was planning to attack Poland, but was hoping through 'dexterous diplomacy' to isolate Poland and avoid war with the Britain and France. War with these two countries was viewed as a possibility, but nevertheless something to be avoided if at all possible. By 22 August, however, the situation was radically changed by Stalin's decision to sign a pact with Germany. This removed the need for 'dexterous diplomacy' and convinced Hitler that Britain and France would at the very most blockade Germany, but not attack it with land forces. The blockade would now be rendered ineffective by the supply of Russian raw materials. War with the Western allies was therefore something that need no longer be avoided. In both sources Hitler's intention to destroy Poland is made clear, but in Source D Stalin's readines to sign the Nazi-Soviet pact has made Hitler more confident of victory and led him on to reveal more of his long term aims in Poland and eastern Europe. In May he refers to expanding 'living space in the east', and in August he reveals that this will lead to the depopulation of Poland and settlement with Germans. In May he was certainly resolved to go to war against

Poland, but hoping that the war could be localized. By 22 August the imminence of the Nazi-Soviet Pact had given him the confidence to dismiss the threat from Britain and France, and to talk of 'the dawn of German rule of the earth'.

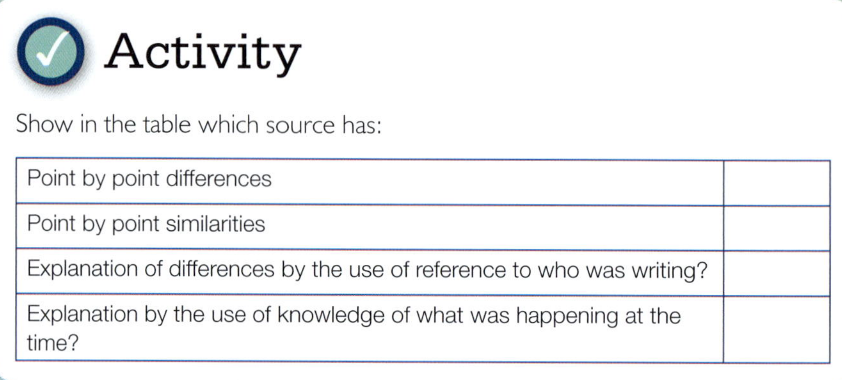

Activity

Show in the table which source has:

Point by point differences	
Point by point similarities	
Explanation of differences by the use of reference to who was writing?	
Explanation by the use of knowledge of what was happening at the time?	

Paper 2 guidance: essay questions

Avoiding descriptive answers and writing analytically

What is meant by a descriptive answer? This is when an answer has relevant supporting knowledge, but it is not directly linked to the actual question. Sometimes the argument is implicit, but even here the reader has to work out how the material is linked to the actual question. Instead of actually answering the question, it simply describes what happened.

It is important that you write an analytical answer rather than simply tell the story. This means you must focus on the key words and phrases in the question and link your material back to them, which is why your essay plan (see pages 55–56) is crucial as it allows you to check you are doing it. You can avoid a narrative answer by referring back to the question as this should prevent you from just providing information about the topic. If you find analytical writing difficult it might be helpful to ensure that the last sentence of each paragraph links back directly to the question.

Consider the following question:

> 'The foreign policy pursued by the Nazi government under Adolf Hitler was the main reason for the outbreak of war in 1939.' How far do you agree?

In order to answer this question you would need to consider the following issues about Nazi foreign policy:

- What were Hitler's ideas and programme for restoring German power?
- In what ways did they help cause a major war with Britain and France?
- How important was Chamberlain's appeasement policy in causing the war?

Then you would need to consider other factors such as:

- the Munich agreement
- the Anglo-French Polish guarantee
- the Nazi-Soviet Pact.

The following is part of a descriptive answer for the question above:

Hitler's first act of aggression was to support a Nazi coup in Austria in 1934. Two years later he remilitarized the Rhineland. Then, after a two-year pause, in quick succession he annexed Austria and the Sudetenland. The British and French Prime Ministers responded to German claims and threats with the policy of appeasement and agreed to these annexations. In March 1939, Hitler, despite the Munich agreement, occupied Bohemia, and Britain and France guaranteed the independence of Poland. The Second World War began on 1 September 1939 after the Nazi-Soviet Pact and the German invasion of Poland.

This paragraph outlines some of the facts about Hitler's foreign policy and actions and is quite well informed but there is little explanation. In what ways could Hitler's foreign policy be seen as the major causes of the war? Could one also blame Chamberlain's appeasement policy or the arms race? The reader has to do a lot of work to find any answers for the question set.

The opening sentence of each paragraph

One way that you can avoid a narrative approach is to focus on the opening sentence of each paragraph. A strong opening sentence will offer a view or idea about an issue relevant to the question, not describe an event or person. You should be able to read the opening sentence of each paragraph and see the line of argument that has been taken in the essay. It is therefore worth spending time practising this skill.

Activity

'The League of Nations had little chance of halting Italy's invasion of Abyssinia in 1936.' How far do you agree?

Look at the following ten opening sentences. Which of these offer an idea that directly answers the question above and which simply give facts?

- Italy had long had ambitions to annex Abyssinia.
- The League possessed no armed forces; it was the responsibility of its members to supply them in order to prevent aggression.
- In December 1934, a clash occurred between Italian and Abyssinian troops at the small oasis of Wal-Wal, some 50 miles (80 km) on the Abyssinian side of the border with Italian Somaliland.
- In March 1936 Hitler remilitarized the Rhineland.
- The Mediterranean was an area where both France and Britain could deploy force and consequently they could have brought pressure on Italy to have negotiated a peaceful settlement with Abyssinia.
- Public opinion in Britain supported the League.
- The Italians had conquered Abyssinia by May 1936.
- Britain and France wanted Italy on their side against Germany, and therefore they were reluctant to condemn Italian aggression in Abyssinia.
- On 18 October the League condemned Italian action.
- The Hoare-Laval Plan proposed placing two-thirds of Abyssinia under Italian control.

QUESTION PRACTICE

In order to practise the skill of directly answering the question, write opening sentences for the following essays:

1 How successfully did Stalin defend the USSR from the Nazi threat between 1933 and 1939?
2 How far was Mussolini a potential ally of Britain and France against Hitler?

EXPLAIN QUESTIONS

It might be helpful also to write opening sentences for the short answer essays below:

1 Explain why appeasement failed.
2 Explain why Chamberlain guaranteed Poland in March 1939.
3 Explain why the Nazi–Soviet Pact was signed in 1939.

China and Japan, 1912–45

This chapter considers the very different histories of China and Japan between 1912 and 1945. It analyzes, on the one hand, the disintegration of China as a unified state and the competing efforts made to restore Chinese power by the **Kuomintang** and the communists, which led to periods of civil war. On the other hand, it looks at the rise of the Japanese Empire, its efforts to subdue China and its ambitions in south-east Asia, which eventually brought it into conflict with and ultimate defeat by Britain and the USA. It considers the history of both these countries under the following headings:

★ What were the implications of the 'warlord era', which affected China 1916–27?

★ How effectively did Chiang Kai-shek deal with the communists in the period 1927–36?

★ Why did the Chinese Communist Party gain support up to 1945?

★ Why did Japan become a military dictatorship in the 1930s and with what consequences?

KEY TERM 

Kuomintang (KMT) Chinese Nationalist party founded by Sun Yat-sen in 1912 and led by General Chiang Kai-shek, 1925–49. It then became the governing party of Taiwan up to 1987.

KEY DATES

1905		Sun Yat-sen announces the Three Principles
1912	**February**	China becomes a republic
1913		Kuomintang (KMT) founded
1916	**June**	Death of President Yuan Shikai
1916–27		Height of 'warlord era' in China
1919	**May**	Protests in Paris and Beijing lead to the May the Fourth Movement
1921		Chinese Communist Party holds first meeting.
1921		Sun sets up revolutionary government in Guangzhou (Canton)
1926 –27		Northern Expedition
1927	**April**	Shanghai falls to KMT and most known communists are massacred (Shanghai massacres)
1928		Chiang becomes Director of the State Council
1929–31		Impact of Great Depression: total Japanese exports fall from 2513 to 1426 million yen
1930		Japanese Prime Minister assassinated by member of right-wing patriotic society
1934–35		Chinese Red Army undertakes the Long March
1937	**July**	Japan attacks China
1940	**27 September**	Tripartite Pact signed by Germany, Italy and Japan
1941	**8 December**	USA declares war on Japan after Pearl Harbor attacks

What were the implications of the 'warlord era', which affected China 1916–27?

For Chinese statesmen seeking to modernize and strengthen the Chinese Republic, the warlords posed a major challenge, which was not overcome until Communist China was established in 1949. The warlords were in effect independent rulers, who could thwart efforts by the central government to reform the state. Individually they could be defeated, but the central government lacked the resources to overthrow them all and to create a strong united Chinese Republic.

The revolution and creation of the Chinese Republic, 1911

In the decade after the defeat of the Boxer Revolts (see page 25), the pressure for reform and change in China grew ever more powerful. Chinese intellectuals increasingly looked to Japan as an example of an east Asian state that was modernising successfully, and could stand up to the Western powers. Chiang Kai-shek (see page 183), the future leader of Nationalist China, for example, studied military strategy in Japan. It was in Japan, too, that Sun Yat-sen formed the United League (*Tongmenghui*) whose policy of the 'Three Principles of the People' was eventually to become the inspiration of Chinese nationalism.

Sun Yat-sen

1866	Born in Guangdong
1886–92	Studied medicine
1905	Formulated the 'Three Principles'
1911	Elected Provisional President of China
1915	Retreated into exile
1919	Refounded the KMT
1921	Set up an independent republic in Guangzhou
1925	Died

Sun Yat-sen was born in Guangdong, the son of a tailor. He then lived with his brother in Hawaii and returned to Hong Kong to study medicine where he became increasingly involved in revolutionary politics and formed the 'Revive China Society'. In 1895 and 1900 Sun was involved in two unsuccessful uprisings and had to escape to Japan and Europe to avoid arrest.

In 1905 he formulated his 'Three Principles' (see page 182), which became his major revolutionary legacy. In 1911, after the uprising in Wuhan (see below), he returned to China and was elected 'Provisional President', but surrendered the position to General Yuan Shikai. When the latter declared himself Emperor of China in 1915, Sun supported his unsuccessful opponents and again had to seek asylum in Japan.

He returned once more to China in 1917 and in 1919 refounded the Kuomintang (KMT), which Yuan had banned. In 1921 he created an independent republic in Guangzhou (Canton) from which he hoped to launch a military expedition to defeat the warlords, who then effectively controlled China. This was unsuccessful, but he did forge links with the USSR, which supplied him with weapons, and he also accepted Chinese communists into the KMT. By 1923 Sun was more interested in propagating the doctrine of the 'Three Principles' than in the practicalities of governing Guangzhou. He died in Beijing in 1924. Posthumously he became a cult figure and 'the father of the nation'. In 1929 Sun's remains were interred in a specially constructed mausoleum in Nanjing.

In November 1908, both the Emperor and the real power behind the throne, the **Empress Dowager Cixi,** died. As the new Emperor, **Puyi**, who had been appointed by Cixi on her deathbed, was only two years old, China was governed by his father, **Prince Chun**, who acted as Regent. Chun sacked the modernizer, General Yuan Shikai, and formed a deeply unpopular and unrepresentative '**clan cabinet**'.

Not surprisingly, this was to meet mounting opposition throughout China. In 1911 the city of Wuhan and seven provinces in southern China declared their independence of the Empire. Initially China was divided: in the south a republic was formed under Sun Yat-sen with its capital in Nanjing, while in the north in Beijing the Empire still existed. Yuan Shikai had been recalled by Chun with instructions to defeat the revolution, but under pressure from the provincial army commanders Puyi was forced to abdicate and the Chinese Republic, which claimed to represent the whole of China, was declared. Sun Yat-sen handed over the presidency to the experienced soldier and politician Yuan Shikai.

General Yuan Shikai

1859	Born
1885	Commander of the Chinese garrison in Korea
1895	Commander of the Beiyang Army
1911	Prime Minister of the Republic of China
1915	Proclaimed himself Emperor of China
1916	Died

KEY FIGURES 

Empress Dowager Cixi (1835–1908) Concubine to the Xianfeng Emperor and, from 1861–1908, as Regent, the effective controller of the Chinese government.

Puyi (1906–67) Last Emperor of China, 1908–12 and July 1917; appointed by the Japanese Emperor of Manchukuo (Manchuria), 1934–45. In 1949 he was imprisoned as a war criminal for ten years.

Prince Chun (1883–1951) Served as Prince Regent, 1908–11. He advised his son against becoming the Emperor of Manchukuo.

KEY TERM 

Clan cabinet A cabinet composed of relatives.

Yuan was born into a reasonably affluent family in Henan and joined the Imperial Army in 1880. Five years later he became the Imperial Resident (or representative) and commander of the Chinese garrison in Korea, but was recalled to Beijing days before the Sino-Japanese war broke out in 1895 (see page 33).

After China's defeat Yuan was appointed to the influential position of Commander of the **Beiyang Army** or First New Army, which was a newly formed elite military force. Thanks to his close links with the influential Dowager Empress Cixi, he was appointed governor of Shandong and defeated the Boxer Rebels (see page 25) in his province. He then became viceroy of the northern Chinese province of Zhili, and turned the Beiyang Army into the strongest force in China. Shortly after Cixi's death in 1908, he was dismissed from these posts, but after the Wuhan uprising he was recalled to court to become Prime Minister.

In 1911 he became President of the newly declared republic of China. Over the next three years Yuan emerged as a dictator, yet his reorganization of the provinces, which gave each governor control of their own armed forces, was to facilitate the emergence of the warlords (see page 179) over the next decade. On 12 December 1915 he had himself proclaimed Emperor, but such was the opposition to this step that he rapidly reappointed himself President on 22 March 1916. Yuan died on 6 June 1916.

KEY TERMS 

Beiyang Army Literally 'North Ocean Army'. A modern Western-style army created in late nineteenth-century China.

Absentee landlord A landlord who owns a property but rents it out to tenants.

Issues facing China: Yuan Shikai and the disintegration of China

Yuan, like Sun Yat-sen, aimed to bring about a revival of Chinese power and to do for China what the Meiji restoration did for Japan after 1868 (see page 32). His failure to achieve this indicates the scale of the problems facing a Chinese government anxious to centralize and reform a disintegrating China. He and his successors faced formidable challenges:

- The countryside was poverty stricken: land prices were dropping, farmers were hit by inflation and **absentee landlords** were driving up rents. Hundreds of thousands of peasants were also rendered homeless by floods and droughts, which led to the formation of secret societies and revolts. Between 1896 and 1911 there were, for instance, 653 insurrections throughout China.
- In the cities bad conditions led to strikes and riots, and it was only in the territory controlled by the foreign concessions (see page 23) that modern industry could flourish independently of the Chinese government.
- The Republic also faced a chronic shortage of money. The provincial governments (see below) retained money which should have gone to the central government in Beijing, and inefficient collection of taxation only yielded about a third of what it should have.
- There was a pressing need for the Beijing government to extend central control over the provinces, but poor communications made this difficult to achieve. In Sichuan, for example, the local gentry were able to ensure that official posts went only to those born in the province, while in the province of Guangdong **Hu Hanmin** and **Chen Jiongming** were able to draw up, independently of Beijing, their own reform programmes.

KEY FIGURES 

Hu Hanmin (1879–1936) Later supporter of Sun Yat-sen and the Kuomintang.

Chen Jiongming (1875–1933) A warlord in Guangzhou. Initially a revolutionary and supporter of Sun Yat-sen, but refused to support his plans for advance in central China in 1920. In 1925 his forces were defeated by the KMT.

- Neither could Beijing rely on the loyalty of the army. After China's defeat by Japan in 1895 new armies had been created, but their loyalty was to their commanders rather than to the government.

Yuan Shikai in power, 1912–16

Once appointed President of China in 1912, Yuan attempted to centralize power in Beijing. He held elections for a national parliament, but when the newly formed Kuomintang Party won, he had its most active campaigner **Song Jiaoren** assassinated and the party banned in 1913. A year later he changed the constitution so that there were no limits to his term of office. He also made enemies of the local gentry and the provincial military commanders by attempting unsuccessfully to abolish China's historic provinces and to place the Republic's armed forces under a central military command.

KEY FIGURE

Song Jiaoren (1882–1913) Founder member of KMT, responsible for its 1913 election victory, but assassinated before he could become Prime Minister.

Nor was he able to solve China's financial problems. The financial situation continued to deteriorate and the annual budgets were works of fiction that bore no relation to reality. The only way to solve the problem was to negotiate foreign loans, but these came at a high cost to Chinese independence. In April 1913 Yuan raised a loan of £10 million with a consortium of six European nations, but this involved the creation of a new **audit office** headed by a European official, whose agreement the Chinese government had to seek before spending any money.

KEY TERM

Audit office A government office that checks how money has been spent.

These policies failed to unite or rejuvenate China, and stirred up intense hostility among patriots and radicals. In 1913, in what was called the 'Second Revolution', seven provinces declared their independence, but were defeated by loyalist troops, causing Sun Yat-sen, who was now highly critical of Yuan, to flee to Japan. Unrest rumbled on and some revolutionaries joined 'the Citizens' Punitive Army', which carried out a guerrilla campaign in central China until it was defeated in 1914. Yuan's restoration of the Empire with himself as Emperor in December 1915 led to the formation of the Anti-Monarchy Army in southern China. Yuan, ill and lacking support from the northern generals who had up to now been loyal to him, had already decided to abdicate just before he died in June 1916.

Power shifts to the warlords, 1916–20

The four years ending in the Five-Day War in July 1920 were a period of accelerating chaos for China. Governments in Beijing could only remain in power with the support of the northern generals, who were increasingly divided among themselves. The key figure during this increasingly anarchic period was the commander of the Beiyang Army, Prime Minister Duan Qirui (see page 38), but his attempts to overcome provincial rivalries and centralize China were opposed by the warlords.

A reconciliation conference in Shanghai aimed at overcoming the divisions between Duan and the warlords failed, and in July 1920 Generals Zhang Zuolin of Manchuria and Wu Peifu of Hunan (see below), in what became called the 'Five-Day War', forced Duan to flee for protection to the Japanese concession in Tianjin. As the historian Jonathan Fenby (2008) has pointed out, the Zhang-Wu victory 'launched the full warlord era that had been brewing since Yuan Shikai's death'.

The warlords

Arguably the independence of the warlords and the need to subdue them were the greatest problems facing Yuan and his successors.

The warlords acted like sovereign monarchs and ruled the territories they controlled as if they were their own kingdoms. They raised taxes, negotiated loans from foreign bankers and waged war or negotiated alliances with other warlords. Above all they had their own armies composed of their followers and sometimes strengthened by mercenaries. By 1925 the warlord armies totalled some 1.5 million men. Whichever warlord temporarily controlled Beijing controlled the central government. Not surprisingly, between 1916 and 1928 there were 26 prime ministers. However, no warlord was strong enough to control China by himself, and so China became what was effectively a patchwork of independent territories each controlled by an individual warlord.

The warlords

The most important warlords during the period 1916–27:

- **Zhang Zuolin** (1875–1928) of Manchuria ('the Old Marshall') who had initially been a bandit and controlled some 300,000 square miles (780,000 km^2) of north-east China. Thanks to Japanese investment, Manchuria was one of the more wealthy areas of China, and consequently Zhang attempted to remain on good terms with the Japanese. However, after his defeat by the KMT in 1928, he was assassinated by the officers in the **Kwantung Army**, who hoped that this would provoke Zuolin's army into taking action against the Japanese and so provide them with an excuse to annex Manchuria.
- **Zhang Zongchang** (1881–1932) of Shandong, the so-called **'Dogmeat General'**, had also been a bandit chief, but after being defeated by his rivals he sought protection from Zhang Zuolin. He became an effective military strategist, who made particularly good use of armoured trains. In 1925 he conquered Shandong, but three years later was forced to seek Japanese protection after being defeated by KMT forces.

KEY TERMS

Kwantung Army
Japanese army guarding south Manchurian railway and stationed in Liaodong Peninsula since 1907.

'Dogmeat General'
Nickname given to Zhang Zongchang because he liked a gambling game called Pal Gow, which in north-eastern China is called 'eating dog meat'.

- **Yan Xishan** (1883–1960) controlled Shanxi province from 1911–49; unlike many of the other warlords, he attempted to modernize and build up its industry.
- **Feng Yuxiang** (1882–1948), the son of a peasant, who had converted to Christianity. In contrast to most of the other warlords he had no territorial base. In 1924 he turned against his main ally, Wu Peifu, and enabled the KMT to seize Beijing.
- **Wu Peifu** (1874–1939) controlled a large area of central China and for a time the government in Beijing. In 1927 he was defeated during Chiang Kai-shek's Northern Expedition and forced to retreat into the interior of Henan.
- In the province of Guangzi, power was exercised by the three-man **Guangzi Group**, which made considerable efforts to modernize the province. Its forces played an important role in the Northern Expedition (see pages 186–88), but the three warlords broke off relations with Chiang Kai-shek, who defeated them in 1929. After the Japanese occupation of Manchuria and invasion of China (see page 210) the Guangzi Group again co-operated with the KMT.
- In Xinjiang, an extensive and predominantly Muslim territory in the west of China, **Yang Zengxin** (1864–1928) ruled quite independently of Beijing. He supported the restoration of the Empire and was so hostile to Bolshevik Russia and communism that he actually banned the construction of factories as these would lead to the growth of a radical working class.
- One of the most savage of the warlords was **Ma Fushing** (1864–1924), who served as commander under Yang Zengxin. He controlled the area around Kashagar, one of the westernmost cities in China, and claimed the region's oil and mineral rights as his personal property. He would kill his enemies by feeding them into a hay-making machine. In the end Yang Zengxin had him executed and his dead body tied to a crucifix for his former subjects to mock and violate.

Some warlords, such as the Guangzi Group, provided a stable government for the provinces they controlled, but they were in a minority. It was quite common for undisciplined warlord troops to work with bandit gangs to terrorize and rob the population. Some of these gangs were small groups; others could number as many as 10,000. Often bandits would co-operate with the warlords, or warlord soldiers might become bandits. Secret societies such as **'The Red Spear' Society** and the anti-Christian **'Big Sword' Society** were formed, which attempted to protect the villages from the ravages of the bandits and warlords.

KEY TERMS 

'The Red Spear' Society Formed by peasants and farmers to protect villages primarily from the warlords, but also from tax collectors and later from communists and the Japanese.

'Big Sword' Society Formed in the 1890s and revived to protect the peasantry against the warlords.

Key
① Yang Zengxin
② Fifty rival generals
③ Long Yun
④ Yan Xishan (The Model Governor)
⑤ Feng Yuxiang (The Christian General)
⑥ Wu Peifu (The Philosopher General)
⑦ Guangxi Clique
⑧ Chen Jiongming/Kuomintang
⑨ Sun Zhuangfang
⑩ Zhang Zongchang (The Dogmeat General)
⑪ Beijing was controlled by Zhang, Wu and Feng at different times
⑫ Zhang Zuolin (The Old Marshall) and Zhang Xueliang (The Young Marshall)
N
Liaoning
Jilin
Inner Mongolia
Liaoing
Xinjiang
Beijing
Tianjin
Hubei
Ningxia
Shanxi
Shandong
Qinghai
Gansu
Jiangsu
Shaanxi
Henan
Anhui
Tibet
Shanghai
Hebei
Zhejiang
Sichuan
Chongqing
Jiangxi
Fujian
Guizhou
Taiwan
Guangdong
Yunnan
Guangxi
Xianggang
Aomen
Hainan
0 100 miles
0 400 km

Figure 4.1 China under the warlords.

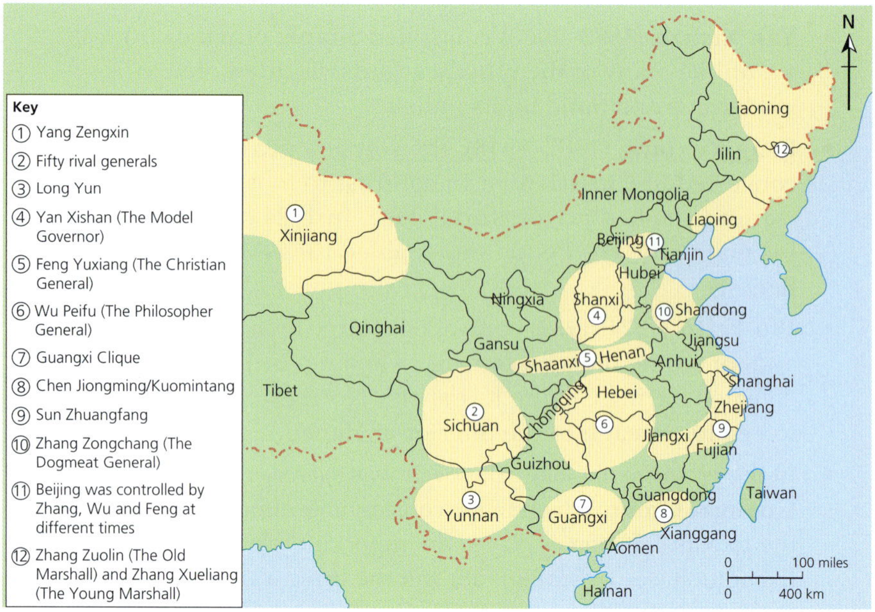

ACTIVITY

To what extent does this map explain China's divisions and weaknesses during the warlord era?

However, the sheer size of China ensured that there were considerable areas that were left untouched by the warlords. Business and industry throve in Manchuria and in the foreign concessions in Shanghai and Guangzou, for example. Elsewhere, however, the picture was much bleaker: unemployment in the countryside was estimated to be around 87 million, the transport infrastructure was primitive and after the end of the First World War the **trade deficit** grew annually. At the Washington Conference in 1922 the Western powers and Japan were ready to assist China to reorganize its finances, but they would not commit themselves to a detailed plan until an effective central government had been formed.

KEY TERM

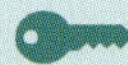

Trade deficit A situation that occurs when a country imports more than it sells.

As we shall see in the next section, the creation of an effective government that could unify China was exactly what the Chinese Nationalists and the young radicals wished to bring about by defeating the warlords and reclaiming the foreign concessions for a new strong, modern Chinese state.

Reasons for and impact of the May the Fourth Movement

Mao Zedong later claimed, when he was the leader of the Chinese Communist Party (see page 193), that it was the workers who had founded the May the Fourth Movement, and at that point took over the leadership of the Chinese revolution. This claim, to quote the historian Jonathan Fenby, was 'utter nonsense'. The Movement, whose intellectual powerhouse was Beijing University, was a result of the frustrations and desire for reform of young Chinese intellectuals, who looked with despair at the state of their country. The movement's members were intent on modernizing China and

ACTIVITY

Prepare a presentation to show the problems facing China in 1920. Write a paragraph on the most challenging problem.

inspired students and intellectuals with the message that China needed to get rid of its **Confucian past** and embrace the values of the modern Western world – democracy, welfare and equality for both sexes and all nations, which were summed up by Sun Yat-sen's 'Three Principles' (see page 182). It sought to replace the old Chinese culture with the most advanced Western ideas and supported the equality of the sexes and female liberation. One leading member, the academic **Chen Duxiu**, argued that what China needed was a 'Mr Science and a Mr Democracy' to enable it to compete with the West.

It was the widespread protests in Beijing on 4 May that led to the formation of the May the Fourth Movement. Young Chinese Nationalists were incensed that in 1919 the former German concessions in Shandong (see page 65) were to be given to Japan rather than returned to China. Japan, after all, had sent no troops to France, while China had sent 100,000 labourers to the Western Front. In Beijing on 4 May some 3000 students rioted in protest against the decision and beat up a former Chinese ambassador to Tokyo. The following month in Paris Chinese students surrounded the hotel where the Chinese delegation were staying in order to prevent their country's diplomats from going to Versailles to sign the treaty.

KEY TERM

Confucian past The philosophy of Confucius (551–479 BC), which stresses the importance of practical moral matters, was adopted by the Chinese Empire as the basis of its education system and the imperial exam system for the civil service.

KEY FIGURE 

Chen Duxiu (1879–1942) Revolutionary socialist, teacher, philosopher and writer; one of the founders of the Chinese Communist Party, and its General Secretary, 1921–27. He was expelled from the party in 1929.

SOURCE A

The Manifesto of the students of Beijing (1919).

Japan's demand for the possession of Qingdao [Tsingtao] and other rights in Shandong is now going to be acceded to in the Paris Peace Conference. Her diplomacy has secured a great victory – and ours has led to a great failure.

The loss of Shandong means the destruction of the integrity of China's territory. Once the integrity of her territory is destroyed, China will soon be annihilated. Accordingly we students today are making a demonstration march to the Allied legations, asking the Allies to support justice. We earnestly hope that all agricultural, industrial, commercial and other groups of the whole nation will rise and hold citizens' meetings to strive to secure our sovereignty in foreign affairs and to get rid of the traitors at home.

This is the last chance for China in her life and death struggle. Today we swear two solemn oaths with all our countrymen. First China's territory may be conquered, but it cannot be given away. Second, the Chinese people may be massacred but they will not surrender.

Our country is about to be annihilated. Up brethren!

How useful is Source A for showing why there was discontent in China by 1919?

Impact of the Movement

By the early 1920s some of the Movement's members hoped that a Chinese equivalent of Mustafa Kemal, the Turkish leader (see page 72), or even Gandhi in India, would emerge to lead China. Others, like Chen Duxiu, looked to communism. Bolshevik Russia quickly exploited this and sent agents to help organize the new party. In 1921 the Chinese Communist Party (CCP) held its first congress. Among those who attended was the future Communist ruler of China, Mao Zedong (see page 193). Although the Movement stood little chance against the power of the Chinese warlords, its ideals would help transform Chinese society and culture in the coming decades.

Reasons for the growth of the Kuomintang Party under Sun Yat-sen

As Provisional President of China in 1912 and then head of the KMT administration in Guangzhou in 1923, Sun Yat-sen (see page 174) had proved to be an ineffective politician and was known as 'Sun the Windbag' among the merchants in Canton. Nevertheless, for all his inadequacies, he became the symbol of Chinese nationalism and his Three Principles, which were formulated in 1905, its slogan. After his death in 1925 he became a legendary figure, whose ideological legacy seemed to offer China the chance of escaping what Jonathan Fenby calls 'the warlord jungle'.

SOURCE B

Extracts from the 'Three Principles of Sun Yat-sen', which were repeated in his book, *Fundamentals of National Reconstruction* (1923).

The principles which I have held in promoting the Chinese revolution were in some cases copied from our traditional ideals, in other cases modelled on European theory … they are described as follows:

1 The Principle of Nationalism

…Externally we should strive to maintain independence in the family of nations, and to spread our indigenous civilization as well as to enrich it by absorbing what is best in world civilization, with the hope that we may forge ahead with other nations towards the goal of ideal brotherhood.

2 The Principle of Democracy

…All through my revolutionary career I have held the view that China must be made a republic. While a constitutional monarchy may not arouse deep resentment in other countries … it will be an impossibility in China. This is from a historical point of view. If a republican government is adopted, there will be no contention; a constitution must be adopted to ensure good government…

Re-write this extract from the 'Three Principles' in your own words. What does Source B reveal about Sun's ambitions for the future of China?

3 The Principle of Livelihood

With the invention of modern machines, the phenomenon of uneven distribution of wealth in the West has become all the more marked. I saw with my own eyes the instability of their economic structure … I felt that, although the disparity of wealth under our economic organization is not as great as in the West, the difference is only in degree, not in character.

The situation will become more acute when the West extends its economic influence to China … After comparing various schools of economic thought; I have come to the realization that the principle of state ownership is most profound, reliable and practicable. I have therefore decided to enforce the principle of the people's livelihood simultaneously with the principles of nationalism and democracy, with the hope to achieve our political objective and nip economic unrest in the bud.

Sun Yat-sen and the Nationalist Republic of Guangzou

In 1919 Sun refounded the Kuomintang (KMT), and three years later he returned to Guangzou together with his military adviser Chiang Kai-shek. Guangzou was the most radical and revolutionary city in China and under the control of the warlord and former revolutionary Chen Jiongming, who initially welcomed Sun to use Guangzou as his base. Chen Jiongming was himself a reformer. He tightly controlled military expenditure, and Chen Duxiu, one of the key figures in the May the Fourth Movement (see above), was in charge of education, which was allocated 20 per cent of the government's budget.

Chiang Kai-shek

1887	Born
1906	Entered military academy
1919	Joined Sun Yat-sen at Guangzhou
1925	Leader of KMT
1928–34	Head of Nanjing government
1937–45	Led war against Japan
1949	Defeated by Communists in civil war and fled to Taiwan
1975	Died

Chiang was born into a prosperous middle-class family of salt merchants. He studied at the Baoding Military Academy in China and then in Japan where under the influence of his fellow Chinese students he became convinced that a Chinese republic needed to replace the Empire. He subsequently joined the Tongmenghui (see page 174). From 1909–11 he served in the Japanese army, returning to China in 1911 where he became one of the founder members of the KMT.

Chiang was a loyal ally of Sun Yat-sen, who appointed him commandant of the Whampoa military academy. In 1926 he became the leader of the KMT and launched the successful Northern Expedition. In 1927 he broke with the Communists and had thousands of them in Shanghai and elsewhere murdered. By 1928 the KMT theoretically controlled much of China, but Chiang continued to be challenged by the Communists, warlords and then, after 1937, the Japanese.

In 1941, after Pearl Harbor (see page 213), Nationalist China under the KMT became one of the major Allied powers, and in 1946 was given a permanent seat on the **Security Council** of the United Nations, which had replaced the League of Nations. Chiang was, however, faced with a renewed challenge from the Communists in 1945 and China was again plunged into a civil war. In December 1949 Chiang was forced to flee to Taiwan, where under protection of the USA he appointed himself President of China, but he never set foot on mainland China again and died in 1975.

KEY TERM

Security Council One of the most important councils of the United Nations, with powers to authorize peace-keeping operations and sanctions.

Sun's aim was to use Guangdong as a base from which to launch a military expedition in an ambitious attempt to unify China. In this he anticipated the intention of Chiang's Northern Expedition of 1926 (see page 186), but instead of advancing over land with overwhelming force, he organized small flotillas of boats on the rivers leading towards northern China. The 1922 expedition was to prove a complete failure. Sun retreated back to Guangzhou where he quarrelled with Chen and to save his life had to escape to Hong Kong.

However, with money from expatriate Chinese in the USA he was able to stage yet another comeback. He exploited Chen's growing unpopularity in Guangzhou, which was caused by ever increasing taxes, and paid a mercenary army to drive him out of the city. In February 1923, together with Chiang, he returned to the city and formed a new government. Sun left the day-to-day administration to Chen Duxiu and his colleagues and concentrated on spreading the doctrine of the Three Principles, which the KMT in January 1924 adopted as its guiding ideology. Sun became the KMT's life president.

Sun's priority was still to defeat the warlords. To achieve this he optimistically hoped that he would be able to gain the support of the Western powers. In December 1923, in apparent contradiction to his Nationalist convictions, he even suggested privately that the USA, Italy, Britain, Germany and France should occupy the main cities in China. Then, after national elections had been held, they would gradually revert back to Chinese control, once the Chinese were capable of self-government. The suggestion was rejected as impracticable by the Western powers, who had no desire to be sucked into the complexities of Chinese politics.

KEY FIGURES 

Borodin (Michael Gruzenberg) (1884–1951) Soviet adviser to the KMT. In 1927 he returned to the USSR after Chiang purged the communists in his party.

Galen (Vasily Blyukher) (1889–1938) Soviet military adviser to KMT, who played a key role in its military successes, 1925–27.

Soviet aid to the Kuomintang

Like the Western powers, the USSR also refused to intervene militarily to defeat the warlords. Nevertheless, it offered to send two advisers, with the code names **Borodin** and **Galen**, to organize the KMT along the lines of the Russian Communist Party and to form a modern army based on the Soviet model. He hoped that this would strengthen Soviet influence in China.

At the KMT Party Congress in January 1924, Sun agreed to model the KMT along Soviet lines. This ensured that essentially an undemocratic party dictatorship was created which dominated the Guangzou government, but Sun was careful to limit Soviet influence as he had no intention of the KMT becoming a communist party. Communists were therefore allocated only 10 out of 41 seats on the **Central Executive Committee**, but they did head the influential Organization Department, and in 1926 a communist, Mao Zedong, the future communist leader of China (see page 193), took over the Propaganda Department.

KEY TERM 

Central Executive Committee The governing committee of the KMT.

Creation of the National Revolutionary Army

Galen played a key role in advising Chiang on the formation of the National Revolutionary Army (NRA), which after 1928 was simply known as the

National Army. Galen optimistically believed that a small well-trained army modelled on the Soviet Red Army would rapidly defeat the warlords. A military academy was set up on Whampoa Island just outside Guangzou under Chiang to train the officers for the NRA. In 1925, Chiang, who was appointed commander-in-chief of the NRA, also made sure that it was politically independent of its Soviet advisers.

Chiang Kai-shek becomes head of the KMT

Chiang was dismissed by his rivals in the KMT as a soldier with no experience of the intricacies of civilian government. However, this was seriously to misjudge his political skills. His control of the NRA gave him a unique position in Chinese politics, which enabled him to become the leader of the KMT and ultimately of Nationalist China.

Initially after Sun's death in March 1925 the 'National Government of the Chinese Republic' was proclaimed in Guangzou under **Wang Jingwei**. Yet Chiang as the head of the newly formed NRA rapidly emerged as the real power in the city, as was shown by the events of the summer of 1925 when he had in quick succession to defeat a mutiny by mercenary troops, keep order in Guangzou at a time of strikes and demonstrations against the foreign concessions, and then defeat an attempt by Chen Jiongming to reoccupy the city.

Chiang's success ensured that he now became part of the **triumvirate** together with Wang and Borodin, the Soviet political adviser, which now controlled Guangzou. In March 1926 Chiang skilfully exploited the absence of Borodin in northern China and the onset of Wang's diabetes to strengthen his position. He removed key Communist officials, including Mao, from their positions and allegedly for their own good put the Soviet advisers into protective custody. Borodin on his return had no option but to accept Chiang's **coup d'état** and Wang fled to France.

KEY FIGURE 

Wang Jingwei (1883–1944) Member of the left wing of the KMT and critic of Chiang. In 1940 he formed a pro-Japanese government in Nanjing in opposition to both the communists (CCP) and KMT.

KEY TERMS 

Triumvirate A ruling group of three people.

Coup d'état A sudden action resulting in a change of government.

The KMT in 1926: poised to go on the offensive

Since being refounded in 1919, over the next seven years the KMT developed into a formidable political and military force. Sun Yat-sen may well have been an ineffective politician and an even worse military leader, but his role in building up the KMT was of key importance:

- By 1923 Sun had secured Guangzou, one of the wealthiest cities in China, as a base for the KMT and set up a republican government there.
- He failed to gain support from the West, but accepted advisers from the USSR. He accepted much of their political and military advice, but made sure that the KMT would not become dominated by them.
- He also agreed to create the elite military school for officers at Whampoa under the leadership of Chiang in 1924, with the express aim of strengthening the KMT as a revolutionary, nationalist force.
- These officers were to become the leaders of the NRA, which was founded in 1925.

ACTIVITY 

Write a paragraph about Sun Yat-sen. Make sure you include a supported judgement as to why he played an important role in China.

- Above all Sun's Three Principles became the official ideology of the KMT, which potentially enabled it to appeal to a wide cross-section of Chinese opinion. Sun, to quote historian Jonathan Fenby (2008), was 'the figurehead round which the regime in Guangdong [province] and Kuomintang supporters elsewhere in China gravitated'.

By March 1926 both the KMT and NRA were controlled by a single individual – Chiang – and together formed the strongest force in China.

The Northern Expedition

The Northern Expedition was a determined attempt to destroy the warlords and unify China. Chiang did succeed where Sun had failed in fighting a brilliant campaign. As the *North China Daily News* observed, the KMT achieved amazing things. No longer were the northern warlords the dominant force in China. At the cost of 25,000 casualties the KMT won control of half a million square miles (1.3 million km^2) and 170 million people (see the map on page 180), but Chiang's very success led to major splits in his government and also attempts to eliminate the Communists, which eventually escalated into a full civil war.

What can we learn from Source C about the aims of the KMT?

SOURCE C

Extract from a KMT government statement. Chiang as head of the KMT government announced on 1 July 1926 that:

To protect the welfare of the people we must overthrow all warlords and wipe out reactionary power so that we may implement the Three People's Principles and complete the National Revolution.

The KMT gave Chiang full command of the military expedition, the aim of which was to carry out Sun Yat-sen's ambition of unifying China by advancing north and wiping out the power of the warlords. On the face of it the Northern Expedition seemed an overambitious plan. The warlords had far larger armies, the financial resources of KMT were limited and its base in Guangzou was still in a state of turmoil as a result of labour unrest. Despite his coup, Chiang also had bitter critics within the KMT, who mistrusted his dictatorial tendencies.

On the other hand Chiang did have some major advantages over the warlords:

- The KMT was a dynamic political force with an ideology, which potentially attracted all those who wanted to see a strong modern China – such as nationalists, democrats, communists, modernizers, liberals, businessmen and financiers in Shanghai.
- The NRA was well organized and trained and generously supplied with equipment by the USSR.
- The Communist wing of the KMT was able to win the support of the peasants to turn them against the warlords by promising land reform.
- Chiang also appealed to many of the enemies of the central and northern warlords such as Tang Shengzi, a former regional commander in Hunan, who had been defeated by allies of Wu Peifu.

ACTIVITY

Write a brief explanation of the following terms: War Lords, The 'Three Principles', Kuomintang Party, the May The Fourth Movement.

The successful advance from Canton to Wuhan, July–October 1926

In three months the KMT achieved impressive success. It first defeated the warlord Wu Peifu and his allies in Hunan and then advanced northwards towards Wuhan, which was captured on 10 October 1926 (see the map on page 180). The KMT administration and Borodin, its Soviet adviser, who had now moved up from Guangzhou to Wuhan, advised Chiang to advance further northwards and capture Beijing. Chiang, however, preferred to capture Nanjing, as it was where Sun Yat-sen had proclaimed the first Chinese republic in 1912 (see page 178), and then move on to occupy the wealthy city of Shanghai.

The NRA and its allied forces now numbered some 260,000 soldiers, among whom there was a particularly effective female group, the '**Dare to Die Unit**' led by 'Canton's Joan of Arc'. Chiang advanced eastwards into Jiangxi where he met stiff opposition from the local warlord, **Sun Chuanfang**, and victory was only assured after Galen drew up new plans for a counter-offensive with air support. On 18 December the NRA seized Fuzhou, the capital of Fujian.

Later the CCP would claim that it was the Communists who had achieved these successes. Certainly there were Communist-inspired peasant uprisings and in places workers' strikes – in Changsha in Hunan, for instance, workers' organizations expelled Wu Peifu's forces. Yet in the final analysis it was a combination of the NRA's military power and Chiang's bribery of the warlords' generals, persuading some of them to defect to the KMT, that was decisive in his military successes.

Preparations for the advance to Nanjing and Shanghai

In his preparations for the advance Chiang showed himself to be as much part of the warlord culture of his times as the representative of a new liberal China. This can be seen in the way he dealt with the threat to the KMT posed by the Communist trade unions in Shanghai. The unions were planning to exploit the chaos that would follow the initial liberation of the city by the NRA, to set up a **soviet** which would effectively rule the city. To counter this, Chiang was offered support by **'Pockmarked' Huang**, the most powerful figure in Shanghai's underworld, in exchange for giving him a free hand to develop his businesses in prostitution, the opium trade and gambling. An offer, as we shall see below, he later accepted.

He was also advised by the wife of H.H. Kung, the financier and Industry Minister in the KMT government in Wuhan, that if he did not gain the support and protection of the Shanghai businessmen, he would be assassinated by the Communists. To win their support Chiang agreed to appoint H.H. Kung to the post of Prime Minister and marry his wife's younger sister, **Soong Meiling**.

KEY TERMS 

'Dare to Die Units' Suicide squads, which volunteers joined to achieve martyrdom in fighting the enemies of China. In Guangzou such a unit was led by a woman, who was compared to Joan of Arc (1412–30), the French heroine of the Hundred Years' War.

Soviet Communist elected council after the model of those initially set up in the USSR.

KEY FIGURES 

Sun Chuanfang (1885–1935) Warlord, who controlled Jiangsu, Fujian, Anhui and Jiangxi and was defeated by the NRA.

'Pockmarked' Huang (Huang Jinrong) (1868–1953) A prominent gangster in Shanghai, who exploited contacts with the police force in the French concession to further his criminal activities.

Soong Meiling (1897–2003) Sister-in-law of Sun Yat-sen. As the 'First Lady of China' she later rallied the Chinese against Japan and made speaking tours of the USA during the Second World War.

ACTIVITY 

Write a paragraph about the Northern Expedition. Make sure you explain the decisive factor(s) in its success.

The advance to Shanghai and Nanjing, January–March 1927

In the first months of 1927 the NRA advanced steadily towards Nanjing and Shanghai. Opposition from the 'Dogmeat General', Zhang Zongchang, who controlled the province of Shandon, was broken in early March, and it was now only a matter of time before both cities fell to Chiang. Yet just as he was on the brink of success, the civilian government in Wuhan attempted to subject him to stricter control, accusing him of being a dictator. After a momentary failure of nerve Chiang decided that he could best defend himself by stepping up the pace of his advance. He won the support of key officials and regional commanders of the Dogmeat General through bribery, which allowed his troops to advance unchallenged further down the Yangtze. He also eliminated potential Communist opposition by allowing his soldiers to execute any CCP members who fell into their hands.

The situation in Shanghai on the eve of occupation by the KMT

With relations between the Communists and Nationalists rapidly deteriorating, the strong Communist influence in Shanghai represented a considerable threat to Chiang. In theory the Shanghai Communists were allies, but in reality they had their own aims and wished to set up an independent soviet in the city. When Chiang's forces approached Shanghai two general strikes broke out in quick succession, involving some 100,000 workers in an attempt to undermine the Dogmeat General's defences of the city. To ensure the strikers' defeat:

- Chiang delayed his advance until the warlord had defeated the first strike and executed hundreds of workers.
- When the second general strike broke out Chiang agreed to the plan that he had already discussed with 'Pockmarked' Huang (see above): a private army formed by the gangland boss, Du Yuesheng (nicknamed 'Big Ears'), would suppress the strike before the Nationalists reached the centre of the city.

KEY FIGURE 

General Bai Chongxi (1893–1966) Chinese general in the NRA and ruler of Guangzi province as warlord.

The fall of Shanghai and Nanjing, March 1927

Little resistance was offered to the 3000 NRA troops under **General Bai** when they advanced into the southern suburbs of Shanghai on 18 March. The Dogmeat General's soldiers put up no resistance, and tried to escape to the foreign concessions. The following day the Nationalist Sixth Army entered Nanjing. Again the warlord's army broke and its soldiers looted, raped and burnt as they fled.

Chiang had indeed won two great victories, but their consequences were to enflame the divisions within the KMT between the Communists and Nationalists, as we shall see in the next section.

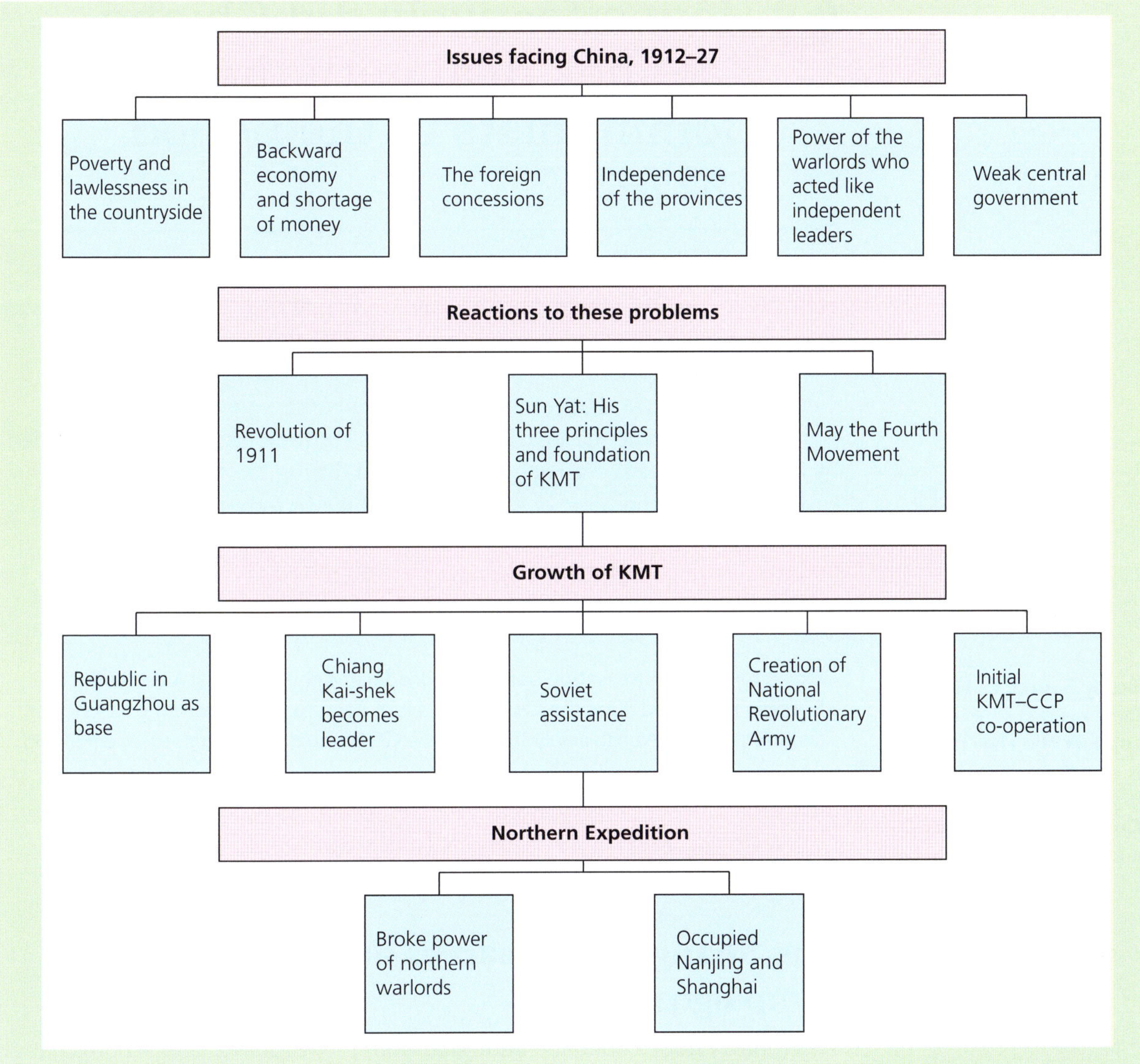

SUMMARY DIAGRAM

What were the implications of the 'warlord era', which affected China from 1916–27?

ACTIVITY

Using information in this section, write down information to support the following views:

1 'Chiang was a divisive and ineffective leader.'

2 'By 1927 the KMT under Chiang had the potential to unite China.'

Then write a paragraph explaining which view you support.

2 How effectively did Chiang Kai-shek deal with the Communists in the period 1927–36?

The Communists presented a major challenge to Chiang as they were subtle political opponents, who did not hesitate to change their tactics when this was required. Essentially they were opportunists. If they saw a chance to seize power, they would take it, but equally they were able to take the long-term view and work towards a revolution that might take a decade or more to achieve. On the other hand, compared to the battle-hardened Nationalists led by Chiang, they lacked an effective army and during the decade 1927–36 were several times on the verge of complete defeat by his forces. They were saved from elimination by the fact that Chiang faced other enemies, the warlords and the Japanese, as well as challenges within the KMT.

Study Source D. How far does this source support the view that it was the organization of the Communists that was a key to their survival?

SOURCE D

Extract from a conversation between Borodin and the journalist Vincent Sheen. Borodin remarked after the Communists had been expelled from the KMT administration in Wuhan in July 1927 that the CCP would continue to survive. He said:

It will go underground. It will become an illegal movement, suppressed by counter-revolution and beaten down by reaction and imperialism, but it has learnt how to organize, how to struggle. Sooner or later, a year, two years, five years from now, it will rise to the surface again. It may be defeated a dozen times, but in the end it must conquer…

The Shanghai massacres and extermination campaigns

When NRA troops liberated Shanghai from the warlord Zhang Zhongchang, Chiang feared an immediate challenge. A general strike had been called (see page 188) and it was feared that the CCP would form a soviet and seize power. In anticipation of this, foreign Communists flocked into the city. Tension was further raised when a raid on the USSR's legation in Beijing in early April not only resulted in the arrest of several Chinese Communists but also the seizure of documents, which apparently revealed plans for a Communist revolution in China.

Chiang's response to these threats had already been prepared (see page 188). On 12 April 1927 Nationalist soldiers and the militia formed by the Shanghai gang leader, 'Big Ears' Du attacked the Communists' strongholds, and shot and bayoneted on the streets anyone suspected of being a Communist. Altogether between 5000 and 10,000 people were killed in Shanghai. The **'White Terror'** rapidly spread to the neighbouring regions Huangzhou, Hunan and Guangzhou.

KEY TERM 

'White Terror' Terror practised by nationalist or reactionary forces.

The consequences of the massacres

The massacres failed to crush the Communists and started in the long term, to quote the historian Jonathan Fenby (2008), 'a violent power struggle between **left** and **right** that would take millions of lives in 22 years of national dislocation'. The Shanghai massacres also intensified the split within the KMT. In Wuhan, Chiang was expelled from the party and denounced as a counter-revolutionary, while the policy of the united front with the Communists was affirmed. This policy was, however, rejected by Stalin, who drew the conclusion from the Shanghai massacres that the CCP should build up an independent Red Army and effectively take over the KMT. This decision was to weaken the CCP still further and to play into Chiang's hands:

- It paved the way for the two wings of the party to unite and to accept Chiang as its leader (see page 197).
- The CCP was weakened even further by attempting to carry out Stalin's instructions for a more aggressive policy. Uprisings in Nanchang and the port of Shantou were rapidly defeated in July 1927.
- In December, again on Stalin's orders, the Communists rose up in Guangzhou, but were ruthlessly crushed. Altogether some 5700 Communists or alleged Communists were murdered.
- The KMT broke off relations with Moscow and closed Soviet legations and offices in China, which ensured that no money reached the CCP.

KEY TERMS 

Left Term used to denote parties stretching from the Liberals to the Communists.

Right Term used to denote parties stretching from Conservatives to Nazis or Fascists.

SOURCE E

On 11 December 1927 the CCP under Stalin's orders staged an uprising in Guangzou. A soviet was set up, police stations seized and officers and merchants were shot. However, the uprising lacked popular support and was ruthlessly crushed.

What information does Source E convey about Chinese politics in 1927?

KEY FIGURES 

Li Lisan (1899–1967)
Leader of the CCP, 1928–30.

Zhou Enlai (1898–1976)
Key ally of Mao and later Prime Minister of Communist China, 1949–76.

The year 1927 was a disastrous one for the CCP. According to one CCP source nearly 38,000 Communists had been killed. The chances of the party's survival were also not helped by the advice they received from Moscow. Galen and Borodin had been both replaced by new advisers and the CCP was firmly under Soviet influence. Its new leaders, **Li Lisan** and **Zhou Enlai**, were based in Shanghai. Li, following the example of the Russian Bolshevik Party, imposed an iron discipline on the CCP, rebuilt the Red Army and argued that the party should concentrate its efforts chiefly on the cities. Here the leadership was obediently following the orthodox Marxist belief that revolution would start in the cities. In fact the CCP was at its weakest in the big cities where it was persecuted by the KMT and its gangland allies.

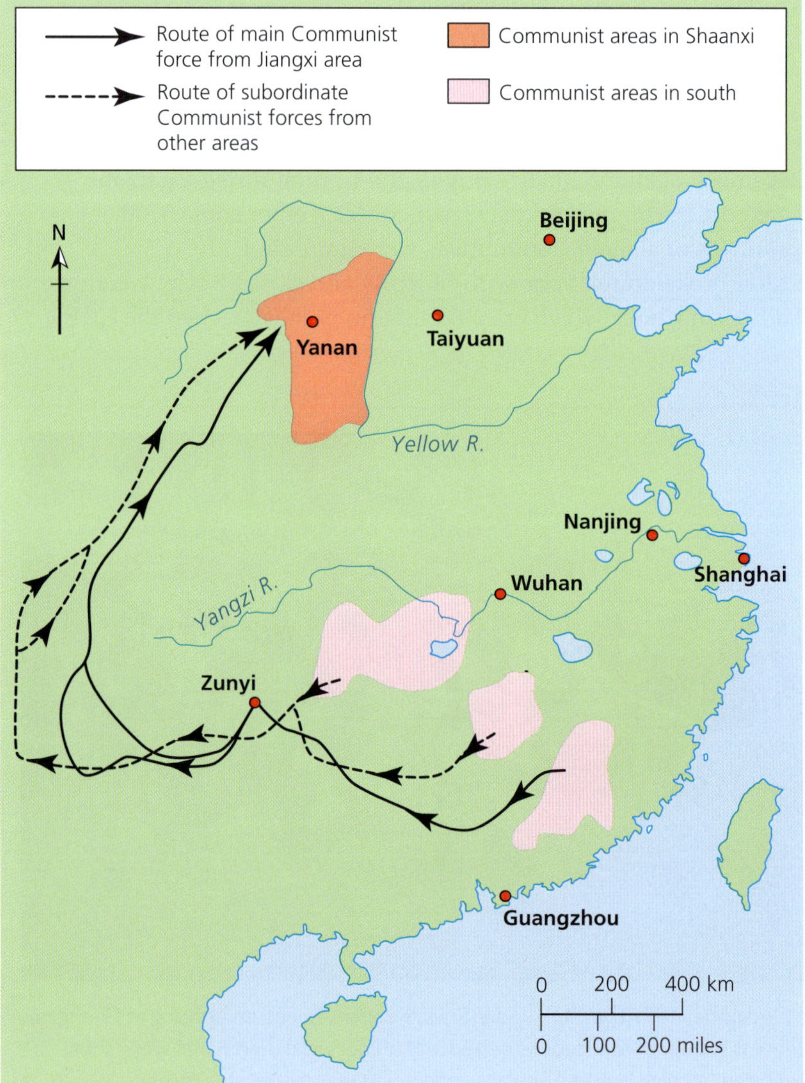

Figure 4.2 The route of the 1934–35 Long March.

ACTIVITY

What does this map reveal about the CCP's tactics in 1934–35?

The Long March, 1934–35

The key to the survival of the CCP during the years immediately after the Shanghai massacres was the creation of some 12 rural bases in remote regions in the countryside. In the mountains of southern Hubei, for example, 200 Communist **partisans** fortified a small area which later expanded into the large base of **E-yu-wan** and were able to recruit thousands of local peasants made desperate by bad harvests and heavy rain. In south-east China, Mao himself set up a base in the mountains of Jiangxi. So while the Long March was unique in scale, it was in fact following earlier precedents. To escape elimination the CCP could only survive by withdrawing to remote areas, where Nationalist troops would find it difficult to subdue them.

KEY TERMS 

Partisans Resistance fighters or guerillas.

E-yu-wan The name is an abbreviation for the area the Yenan base eventually covered on the frontiers of Henan and Anhui.

Politbureau The political Bureau of the Central Committee of the Communist Party.

Five-Year Plans Plans to modernize and expand the economy over a five-year period.

The CCP on the defensive, 1928–34

Mao Zedong

1893	Born
1921	Founder member of the CCP
1934	Led the Long March
1935–45	Created Yenan soviet
1945–49	Defeated the Nationalists in the civil war
1949	Founded the People's Republic of China
1976	Died

Mao was the son of a prosperous small-scale farmer. As a young man he was influenced by the Chinese revolution of 1911, Sun Yat-sen, and then the May The Fourth Movement of 1919. He became a Communist while working as a librarian at Beijing University and was appointed Party Secretary for the Hunan province branch of the CCP. He was willing to collaborate with the Kuomintang, and during 1922–27 headed the Peasant Department. After the Shanghai massacres and the KMT's break with the Communists, Mao was appointed the commander-in-chief of the Red Army and led the unsuccessful 'Autumn Harvest uprising'. He then went on to establish the Communist base in Jiangxi, which by 1931 covered 10,000 square miles (26,000 km^2). There he exercised a ruthless control, purging thousands of his enemies.

In 1930, after a series of defeats by the Nationalists, Mao was declared Chairman of the Soviet Republic of China, but three years later he was marginalized by Bo Gu, who had been sent to ensure that he obeyed Stalin's instructions. In 1934 he took part in the Long March and defeated his political rivals to become the effective head of the CCP as Chairman of the **Politbureau**.

After the outbreak of war with Japan Mao agreed to an alliance with the Kuomintang to form a united front to defend China. It was an uneasy truce, which after increasing tension and clashes broke down in 1946. Chiang was defeated in 1949 and the People's Republic of China was proclaimed on 1 October with Mao as Chairman of the ruling CCP. Over the next 25 years he turned China into a Communist society, ruthlessly eliminating 'class enemies', collectivizing agriculture and through a series of **Five-Year Plans** building a state-controlled industrial base.

Between 1930 and 1934 Nationalist pressure on the CCP intensified. Its organization in Shanghai was smashed in 1931 and many leading Communists were killed. Chiang also planned a further major campaign against the CCP's bases but at the last moment his attention was distracted by the Japanese occupation of Manchuria in September 1931 (see page 146). A year elapsed before he could resume the campaign with an attack on the E-yu-wan base. This was so effective that, to survive, the Communist forces led by **Zhang Guotao** had rapidly to evacuate E-yu-wan. In an operation that anticipated the Long March they set up a new base in the security of the remote region of Sichuan. Ironically Mao, who was later to use similar tactics with the 'Long March', denounced Zhang for running away, accusing him of 'warlordism and flightism'. One reason for this accusation was that Zhang was one of his political rivals for the control of the party.

KEY FIGURE 

Zhang Guotao (1897–1979) Leader of E-yu-wan base and rival of Mao. Zhang later defected to the Nationalists.

In 1933 Chiang's campaign against the Communists was again interrupted when the Japanese occupied Jehol and it was not until he negotiated a ceasefire with them, the Tanggu Truce of May 1933, that he was free to continue his campaign against the CCP. This time the Nationalists launched a well-prepared attack on the Jiangxi base: a blockade cut off its food supplies, new roads were built for the movement of Nationalist forces and some 150 planes were deployed. By the end of September 1934 Chiang's troops were poised to overrun the base, and the Jiangxi soviet came to the conclusion that the only option for the Red Army was to find a safer and even more remote base. It was this quest that was to become 'the Long March'.

ACTIVITY

Further research: Find out more details about the Japanese threat to China, 1931–37. Read pages 146–48 and 209–10 and then use the further reading section. Consider how serious the threat was and what forms it took.

The Long March

The Long March lasted for a year and covered some 5000 miles (8000 km^2). The initial chances of it succeeding were not high. The participants had to traverse a hostile terrain interrupted by mountain ranges, rivers and swamps (see page 192), defend themselves from superior Nationalist forces, which inflicted frequent defeats on them, guerrilla attacks from warlords, disease, starvation and the bitter cold in winter. Somewhere between 80,000 and 100,000 men, women and children began the March in October 1934 and only about 10,000 reached Yenan a year later. The history of the March rapidly became the great epic story of Chinese communism and was used as evidence that the CCP and particularly its leader Mao possessed a heroic strength, which would ultimately overcome all its enemies.

SOURCE F

In this extract from a conversation with Li Weihan, a Long Marcher recalled later: (quoted in Chang and Jon Halliday, *Mao*, Vintage, 2007, p.197)

I once saw several men under a blanket and thought they were stragglers. So I tried to rouse them. [The men were dead. There was little to eat.] When a horse died, we ate it: the troops at the front ate the meat, the ones at the back gnawed the bones, and chewed leather belts.

How useful is Source F in adding to our knowledge of the Long March?

Why was it that against all the odds the March succeeded and that Chiang was unable to capture Mao and the other Communist leaders?

- Chiang's allies, the warlords, could not be relied upon. At a crucial moment in his campaign against Mao, some withdrew their co-operation. Right at the beginning of the March, for instance, the local warlord, the Governor of Guangdong, allowed the Communists to slip round the ring of block houses, which had been constructed by the Nationalists to keep them penned in, and move on to Guangzi.
- Chiang's operations were also sometimes disrupted by bad weather, which enabled the Red Army to escape defeat. For example, the Nationalists won the battle of Guiyang, in February 1935, but thanks to rain and cloud which prevented the effective deployments of air power, Mao and the survivors again escaped and made for the Yunnan province, where they were helped by the warlord Long Yun to move on and cross the Yangzi.
- Chiang again had a good chance of destroying the Communist forces as they crossed the turbulent Dadu River in Sichuan province in May 1935. Communist propaganda was later to spread the myth of an epic victory there, but recent historians have concluded that it was only a minor skirmish because the main part of the Nationalist army failed to arrive on time. However, the crucial point is that the Red Army was once again able to escape, and on 12 June 1935 to join up with Zhang Guatao's soviet in northern Sichuan.
- In Mao Chiang had a ruthless opponent, who knew what he wanted and during the March was able to neutralize his critics in the party (see page 200) and enforce his will over the party.
- Chiang also faced the constant threat by the Japanese Kwantung Army (see page 178) in Manchuria to control northern China. This distracted from his campaign against the Red Army at crucial moments.

ACTIVITY 

Using the further reading section find out more details about the 'Long March'. Then hold a class debate on its importance. One group will stress its achievements and importance; the other will minimize these in contrast to other factors affecting the survival of the CCP. Each group should use cards with clear debating points on one side and supporting evidence on the other.

SOURCE G

The bridge over the Dadu River at Luding.

Study Source G. How justified was the CCP in claiming that the Dadu crossing was a major victory for them? Why was it important for the CCP to claim the crossing as a great feat of courage and endurance?

The Xi'an incident

Despite reaching Yenan, the CCP was not yet safe from further Nationalist attacks, but then its position was unexpectedly strengthened when General Chang Kai-shek was kidnapped in Xi'an in December 1936. How did this extraordinary turn of events happen?

Chiang accused of appeasement

In Yenan, Mao skilfully played the patriotic card and argued that the KMT government was appeasing Japan and not defending China from Japanese aggression. In fact Chiang was seeking to prepare China for the coming war against Japan by strengthening its defences and buying armaments in Germany and the USA, but all this had to be done secretly for fear of provoking Japanese retaliation. Consequently Chiang could not openly refute Mao's accusations, which increasingly won support both from Chinese patriots and Chiang's enemies, the warlords. The well-known Chinese philosopher and member of the May the Fourth Movement, **Hu Shih**, described the Kuomintang as 'dead but not buried, and all unburied dead things cause trouble for the living'.

KEY FIGURE 

Hu Shih (1891–1962) Poet, intellectual and university professor; ambassador to the USA, 1938–42.

Chiang, however, was convinced that he needed to eliminate the CCP before he confronted the Japanese. Mao responded to this threat by advocating a **united front** composed of the KMT, CCP and even the warlords against the Japanese, and was able to gain the support of the warlord of Shanxi, Yan Xishan, and Zhang Xueliang of Manchuria, both of whom feared that if Chiang crushed the CCP he would then be in a position finally to reduce their power by incorporating their armies into the Nationalist forces. In September 1936 the CCP signed a secret agreement with Zhang 'to Resist Japan and Save the Nation'.

KEY TERMS 

United front A coalition of parties, usually to oppose a foreign aggressor.

People's Court A special court set up to try 'enemies of the people'.

The kidnapping of Chiang and its consequences

At the suggestion of General Yang, commander of the Kuomintang's North-West Army, who was impressed by Mao's apparent patriotism, plans were drawn up to kidnap Chiang when he visited Xi'an, the provincial capital of Shaanxi in December. On 12 December Chiang and all the KMT members accompanying him were rounded up and imprisoned.

Mao, of course, was delighted and demanded Chiang's 'elimination' and trial by a **People's Court**, but here he was overruled by Stalin, who believed that Chiang was the best man to lead China in a war against Japan. Chiang was therefore released and instead a united front between the KMT and CCP was formed.

ACTIVITY 

List five reasons why the CCP came near to defeat at the hands of the KMT. Write a paragraph on why it survived.

Chiang's release and the creation of the united front were received with relief by many Chinese, who were convinced that the Japanese threat required national unity. The united front saved the CCP from possible elimination, as Chiang could hardly now go ahead with his plans for sending a military expedition to Yenan.

Attempts at modernization and reform

Briefly between 1928 and 1930 it seemed that Chiang would be able to modernize and reform China, but these hopes proved to be a mirage as Chiang struggled to defeat the CCP and prepare for eventual war against Japan.

Chiang reappointed head of the Kuomintang government

After the left wing of the KMT, which was based in Wuhan, decided to cut its links with the Communists in July 1927, the two wings of the KMT reunited. Initially the reunited party hoped to form a government without Chiang, who was forced to resign and withdrew to his ancestral home. Yet in December, after the failed Communist uprising in Guangzhou (see page 191), in response to calls for a strong leader, Chiang was reappointed head of the KMT. He launched a second stage of the Northern Expedition and conquered both the province of Shandong and the old imperial capital of Beijing, but Chiang broke with tradition and kept his government in Nanjing. With the establishment of the united Nationalist administration in Nanjing, it seemed momentarily as if China would at last be able to modernize and reform itself. Chiang won the support of the intellectuals, many members of the May The Fourth Movement, key businessmen and even of some of the warlords. The Communists seemed to be marginalized.

The new government and administration

Chiang, as Chairman of the State Council, created in 1928 a new blueprint for China's government, which was now to consist of five departments, or yuan, which controlled the business of government. The closest approximation to a parliament was the legislative yuan, which had the powers to debate and approve legislation, national budgets and foreign policy. It was, however, an unelected body, which initially had only 51 members, later increased to 194, who were appointed by the government and not chosen in free elections by the people. Despite frequently referring to Sun Yat-sen's Three Principles, Chiang was more of a dictator, who sought to rule through the KMT rather than as a democrat. The fifth yuan, for instance, was called the 'Control Yuan'. Its task was to enforce discipline and obedience to the ideology of the KMT, which was entrusted to rule on behalf of the people until 1936, when elections would be held for a new government. In practice the outbreak of the second Sino-Japanese war in 1937 ensured that this period was extended indefinitely.

A party dictatorship was established, which attempted, despite the fragility of the KMT regime, to impose its regime on the country. There were tight controls on the press, education and the arts. The political police, backed by the **Blue Shirts**, conducted a reign of terror against dissidents, especially communists.

KEY TERM

Blue Shirts Created in 1924 by a group of army officers. By the 1930s the Blue Shirt Society was increasingly influential in the KMT.

Economic, social and financial reforms

KEY TERMS 

Central bank A national bank, which controls a nation's currency and interest rates.

Foot binding Traditional Chinese custom whereby young girls' feet were tightly bound to control their growth. Small feet were considered a mark of beauty.

Monopolies Sole control of supplying a commodity exercised by a company or group of companies.

In the early years of the KMT, ambitious plans for financial reform, agricultural improvements and industrial expansion were launched. A **central bank** was created, attempts were made to standardize weights and measures and taxes, while a National Reconstruction Commission was formed to build power stations and oversee the modernization of the economy.

There were, too, a series of enlightened reforms, which had they been effective, would have undermined support for the Communists:

- An eight-hour working day was introduced and workers were to share in the profits made by their employers.
- Child labour was prohibited.
- **Foot binding** was to be banned.
- Health care and education were to be greatly expanded.
- Civil servants were to be given higher salaries in an attempt to eliminate corruption by government officials.

In practice these ambitious reforms were impossible to implement. Despite Chiang's victories, China was still a deeply divided state, and several warlords, despite Chiang's victories, managed to retain considerable independence. Chiang could defeat an individual warlord, but he lacked the power to eliminate them completely and so create a uniform modern state. The money and time that was spent on military operations against the Communists and defiant warlords meant that there were neither the financial resources nor the time to concentrate on effectively building a modern China. Thus in 1935, for a population of 450 million, there were only 30,000 hospital beds and just 500,000 children attended schools. Some progress was made in the development of modern coal and iron industries, but overall only between 1.5 and 2 million workers were employed in modern factories.

In the countryside, which was a fertile recruiting ground for the CCP, relatively little had changed since the beginning of the century. The majority of farmers used the traditional methods of cultivation, and in 1933, for example, the average farmer's income was less than his outgoings. They were, too, burdened with heavy taxes, much of which were embezzled by the tax collectors, and those who grew tea, tobacco or silk crops were at the mercy of **monopolies** run by big business or large landowners. It is not surprising therefore that the British economic historian, R.H. Tawney, compared the life of the typical Chinese peasant to 'a man standing permanently up to his neck in water so that even a ripple is sufficient to drown him'.

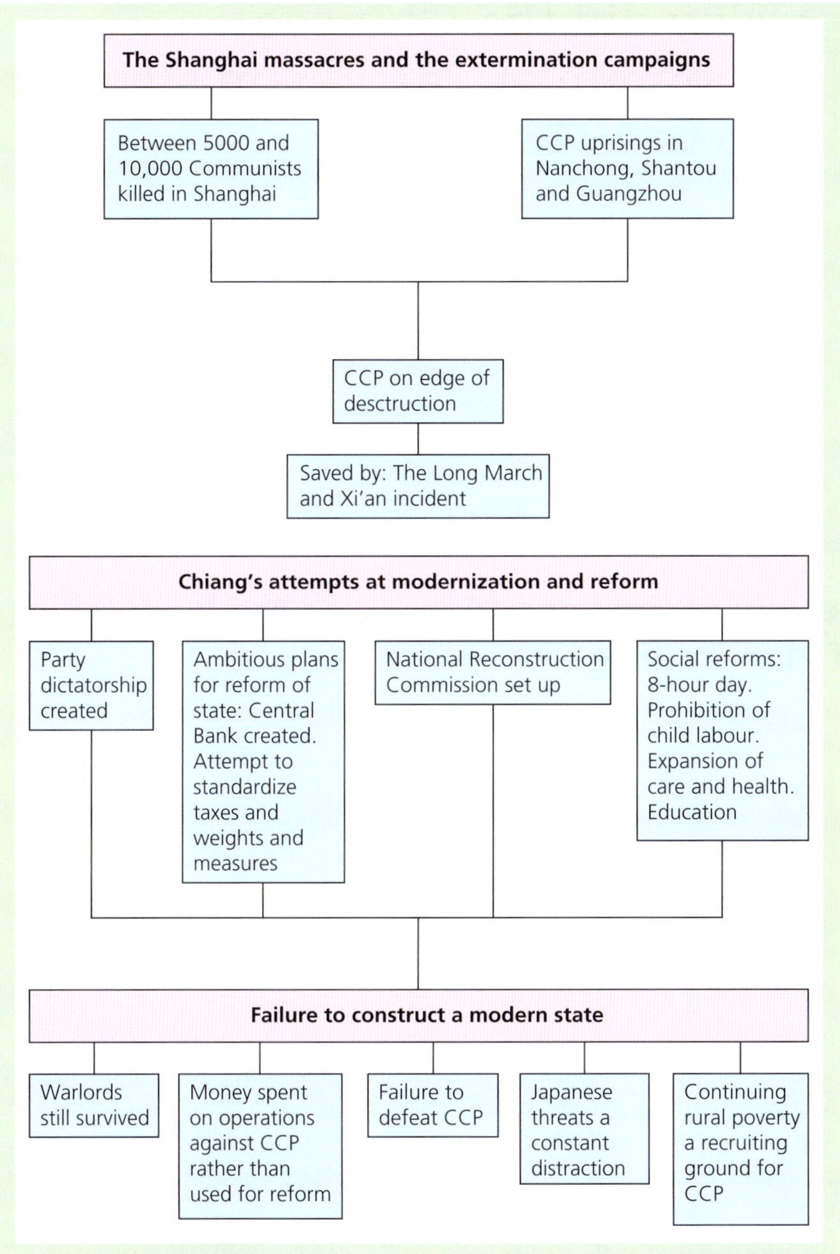

SUMMARY DIAGRAM

How effectively did Chiang Kai-shek deal with the Communists in the period 1927–36?

ACTIVITY

Re-read section 2 and then copy this chart briefly to summarize, as indicated, Chiang's efforts to solve the problems facing China 1927–36.

Problem	Action taken	How effective

Now write a concluding paragraph assessing Chiang's overall success in this period.

Why did the Chinese Communist Party gain support up to 1945?

ACTIVITY 

Read Section 3 and then copy the chart and its headings on page 199 to summarize, as indicated, how Mao built up his power base in the CCP. Write a concluding paragraph assessing why Mao was successful.

Although the Long March and the Xi'an incident saved the CCP from immediate destruction, it was still in considerable danger from the Nationalists. The situation, however, was transformed by the large-scale invasion of China by Japan, which resulted in a war that lasted until 1945. Mao was able to expand the Yenan base into the provinces of Gansu and Ningxia, even though its borders remained under constant surveillance from the Nationalists. It was here, as we shall see below, that Mao was able to set up, in comparative security, the Yenan soviet. The Red Army was also greatly expanded to 184,000 by 1938, and now consisted of a force in Shaanxi (the Eighth Army) and the newly formed Fourth Army in the Lower Yangzi.

Results of the Long March and the leadership of Mao Zedong

During the Long March Mao was able to defeat two challenges to his position:

1 In January 1935 an 'Enlarged Meeting of the Politburo' was called to hold an inquiry into the disasters that had befallen the CCP over the last few years. Mao successfully led the criticism directed at Bo Gu, the head of the CCP, and Zhou Enlai, the political leader in charge of the army. He won the argument and emerged in a much stronger position: he joined the **Standing Committee** of the Politburo and one of his close political allies, Lo Fu, replaced Bo as party leader.

2 In June Mao saw off another challenge when he met up with Zhang Guotao, the former leader of the E-yu-wan base, after crossing the Snowy Mountains. As Zhang's Fourth Army was larger and better equipped than Mao's First Army, he had a strong claim to become the leader of the combined force, but Mao managed to sideline him as deputy chairman of the Military Commission. Zhang ceased to be a threat after his defeat on the Upper Yellow River by the Nationalists in the autumn of 1935.

KEY TERM 

Standing Committee A permanent committee.

KEY FIGURE 

Chen Boda (1904–89) Communist theoretician and Mao's speech writer and later personal secretary.

Even though Mao was the most powerful figure in the CCP leadership by the end of 1935, he still faced considerable criticism within the party from a large group of Russian-trained Chinese Communists, who had returned to Yenan with orders from Stalin to enforce the orthodox Communist teaching that revolution can only occur in the big cities. To combat these arguments Mao, with the help of a brilliant intellectual, **Chen Boda**, learnt to master Marxist philosophy and argue that in China it had to adjust to Chinese reality, where peasants made up 88 per cent of the workforce. Mao managed to defer the meeting of the Seventh Communist Party Congress, which could have overridden his decisions until 1945. By which time with Boda's assistance, he had developed the Mao cult. Through propaganda at every level he was portrayed as the great leader. He became chairman of both the Communist Central Committee and of the Politburo.

SOURCE H

Extract from the CCP's Seventh Party Congress, 1945, declaring that:

The Chinese Communist Party takes Mao Zedong's thought – the thought that unites **Marxist–Leninist theory** *and practice of the Chinese revolution – as the guide for all its work, and opposes all* **dogmatic or empiricist deviations**.

Rewrite Source H in your own words. What can we learn from the source about Mao's leadership of the CCP?

Establishment of the Yenan Soviet, land reform and Mao's Rectification Campaign

In the decade between 1935 and 1945 Mao was able to turn the Yenan base into a soviet, which in many ways provided a blueprint for how the Communists would rule China if they gained power. Above all Mao was able to put into practice his belief that the Chinese revolution would start in the countryside by mobilising the peasantry:

- Units of the Red Army fanned out from Yenan to occupy the countryside. Landlords were evicted and often mercilessly killed. The soldiers were given strict instructions not to behave like warlord troops and plunder the peasantry.
- Land was then shared out among the peasantry and local soviets set up.
- Literacy and education programmes were introduced and basic medical services provided.

KEY TERMS

Marxist–Leninist theory Doctrines of Karl Marx's teaching, which were modified by Lenin to suit the situation in Russia.

Dogmatic or empiricist deviations Opinionated or independent thought.

SOURCE I

Extract from the report by Mao on an *Investigation of the Peasant Movement in Hunan*, 1927.

A revolution is not a dinner party, or writing an essay, or painting a picture, or doing embroidery. It cannot be so refined, so leisurely and gentle, so temperate, kind courteous, retrained and magnanimous. A revolution is an insurrection, an act of violence by which one class overthrows another. A rural revolution is a revolution by which the peasantry overthrows the power of the feudal class. Without using the greatest force, the peasants cannot possibly overthrow the deep-rooted authority of the landlords, which had lasted for thousands of years.

Compare Sources H and I as evidence about Mao's strategy for a communist revolution in China.

The Rectification Campaign

In many ways Mao's policy of confiscating land from the landlords was effective in increasing the popularity of the CCP, which increased its numbers from some 700,000 to well over a million by 1945. However, dissenters and critics of Mao were not tolerated. Villages which did not want to join the soviet had all their crops and livestock seized and were subject to punitive taxation reminiscent of the worst of the warlords.

Similarly, anyone who questioned Mao's interpretation of Marxism or his peasant policy was rapidly marginalized from the party. Mao particularly directed his attention against party intellectuals, who had been trained in Moscow, and who questioned both his authority and policies. A 'Rectification Campaign' was therefore launched against those guilty of:

- 'subjectivism', by which was meant those who did not agree with Mao's interpretation of Marxist-Leninism
- 'sectarianism', by which anybody who did not agree *totally* with and obey the authority of the Central Committee was guilty of 'party formalism'. This referred for the most part to intellectuals who could not communicate with the people in a way that could be understood.

Intellectuals who had joined the Yenan soviet after the Long March were denounced at party rallies and subject to terror. In the autumn of 1942 a '**cadre screening movement**' was organized by Mao's political police in Yenan, allegedly against Nationalist spies, but by December it was widened to include anybody who dared deviate from the official party line and was now called a 'rescue movement'. Those 'rescued' from error had the chance under torture to 'rectify' their mistakes.

By the time the Rectification Campaign was halted, some 40,000 people had been expelled from the party. Its main purpose was achieved. Mao had eliminated anybody who did not agree with him and had created a centralized, obedient revolutionary force, which after 1945 was to be highly effective in defeating the Nationalists.

KEY TERMS

Cadre screening movement A campaign aimed at checking the loyalty of core groups of the CCP.

Marco Polo Bridge incident A minor confrontation between Chinese and Japanese troops near Marco Polo Bridge outside Beijing, July 1937, which rapidly escalated into a major war. The Japanese Kwantung Army was conducting manoeuvres just outside Beijing, when Chinese troops fired into the area.

Nanjing massacres For six weeks in December 1937–January 1938 Japanese troops committed mass murder in Nanjing.

Impact of the war with Japan, 1937–45

War between China and Japan broke out in August 1937 after the **Marco Polo Bridge incident**. It rapidly escalated into a prolonged and savage struggle, which involved terrible incidents like the **Nanjing massacres** by Japanese troops and the destruction of the Yellow River dykes by the Nationalists, which resulted in the drowning of some 500,000 people.

By December 1941, when the USA declared the war on Japan after the Pearl Harbor raid (see page 213), much of eastern China was occupied by Japan (see map, page 211). Yet so long as the Nationalists and Communists were ready to fight, it was a war which Japan could not win. The western provinces remained unoccupied, and even the occupied areas were impossible effectively to police. Neither side was able to win outright and over a million Japanese soldiers were tied down in China until the dropping of atom bombs on Hiroshima and Nagasaki by the USA forced Japan to surrender.

China paid a high price for victory. Some 14 to 20 million Chinese were killed. As the historian Rana Mitter (2014) observed, 'the war … had hollowed China out'. In the eastern part of the country, its cities were in ruins and agricultural land had been destroyed by the **scorched earth policies** practised by both sides, so that much of the population faced starvation. Inflation, too, had ruined the currency. Above all China emerged from the war with Japan still a deeply divided country. It now faced a massive escalation of the conflict between the Nationalists and Communists.

KEY TERM 

Scorched earth policy A military strategy aimed at destroying anything of use to the advancing enemy.

Impact of the war on the CCP

Paradoxically the war saved the CCP from destruction by the Nationalist forces, a point that Mao was to make when the Prime Minister of Japan visited China in 1972! It was on the Nationalists that the main burden of the war fell, even though there was some limited fighting between the Japanese and Communists.

ACTIVITY 

Discussion point: Do you think Mao's policy towards the Japanese 1937–45 was politically defensible?

Wherever possible, Mao sought to avoid conflict with the Japanese and continued to view Chiang as his main enemy, even though, of course, CCP propaganda lost no opportunity to claim that it was the true patriotic party and was doing most of the fighting against the Japanese! In fact, in 1940 Mao hoped that the USSR and Japan would co-operate to divide China along the Yangtze, thereby enabling the CCP to control half the country. Mao also cultivated links with Japanese intelligence in the hope of sabotaging the Nationalist war effort. Despite the agreement to establish a united front with Chiang for the duration of the war with Japan, conflict between the Nationalists and Communists did continue. For instance, in January 1941 large-scale fighting broke out between the Communist Fourth Army and the Nationalists in the Lower Yangzi region, which resulted in the defeat of the former.

Thanks to Mao's strategy of avoiding conflict, the CCP emerged in 1945 much stronger than it had been in 1937:

- It had established control over large areas of northern China and was well placed to make contact with the Russians when they declared war on Japan and invaded Manchuria.
- It had an army of nearly a million supported by an additional militia about 900,000-strong, while party membership was over a million.
- It was recognized by both the USSR and USA as a strong political movement that would play an indispensable role in the future of China. In 1944, for instance, the US set up a mission in Yenan to liaise with Mao.

SOURCE J

In this extract from an interview with Seiichi Koizumi, a CCP intelligence agent recalled that, in 1941:

Our tactic with the Japanese and collaborators was: 'Use the hand of the enemy to strike the other enemy' … Collaborators' organizations were filled with our comrades, who used the knives of the Japanese to slaughter Nationalists … Of the things I knew personally, the Japanese annihilation of the [Nationalist underground army] south of the Yangtze was one of the masterpieces of co-operation between the Japanese and our Party.

What does Source J reveal about the tactics of the CCP during the Sino-Japanese war?

Unpopularity of Chiang Kai-shek and the Kuomintang

With the surrender of Japan in 1945, Chiang had won the war in China, but this victory did little to ensure the popularity of his regime. The Kuomintang was unable to appeal either to the broad mass of the Chinese people or to the intellectuals and the liberals. In an effort to unite the country he set up a National Political Consultative Council in July 1938, but even when it was reformed in 1943, it proved, as the historian Jonathan Fenby (2008) observed, mere 'window dressing' for his own power and was not able to provide a focus for national unity.

Neither was Chiang able to mitigate the impact of the war on the Chinese people. Indeed his tactics often intensified their hardship. When, for example, he ordered the dykes on the Yellow River to be blown, he displaced some 6 million people, possibly killing half a million. The war caused a constant stream of refugees, who, as the state was unable to feed them, were sometimes reduced to eating tree bark or even to cannibalism. The army had first claim to the food supplies; in Henan, for example, which experienced severe drought in 1942, the army requisitioned between 30 and 50 per cent of its meagre food supplies.

As a result of the huge areas lost to the Japanese, Chiang had little option but to increase taxes and to inflate the currency. By 1941 soldiers' wages were 78 per cent lower than they had been in 1937. It was no wonder then that soldiers would often plunder the peasantry and steal their food and property as if they were bandits or warlord troops. Besides, they were often conscripted, ill-disciplined soldiers, who on marches to the front had to be roped together in case they deserted.

ACTIVITY 

Re-read pages 204–5 and 190–98. Hold a class debate about Chiang's leadership of the KMT (1927–45). One group will argue that he was a successful leader in both peace and war, the other the opposite. Each group should use cards with clear debating points on one side and supporting evidence on the other.

Neither did the defeat of Japan in August 1945 bring any relief to the population:

- The government had nothing new or inspiring to offer the cities or the intellectuals. Instead of a democratic 'new deal', a virtual police state came into being. Communists and liberals were arrested and strikes broken up.
- Industry and the transport infrastructure had suffered greatly from the war, and there were no funds to rebuild them.
- In the countryside landlords were able to extract rents and payments from the peasantry at will. If payments were refused, private militias or even KMT troops were used in retribution.
- In the newly liberated areas profiteers and swindlers swarmed in to exploit the helplessness and the misery of the population to make money.
- Corruption and the **black market** existed everywhere. **Blood plasma** made available by the American Red Cross was sold in shops in Shanghai and elsewhere.
- Inflation tipped over into hyperinflation. In Shanghai, for instance, the cost of living index was 900 times higher than it had been in 1937.

KEY TERMS 

Black market Illegal trade in rationed goods and food.

Blood plasma The vital yellowish-coloured liquid component of blood.

- Above all by the end of 1945 China was again engulfed in the civil war between the Communists and Nationalists. With the Nationalists unable to reform and unite the nation, it was no surprise that increasingly the Chinese came to accept Mao.

ACTIVITY 

Draw a spider diagram to show the impact of the war on China.

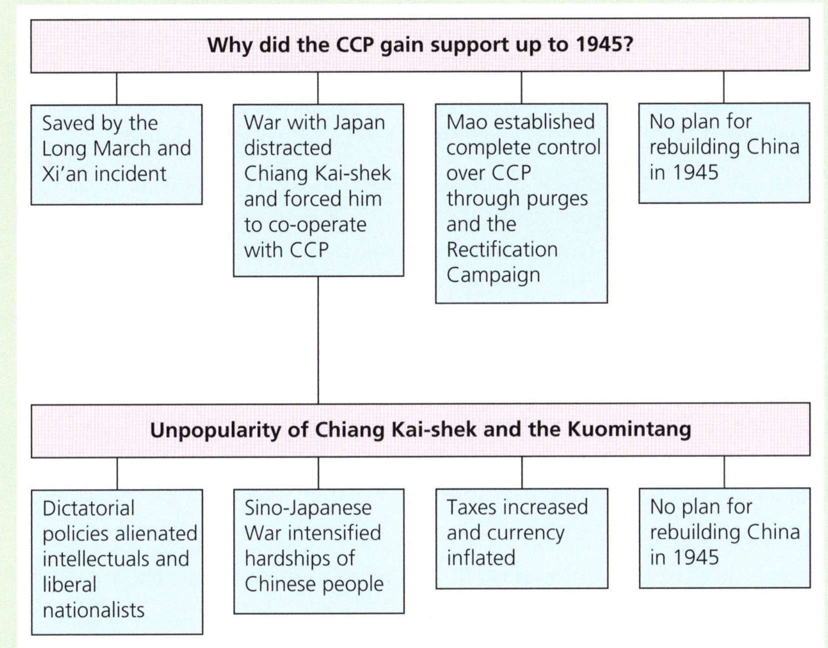

SUMMARY DIAGRAM

Why did the Chinese Communist Party gain support up to 1945?

ACTIVITY

Using the factors mentioned in the diagrams on page 199 and 205 briefly explain why Chiang Kai-shek failed to defeat the Communists, 1927–45.

4 Why did Japan become a military dictatorship in the 1930s and with what consequences?

This section looks at the history of Japan from the end of the First World War until its attack on the American base at Pearl Harbor in December 1941. It was a period in which increasing tensions developed both within Japan and between Japan and the Western powers and the USSR.

Japan's international status in 1919 and its reaction to the Paris peace settlements

When Japan attended the Paris Peace Conference in 1919 as a member of the victorious coalition which had defeated Germany, the USA and the European Allies were unsure whether Japan counted as a great power.

KEY TERM 

GDP (gross domestic product) The financial value of all goods and service produced by a country.

Modern Japan had only emerged as a major power in the early twentieth century. By 1919 it had the world's third largest navy as well as a formidable army, which had been able to defeat Russia in 1905 (see page 36). Its military strength was also complemented by its economic strength. Between 1895 and 1920 its **GDP** had nearly trebled, and the output of mining and manufacturing had increased by almost six times. On the other hand it was still essentially a regional power interested in expanding into Korea, Manchuria and China. In the First World War it had concentrated on seizing the German concessions in Shandong in China (see page 38) and the small German north Pacific islands, and refused to send troops to Europe.

To Asian nationalists Japan was an inspiration and an example. The country had managed to modernize itself. It was both able to resist Western imperialists and, as the Anglo-Japanese Treaty of 1902 showed, even co-operate with them as equals (see page 35) and negotiate alliances with them. Yet, by 1919 Japan's very success made Britain and the USA increasingly apprehensive of the growing Japanese economic and military power in east Asia. Military circles in both Japan and the USA were uneasily aware of a possible future confrontation between the two powers. The Japanese navy, for example, saw the possession of the German north Pacific islands as the key to blocking a future US advance into the area.

Despite its strength, Japan, as an Asian power, experienced considerable racial prejudice by, particularly, the English-speaking powers, Britain, the USA and the 'white Dominions', Australia, New Zealand and Canada. US politicians, for instance, were worried about the impact of possible Japanese immigration on California and the West Coast. The Japanese were sufficiently concerned to fear, in the words of one Japanese elder statesman, 'a white alliance against the yellow peoples'.

Japan's reactions to the Paris peace settlements

Japan came to Paris to achieve certain specific aims:

- To retain the former German concession of Shandong.
- To establish control over the former German islands in the north Pacific.
- As far as possible to co-operate with Britain and the USA and support the Fourteen Points.
- It was lukewarm about the establishment of the League of Nations as it feared that it might be an attempt, as the historian Margaret MacMillan (2001) has put it, 'to freeze the status quo and to keep Japan in the second rank'. If Japan could not delay the League's creation, it would insist on the insertion of a racial equality clause into the League's constitution.

The Japanese retained Shandong and the former German Pacific islands, even though they were made mandates under the League of Nations (see page 104), but the racial equality clause was rejected by Britain as a result of pressure from New Zealand and Australia.

The reaction of the Japanese press to this was highly critical. **Count Makino Nobuaki** warned the USA and the Allies that this might cause Japan to lose faith in the League. Sadly he was correct, and in Margaret Macmillan's (2001) opinion: 'The failure to get the racial equality clause was to be an important factor in turning Japan away from co-operation with the West and towards more aggressively nationalistic policies.'

KEY FIGURES 

Count Makino Nobuaki (1861–1949) Japanese ambassador, Foreign Minister and representative at the Paris Peace Conference.

Hara Kei (1856–1921) Japanese politician and Prime Minister, 1918–21

Kato Takaaki (1860–1926) Japanese politician and Prime Minister, 1924–26.

Political and economic factors in the failure of democracy

As the historian Mary Hanneman (2001) observed, during the 1920s, 'Japan was poised between the promise of greater democracy and the threat of greater control by the government.' By 1930 Japan enjoyed some of the characteristics of a democracy, but the impact of the Great Depression was dramatically to strengthen the anti-democratic forces such as the army and the patriotic societies.

Political developments during the 1920s

By 1918 it seemed as if a new kind of party politics was emerging with the formation of two new political parties, the *Seiyukai* (Association of Political Friends) and the more liberal *Kenseikai* (Constitutional Association), and yet successive governments backed by both groups still failed to democratize Japanese's politics. **Hara Kei**, the leader of the *Seiyukai*, did manage to open up some political posts to members of his party, but he was too dependent on the House of Peers and the **genro** to consider any serious constitutional reform or to extend the suffrage.

KEY TERM 

Genro Term used for a group of Japanese elder statesmen, who were seen as the founding fathers of modern Japan.

It was **Kato Takaaki**, the leader of the *Kenseikai*, who agitated strongly for the introduction of representative government on the British model. In 1924 he won an election fought on this issue, and in 1925 he introduced the Universal Suffrage Act, which gave the vote to all males over 25. The Act did not, however, signal the start of a more liberal regime. It only became law because the Diet, which was under pressure from conservative and nationalist pressure groups such as the *Kokuhonsha* (National Foundation Society), passed the Peace Preservation Law. This sweepingly outlawed any organization that dared demand changes in Japan's imperial constitution or an end to private property.

In 1928, when the first election was held under the new franchise, the Prime Minister, Tanaka Giichi, used the Peace Preservation Law to make over a thousand arrests and dissolve three left-wing parties. Clearly therefore, fear of communism and socialism provoked a reaction from the nationalist right and the government, which did much to stop the development of an effective democracy in Japan in the 1920s.

ACTIVITY

Draw a spider diagram to show the reasons for the failure of democracy in Japan, 1919–33.

The impact of economic factors on the failure of democracy

Between 1923 and 1931 Japan suffered a series of economic crises, all of which triggered anti-democratic reactions from the government. In September 1923 the Kanto earthquake devastated Tokyo and killed over 100,000 people. The large sums needed to recover from this disaster led to inflation and the weakening of the banking system. In 1927 the Japanese banking system was in crisis as the banks had huge debts they could not cover. This led to the collapse of more than twenty banks and an economic recession.

These crises inevitably had political repercussions and fuelled political protests from left-wing groups, whom the government ruthlessly tried to suppress. In May 1928, as we have already seen, over a thousand arrests were made and a permanent police surveillance system was set up.

The economic impact of the Great Depression, 1929–31

Japan had hardly recovered from the 1927 recession when its economy was hit by the great global depression of 1929, which was triggered by the collapse of the US stock market (see page 119). Its impact was made more disastrous by the return of the yen to the gold standard in June 1929, which drove the price of Japanese exports up to uncompetitive levels. The total value of exports fell from 2513 million yen in 1929 to 1426 million in 1931. The textile trade was particularly severely hit, as Japanese exports to the USA almost dried up. By 1930 the price of silk had fallen by 80 per cent compared to 1925. Inevitably this was a devastating blow for farmers, whose incomes dropped by two-thirds.

The political impact of the Great Depression

Rural Japan was the seedbed of the militarism and nationalism that was to dominate Japan up to 1945. The peasants' bitterness and belief that their misery and poverty were not understood by big business and the politicians were exploited by the various right-wing pressure groups such as the Imperial Reservists' Association, for who the countryside and its inhabitants embodied the traditional virtues of Japan. Economic despair fuelled the growth of nationalism and militarism, and increasingly it was to the army that the victims of the Great Depression looked to reform Japan and restore its ancient warlike virtues.

The growth in ultra-nationalist groups

Ultra-conservatives and Japanese nationalists accepted that, to defend itself against Western imperialism, Japan had itself to industrialize and to model itself in many ways on the West, but by doing this it ran the risk of losing touch with its own ancient traditions. To reconcile the ancient and the modern, Japanese patriots looked to the army to achieve victory on the battlefield and the domination of east Asia. This, they believed, would restore national pride in Japanese traditions and also make Japan prosperous. By 1936 well over half a million Japanese belonged to ultra-nationalist organizations. It was these which were to mobilize mass support for the army's expansionist policies in China and weaken the government's ability to control the armed forces.

Implications of military rule for Japanese expansionism

After 1930 the influence of the army and navy in Japanese politics increased to the point where effectively they controlled Japan. They never created an actual dictatorship, but they had the power to veto government policies and bring about the dismissal of ministers they considered hostile to their interests. The military both in Tokyo and in China and Manchuria was the driving force behind Japanese expansionism.

Attempts to bring about the 'Showa restoration'

Ultra-nationalist ideas were particularly strong in the army among junior officers, who were influenced by the ideas of **Kita Ikki** for a **Showa restoration**. By assassinating corrupt civilian politicians they would destroy what they regarded as 'decadent' democracy and restore the power of the emperor. The Showa restoration failed but the five plots against the government and assassinations of its members, 1931–36, nevertheless succeeded in strengthening the power of the armed forces over the government:

- In 1931, there were two unsuccessful attempts by the nationalist *Sakurakai*, or Cherry Blossom Society, to assassinate the Prime Minister and install General Ugaki, the War Minister, as the head of a new government.
- On 15 May 1932, members of the *Ketsumeidan*, or Blood League, who were predominantly young peasants, co-operated with military and naval cadets in a plan to destroy the government and declare martial law. Although they assassinated the Prime Minister, they failed to achieve a military government. Instead a 'cabinet of national unity' was appointed.
- In August 1935 and February 1936, fighting broke out between two rival groups within the army: the Koda or 'Imperial Way' faction and the Tosei, or 'Control' faction. The former believed in direct action to bring about the Showa restoration, while the latter believed that this was a distraction from preparing for an all-out war against China. The Koda was comprehensively defeated in 1936 when the navy, the key military authorities and Emperor Hirohito himself all turned against its plotters.

KEY FIGURE 

Kita Ikki (1883–1937) The leading ultra-nationalist philosopher, whose ideas inspired the 26 February Incident, for which he was executed.

KEY TERM 

Showa restoration Attempts in the early 1930s to restore the power of the emperor. Showa was the title of Emperor Hirohito's reign, 1926–89.

KEY TERM 

Manchukuo The name given to the Japanese-dominated state of Manchuria under Puyi, the deposed Emperor of China.

The army and Japanese expansion, 1931–37

The constant threats by ultra-nationalist officers against the government made it increasingly difficult for ministers to control the army. Even though they knew in advance of the Kwantung Army's plans to occupy Manchuria in September 1931, they were unable to stop them, as the army simply ignored instructions from Tokyo. The plots of October 1931 and May 1932 failed, but nevertheless they intimidated the government into supporting the Kwantung Army's policy in Manchuria and recognizing the creation of the Japanese-dominated state of **Manchukuo**. The government now had no option but to defend the army's conquest of Manchuria in the League of Nations, even though they had not planned it. As Mary Hanneman (2001) stresses, 'from this point forward the military had effective control of foreign policy'.

ACTIVITY

Write a brief explanation of the following terms: Manchukuo, militarism, stock markets, Showa restoration, ultra-nationalist groups.

When the incident at Marco Polo Bridge outside just outside Beijing (see page 202) occurred in July 1937, the Japanese cabinet was divided about how to react, but the War Ministry, backed by the senior General Staff Officer and the Chief of Military Affairs department, were ready to escalate hostilities. In the end, despite cabinet divisions, the Japanese government issued an ultimatum to China demanding the withdrawal of Chinese troops back to KMT territory within 24 hours, but before the time limit had elapsed, the Kwantung Army launched a full-scale attack on the Japanese and began the eight-year war against China.

KEY FIGURE 

Konoe Fumimaro (1891–1945) Japanese Prime Minister, 1937–39, and from July 1940 to October 1941.

Reasons for involvement in the Second World War

The root cause of Japan's involvement in the Second World War was the bitterness of many conservatives about Western imperialism. It was this that had forced Japan to modernize and industrialize and so to lose touch with its historic roots. Nor, once it had done this, did the West greet Japan as an equal. At the Paris Peace Conference it refused to have a racial equality clause inserted into the constitution of the League of Nations and in 1924 the US Congress passed the Exclusion Act limiting Japanese immigration to the USA. To Japanese statesmen such as **Konoe Fumimaro**, the Western powers seemed hypocritical: they had through conquest built up their own empires in the nineteenth century, yet they were stopping Japan from creating its own empire in China. No wonder, in Mary Hanneman's (2001) words, Japanese nationalists 'viewed the West's criticism ...designed merely ... to protect the West's global hegemony'.

Figure 4.3 Manchuria, east Asia and the Pacific, 1931–42. In 1942 Japanese expansion reached its greatest extent.

> **ACTIVITY**
>
> What does this map show about the growth of Japanese power in east Asia and the Pacific 1931–42?

Japan's plans for a 'New Order' in east Asia and the US reaction

On 11 November 1938 the Japanese Prime Minister, Konoe, proclaimed Japan's ultimate intention of creating the 'New Order' in east Asia. Under Japanese leadership this would form a large trading bloc from which the Western powers were to be excluded. It was this aim that was ultimately to cause war with the USA. To the US government it was an article of both faith and practical economics that America should be able to trade and invest freely. Washington thus responded to each fresh extension of Japanese power not only by building up its naval forces in the Pacific, but by restricting more and more tightly the exports of potential war materials to Japan, a measure which in fact only intensified the Japanese drive for economic self-sufficiency. The USA also agreed to extend financial aid to Chiang Kai-shek's government. Japan and the USA consequently seemed therefore to be on a collision course.

What message does Source K seek to convey? Whom do you think is the intended audience for this source?

SOURCE K

Japanese infantry advance while displaying their rising sun flag in China, 1938. The bitter fighting in China was on a huge scale. By the beginning of 1938 the front stretched hundreds of kilometres.

The impact of the war in Europe, 1940

KEY TERMS 

Dunkirk The harbour in northern France from where the British Expeditionary Force was evacuated in May–June 1940.

Hawks Politicians and generals who wanted Japan to follow an aggressive foreign policy.

In September 1939, Britain and France had declared war on Germany when German troops invaded Poland. Hitler rapidly defeated Poland and then in May 1940 turned west to defeat France, occupy the Netherlands and force the evacuation of the British army at **Dunkirk**.

These events in Europe inevitably weakened the position of the European powers in south-east Asia and strengthened the hand of the **hawks** in Tokyo who advocated the occupation of the European colonies in south-east Asia. A relatively pro-Western government, which wished to avoid confrontation with the USA and Britain, was replaced by a more anti-Western regime, once more under Konoe, which again emphasized its intention of creating a Japanese-dominated Asia, and advocated closer co-operation with the victorious Nazi Germany. Washington responded by suspending exports of vital aviation fuel and lubricating oil. To neutralize growing US opposition the Japanese then tried to negotiate a four-power pact with the Axis states and the USSR. They succeeded in reaching an agreement with Germany and Italy in September (the Tripartite Pact) and they signed a five-year treaty of neutrality with Stalin the following spring. But the German invasion of the USSR in June 1941 terminated any prospect of a grand four-power alliance against Britain and the USA. On the other hand it did remove the threat of a Soviet attack on Japan.

Pearl Harbor

In July 1941 the Japanese occupied the southern half of French Indo-China and the Americans responded by imposing a comprehensive oil embargo on Japan. The embargo confronted the Japanese with the alternative of either seeing their war machine paralyzed through lack of oil or launching, within a few months at the latest, a pre-emptive strike against their enemies.

In early December they received verbal assurances from Ribbentrop that, in the event of a Japanese attack, Germany would also declare war against the USA, even though strictly speaking the Tripartite Pact did not commit Germany to such an action as it was a defensive alliance only. Thus, at dawn on 7 December, the Japanese felt sufficiently confident to launch their attack on the US naval base at Pearl Harbor in Hawaii. Their aim was to destroy as much of the US navy as possible, in the hope that a weakened USA would be ready to negotiate a compromise peace, but this was to prove a massive miscalculation. The USA declared war and eventually, in August 1945, after the dropping of atom bombs on Hiroshima and Nagasaki, forced Japan to surrender unconditionally.

SOURCE L

Extract from a statement by Prime Minister Konoe to the Japanese Imperial Conference of 6 September 1941.

As you all know, the international situation in which we are involved has become increasingly strained; and in particular, the United States, Great Britain and the Netherlands have come to oppose our Empire with all available means. There has emerged the prospect that the United States and the Soviet Union will form a united front against Japan, as the war between Germany and the Soviet Union becomes prolonged…

Under these circumstances our Empire must, of course, quickly prepare to meet any situation that may occur, and at the same time it must try to prevent the disaster of war by resorting to all possible diplomatic measures. If the diplomatic measures should fail to bring about favourable results within a certain period, I believe we cannot help but to take the ultimate step to defend ourselves.

How accurate is the evidence in Source L as an explanation of Japan's position in 1941?

SOURCE M

The *USS Arizona* sinks in Pearl Harbor following the Japanese air attack on 7 December 1941. It was this attack that brought the USA into the war.

How useful is Source M in understanding the attack on Pearl Harbor and its consequences?

ACTIVITY

Copy this table and list the causes of Japan's involvement in the Second World War.

Cause	Explanation	Importance on scale of 1–6	Why award

SUMMARY DIAGRAM

Why did Japan become a military dictatorship in the 1930s and with what consequences?

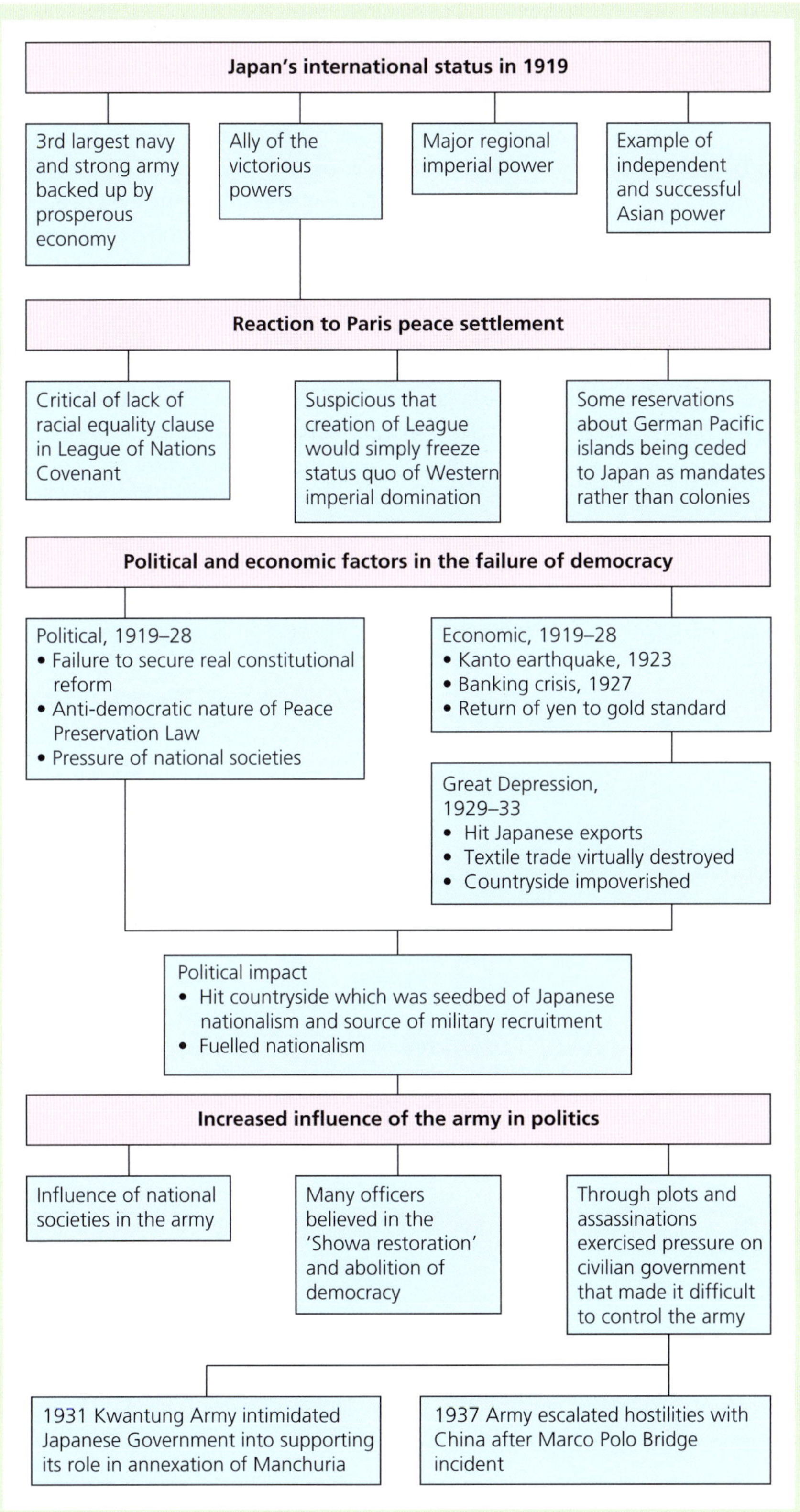

ACTIVITY

With reference to each factor mentioned in the diagram briefly explain why Japan followed a policy of aggression in East Asia, 1931–45.

Chapter summary

By the early twentieth century China seemed to be on the brink of disintegration as the central government was unable to assert its power over the country. It was no wonder that young ambitious officers like Chiang Kai-shek and intellectuals like Sun Yat-sen were urging revolution. Yet when the Empire was swept away, the new republic, despite the authoritarian rule of Yuan Shikai, was unable to implement effective reforms. One of the main barriers to success were the warlords, who controlled large areas of China and acted as independent rulers. China therefore continued to be a 'failed state', which could be exploited by Japan and the Western nations.

The May The Fourth Movement, the CCP and the KMT all attempted to modernize China. In 1926 Chiang Kai-shek's successful Northern Expedition extended the control of the KMT to over half a million square miles (1.3 million km^2) and 170 million people. Over the next ten years Chiang attempted to build a modern Chinese state and eliminate the CCP, which only managed to survive by retreating by the Long March to Yenan. Here Mao consolidated his leadership of the CCP and established the Yenan soviet. By 1945, after the defeat of Japan, he was ready to challenge Chiang.

The CCP further benefited from the outbreak of war with Japan in 1937. As a result of the growth of nationalism, growing disillusionment with the Western imperialist powers and the economic crises of 1923–31, Japan pursued an increasingly aggressive plans for establishing a 'New Order' in east Asia, which was opposed by the USA and led ultimately to the Japanese attack on Pearl Harbor on 7 December 1941 and the American and British declaration of war on Japan.

Refresher questions

1 What was the significance of the May The Fourth Movement?
2 Why were the warlords able to act like independent rulers?
3 How successful was the KMT by 1927?
4 Why did Chiang Kai-shek fail to eliminate the CCP?
5 Why did the 'Long March' save the CCP from elimination?
6 What progress had Chiang Kai-shek made in modernizing and unifying China by 1937?
7 Why was the Kuomintang so unpopular by 1945?
8 What was the impact of the war with Japan on China, 1937–45?
9 Why and with what consequences did democracy fail in Japan?
10 Why did Japan go to war with the USA in December 1941?

Study skills

Paper 1 guidance: sources

Visual sources

You may be asked to use a visual source like a cartoon or a poster. It is important to be able to see its meaning in relation to the issue in the question and to test its validity by considering its purpose and origin and also to use contextual knowledge.

Take this example:

SOURCE C

From *Punch*, a British satirical magazine, 10 December 1916.

How would you assess this source as evidence of the weakness of the League of Nations? Think about the cartoon itself.

Which answer is the more narrative and descriptive rather than answering the actual question set?

Answer A

It shows a bridge, which symbolizes the League of Nations, stretching over a ravine. However, crucially there is a 'gap' in the centre of the bridge. On one side there is a notice stressing that the League of Nations is an American idea – 'designed by the President of the USA', it states in capital letters. On the other side, Uncle Sam, the figure, which symbolizes the USA, is relaxing with his back resting against the 'keystone' of the bridge. The other blocks already in place on the bridge represent the major powers in the League and members of the Council of the League.

Answer B

The source is from the satirical British magazine, 'Punch', and the cartoonist is simplifying a complex matter in order to stress his message. In a crucial debate in November the US Senate rejected the Treaty of Versailles, which also included the League of Nations. Thus the cartoon is communicating and commenting on a vital political truth. Without the full participation of the USA, the League would be deprived of the support of the strongest country in the world at that time. By depicting 'Uncle Sam' apparently relaxing without a care in the world it is emphasizing the detachment of the USA from the vital task of implementing the peace.

Look at the following cartoon and assess how far it supports the view that the League was ill equipped to prevent the outbreak of international strife and war.

SOURCE D

MORAL SUASION.

THE RABBIT. "MY OFFENSIVE EQUIPMENT BEING PRACTICALLY *NIL*, IT REMAINS FOR ME TO FASCINATE HIM WITH THE POWER OF MY EYE."

Cartoon in the British magazine *Punch*, 28 July 1920

The message of the cartoon…

The provenance of the cartoon…

Knowledge to apply to the cartoon…

Paper 2 guidance: essay questions

Writing a conclusion and overall essay writing

What is the purpose of a conclusion? A conclusion should come to a judgement that is based on what you have already written and should be briefly supported. It should not introduce new ideas – if they were important they should have been discussed in the main body of the essay. You must also take care to avoid offering a contrary argument to the one you have pursued throughout the rest of the essay, as that will suggest to the reader that you have not thought through your ideas and are unclear as to what you think.

It might be that you are largely restating the view you offered in the vital opening paragraph, or in stronger answers there might be a subtle variation to the judgement – you confirm your original view, but suggest, with an example, that there were occasions when this was not always correct.

If the question has named a factor then you should give a judgement about that factor's relative importance, either explaining why it is or is not the most important, and the role it played in the events you have discussed. If the question asks you to assess a range of factors, the conclusion should explain which you think is the most important and should support the claim. At first sight a claim might appear to be judgement, but without supporting material it is no more than an assertion and will not gain credit.

Consider the following essay question:

> **'The Chinese Communist Party managed to survive and in time became the ruling party in China as a result of the Sino-Japanese war.' How far do you agree?**

In order to answer this question you may consider:

- Shanghai massacres and extermination campaigns
- Long March and Yenan soviet
- Xi'an incident
- impact of the Sino-Japanese war, 1937–45
- weaknesses of the Nationalists
- impact of the Second World War.

Now consider this sample conclusion:

By 1934 the CCP was on the verge of destruction. The Shanghai massacres in 1927 followed by the disastrous uprising in Guangzhou and repeated Nationalist attacks on their bases at E-yu-wan and elsewhere threatened to annihilate it as a political force. It is true that the evacuation of these bases and the Long March to Yenan 1934–35 saved a small core of the party, but at the cost of tremendous casualties. Even at Yenan the CCP was not secure from attack as Chiang was still determined to destroy the party, and it is likely that, without the

This is an excellent final paragraph because: it focuses immediately on the issue in the question; it provides a clear judgement on that issue; that judgement is supported with good argument and evidence; it briefly summarizes what the author believes was the main reason.

ever growing threat from Japan, he would have succeeded. It enabled Mao and the CCP to pose as the patriotic party ready to defend China, while Chiang and the Nationalists were more concerned with eliminating the CCP. In an attempt to force Chiang to co-operate with the CCP against the Japanese threat, Chiang was kidnapped at Xi'an in December 1936 and forced to agree to a united front with the Communists against the Japanese threat in the north. This effectively prevented him from concentrating on crushing the CCP. In August 1937 the Japanese declared war on China, and Chiang's first concern was the defence of the country. This again took the heat off the CCP, which at times even exchanged secret information with Japanese agents in order to weaken the Nationalists. The war also enabled Mao to build up the Yenan Soviet and the Red Army and to establish his absolute control over the CCP, so that he would be ready, once the war ended, to challenge Chiang's Nationalists. By 1945 when the Japanese surrendered, Chiang was theoretically the victor, but his victory was a mirage. Due to the suffering of the Chinese people and the corruption of the KMT, he was deeply unpopular, while the CCP, which had posed as the patriotic party, had gone from strength to strength and was ready to challenge the Nationalists.

QUESTION PRACTICE

In light of the advice and the sample conclusion, write conclusions to the following questions:

1. 'The warlords were the main factor stopping the unification and reform of China.' How far do you agree?
2. How successful was Sun Yat-sen as a reformer and politician?
3. How important were political and economic factors in the failure of democracy in Japan, 1920–33?

You have now covered all the main skills you need to write a good essay. It is worth looking back at these skills before you write each essay you are set. This will help you to build up and reinforce the skills you need for the examination.

EXPLAIN QUESTIONS

Answer one of the following questions and highlight where you have explained and where you have described.

1. Explain the significance of the Long March.
2. Explain why the May the Fourth Movement was formed.
3. Explain why Chiang was unable to eliminate the CCP as a political force.

Further reading

General texts

Hugh Brogan, *The Penguin History of the USA*, London, Penguin, 2001

A very readable general survey of US history, particularly useful for the period 1865–1945.

J. Fenby, *History of Modern China: The Fall and Rise of a Great Power: 1850 to the Present*, London, Penguin, 2008

An indispensable book for the study of modern Chinese history.

Niall Ferguson, *How Britain Made the Modern World*, London, Penguin, 2004

A broad survey of the history of the British Empire, with informative chapters on Africa.

L. James, *Empires in the Sun: the Struggle for the Mastery of Africa*, London, Weidenfeld and Nicolson, 2016

A good survey of not only the scramble for Africa, but also the history of European power in Africa up to the present.

M. Kitchen, *Europe Between the Wars*, Longman, 1988

A useful survey of Europe, 1919–39.

J. Lowe, *The Great Powers, Imperialism and the German Problem, 1865–1925*, London, Routledge, 1994

A useful account of great power diplomacy.

N. Rich, *Great Power Diplomacy, 1814–1914*, Columbus, OH, McGraw Hill, 1992

Contains excellent analyses of great power relationships and colonial rivalry, 1870–1914.

A.J.P. Taylor, *The Struggle for Mastery in Europe, 1848–1918* (paperback edition), Oxford, OUP, 1971

Inevitably dated, but like all Taylor's work intellectually provocative. Particularly good on the European powers and imperialism.

H.L. Wesseling, *The European Colonial Empires, 1815–1819*, Harlow, Pearson/Longman, 2004

A useful survey of European imperialism in the century after 1815 in all regions of the world.

E. Wiskemann, *Europe of the Dictators*, Fontana, 1970

Still a useful general survey of the period.

Chapter 1

W.G. Beasley, *The Rise of Modern Japan* (third edition), Basingstoke/London, Palgrave Macmillan, 2000

One of the best studies of the emergence of Japan as a great power.

R. Bickers, *The Scramble for China, 1832–1914*, Penguin, 2012

An informative survey of the European powers and their ambitions in China.

H.W. Brand, *The Reckless Decade: America in the 1890s* (new edition), Chicago, University of Chicago Press, 2002

A comprehensive survey of US foreign policy during the key decade of the 1890s.

M.E. Chamberlain, *The New Imperialism* (new edition), Historical Association pamphlet, 2010.

An indispensable guide to the historical debate on the 'New Imperialism'.

M.E. Chamberlain, *The Scramble for Africa* (third edition), London, Taylor Francis, 2010

An excellent and concise analytical account of 'the scramble'.

R.H. Ferrell, *Woodrow Wilson and the First World War, 1917–1921*, New York, Harper and Row, 1985

Covers US policy during the war and afterwards in detail.

A. Gordon, *A Modern History of Japan*, New York, OUP, 2003

Especially good on the period 1868–1918.

George C. Herring, *The American Century and Beyond*, New York, OUP, 2008

Very informative on the period 1893–18.

M. Jansen and P. Duus (eds.), *The Cambridge History of Japan, 1988–89*, Vols. V and VI, Cambridge, CUP

These volumes give a full account of Japanese history in the nineteenth and twentieth centuries.

J. Joll, *The Origins of the First World War* (second edition), Longman, 1992

Helpful assessments of contemporary militarism and imperialism.

W.L. Langer, *The Diplomacy of Imperialism, 1890–1902* (revised edition), New York, Knopf, 1951

The classic study on the complexities of imperial rivalries at the end of the nineteenth century.

John Lowe and Robert Pearce, *Rivalry and Accord: International Relations, 1870–1914* (second edition), Hodder, 1998

A good introduction to great power diplomacy during this period.

Thomas Pakenham, *The Scramble for Africa*, London, Abacus, 1992

A detailed and comprehensive survey of the scramble for Africa.

R. Robinson, 'The Partition of Africa' in Hinsley, F.H. (ed.), *The New Cambridge Modern History XI*, Cambridge, CUP, (reprinted) 1979, pages 593–640

A much briefer summary of the arguments in *Africa and the Victorians*.

R. Robinson and J. Gallagher, *Africa and the Victorians*, London, Macmillan, 1961

The classic study of imperialism, whose central arguments are still controversial.

David Stevenson, *The First World War and International Politics*, OUP, 1998

An invaluable analysis of international politics, 1914–18, which puts US intervention into the context of the war.

W. Appleman Williams, *The Tragedy of American Diplomacy* (new edition), New York/London, Norton Publishing, 2009

A revisionist study which argues that US foreign policy in China, Cuba and elsewhere was motivated by the desire for free trade –'the open door'.

Chapter 2

C. Fischer, *The Ruhr Crisis*, OUP, 2002

A comprehensive study of the crisis.

O.A. Hathaway, *The Internationalists*, New York, Simon and Schuster, 2017

A study of the significance of the Kellogg-Briand Pact and its legacy.

R. Henig, *The League of Nations*, London, Haus Publishing, 2010

Provides a concise guide to the League of Nations in the inter-war period.

R. Henig, *Versailles and After, 1919–33* (second edition), Routledge, 1995

A good summary of the facts and the controversies surrounding the peace treaties.

W.M. Jordan, *Great Britain, France and the German Problem, 1918–39* (new impression), London, Cass, 1971

First written in 1943 but perceptive and well worth reading.

M. Macmillan, *Peacemakers*, John Murray, 2001

Readable and a mine of information on the peace treaties.

C.S. Maier, *Recasting Bourgeois Europe*, Princeton University Press, 1988

A study of the economic and stabilization policies of post-war Europe, 1919–29.

A.J. Mayer, *Politics and Diplomacy in Peacemaking: Containment and Counter-Revolution at Versailles*, Weidenfeld and Nicolson, 1968

Good for detail on 'the new diplomacy' as represented by the USA and revolutionary Russia.

F.S. Northedge, *The League of Nations: Its Life and Times*, Leicester University Press, 1986

A comprehensive and informative study. Arguably the best on the League.

G. Schulz, *Revolutions and Peace Treaties, 1917–20*, Methuen, 1972

A survey of the peace treaties with particular emphasis on Germany and Russia.

Alan Sharp (ed.), *Makers of the Modern World: The Paris Peace Conferences 1919–23*, Haus Publishing, 2009

Helpful for biographies of the main statesmen at the Paris Conferences and also for the international consequences of the treaties.

Zara Steiner, *The Lights That Failed, 1919–1933*, OUP, 2005

A good study of the 1920s and the impact of the Great Depression.

A. Tooze, *The Deluge: The Great War and the Remaking of Global Order, 1916–1931*, Allen Lane, 2014

A study of the emergence of the USA as a financial super power dominating the global financial system and its impact on the other powers.

D. G. Williamson, *The British in Interwar Germany, 1918–30*, Bloomsbury, 2017

A detailed history of British policy in Germany.

J. Wright, *Gustav Stresemann: Weimar's Greatest Statesman*, OUP, 2002

Contains useful chapters on Stresemann as Chancellor and Foreign Minister.

Chapter 3

A. Adamthwaite, *France and the Coming of the Second World War*, Cass, 1977

Excellent book on French foreign policy on the eve of the Second World War.

P.M.M. Bell, *Origins of the Second World War in Europe*, London/New York, Longman, 1986

Excellent on ideological and economic issues as well as rearmament.

R. Boyce, 'World Depression, World War: Some Economic Origins of the Second World War' in R. Boyce and E.M. Robertson (eds), *Paths to War: New Essays on the Origins of the Second World War*, Macmillan, 1989

An informative analysis of the impact of the Great Depression.

A. Bullock, 'Hitler and the Origins of the Second World War' in E. Robertson (ed.), *The Origins of the Second World War*, Macmillan, 1971

Still very useful for understanding the motives behind Hitler's foreign policy.

W.M. Carr, *Arms, Autarky and Aggression*, Arnold, 1972

A clear and incisive analysis of Hitler's foreign policy.

D. Dutton, *Neville Chamberlain*, Hodder, 2001

A revisionist assessment of Chamberlain and his role in appeasement.

R.J. Overy, *The Origins of the Second World War*, Longman, 1987

A brief but authoritative study.

R.A.C. Parker, *Chamberlain and Appeasement: British Policy and the Coming of the Second World War*, Macmillan, 1993, and *Churchill and Appeasement*, Palgrave, 2000

Both books take a critical line towards Chamberlain's foreign policy.

G. Roberts, *The Soviet Union and the Origins of the Second World War, 1933–41*, Macmillan, 1995

A good guide to Stalin's foreign policy.

E. Robertson, *Mussolini as Empire-Builder: Europe and Africa, 1932–1936*, Macmillan, 1979

An important book for understanding the Abyssinian crisis.

R. Shay, *British Rearmament in the Thirties: Politics and Profits*, Princeton University Press, 1977

An important study of the progress made in rearming Britain in the 1930s.

A.J.P. Taylor, *The Origins of the Second World War*, Arnold, 1961

Still an important and stimulating book.

C. Thorne, *The Limits of Foreign Policy: The West, the League and the Far Eastern Crisis of 1931–1933*, Hamilton, London, 1972

A detailed study of the Manchurian crisis.

G. Weinberg, *The Foreign Policy of Hitler's Germany*, Vol. I, *Diplomatic Revolution in Europe, 1933–36*, and Vol II, *Starting World War II*, University of Chicago Press, 1970, 1980

A comprehensive study of Hitler's foreign policy.

J. Wright, *Germany and the Origins of the Second World War*, Palgrave, 2007

A clear, brief and authoritative account of Hitler's foreign policy and motives.

Chapter 4

J. Chang and J. Halliday, *Mao, The Unknown Story*, London, Vintage, 2007

A critical biography, which explores his ruthlessness and punctures many of the myths surrounding him.

L. Eastman *et al.*, *The Nationalist Era in China, 1927–37*, Cambridge, CUP, 1991

A study of Nationalist China at its most powerful.

J. Fenby, *Generalissimo: Chiang Kai-shek and the World He Lost*, London, Allen Lane, 2008

A study of Chiang and the Nationalists with an analysis of why they lost.

M. Hannemann, *Japan Faces the World, 1925–1952*, Longman, 2001

Helpful for understanding Japanese foreign policy and expansion, 1919–45.

M. Lamb and N. Tarling, *From Versailles to Pearl Harbor*, Palgrave, 2001

Especially useful for the Japanese and Far Eastern perspective.

R. Mitter, *China's War with Japan, 1937–1945*, London, Penguin, 2014

An important book for understanding the causes of the Sino-Japanese war and its impact on China during the war with Japan, 1937–45.

J. Spence, *Mao*, London, Orion, 1999

A brief biography of Mao, which gives a good and, on balance, positive overview of his life.

S. Wilson, *Manchurian Crisis and Japanese Society*, Routledge, 2002

Puts the crisis into the context of Japanese society and economy.

Internet sources

- **https://alphahistory.com/chineserevolution/Chinese-revolution-documents** contains some basic source material.
- Michael Duff's First World War.com: **www.firstworldwar.com** Contains a vast amount of material relevant to the causes, course and consequences of the First World War.
- Fordham University's Modern Internet History Sourcebook: **https://sourcebooks.fordham.edu/mod/modsbook.asp** A mine of source material including treaties, speeches, etc.
- Both the British National Archives and the US National Archives contain an enormous volume of material on the events covered by this book: British National Archives: **www.nationalarchives.gov.uk** and US National Archives: **www.archives.gov**
- Yale Law School, the Avalon Project, Documents in Law, History and Diplomacy, **Avalon.law.Yale.edu/** Useful for treaties and other historical documents covering the period of this book.

Glossary

Absentee landlord A landlord who owns a property but rents it out to tenants.

Alliance system The German–Austrian alliance of 1879 was opposed by the Franco-Russian alliance of 1894.

Allies Britain, France, Russia and Italy, which declared war against Germany in 1915.

Anarchist A supporter of anarchism, a political theory advocating small, self-governing societies.

Anschluss The union of Austria with Germany.

Anthropologist Someone who studies human beings and their societies, customs and beliefs.

Arbitration A form of resolving disputes through mediation by a third party.

Associated power The USA was not bound by any treaties with Britain and France, 1917–19, and was free, if necessary, to pursue its own policies.

Audit office A government office that checks how money has been spent.

Autarchy Economic self-sufficiency.

Balfour Declaration A communication to the Zionists by A.J. Balfour, the British Foreign Secretary, declaring British support for establishing a national home for the Jews in Palestine.

'Balkan Prussia' Bulgaria was compared to Prussia, which in the eyes of the Allies had an aggressive and militarist reputation.

Balkans A geographic area in south-eastern Europe; the principal states in 1913 were: Serbia, Romania, Bulgaria, Albania and Greece.

Beiyang Army Literally 'North Ocean Army'. A modern Western-style army created in the late nineteenth-century China.

Benevolent passivity Favouring one side while not officially supporting them.

'Big Sword' Society Formed in the 1890s and revived to protect the peasantry against the warlords.

Bilateral Agreement or action between or by two states.

Black Dragon Society (or the Kokuryukai or Amur Society) Founded in 1901 with the aim of extending Japan's 'imperial mission' to Manchuria, Mongolia and Siberia. It had close contacts with the Japanese officer corps.

Black market Illegal trade in rationed goods and foodstuffs.

Blood plasma The vital yellowish-coloured liquid component of blood.

Blue Shirts Created in 1924 by a group of army officers. By the 1930s the Blue Shirt Society was increasingly influential in the KMT.

Boers Descendants of Dutch settlers who had originally colonized South Africa.

Bolsheviks The Russian Communist Party. It was based on the theories of Karl Marx and Lenin, which predicted the overthrow of capitalism and the creation of socialism.

Bonds Certificates issued by a government or large company promising to repay borrowed money at a fixed rate of interest by a specified date.

Boxer A secret Chinese patriotic and nationalist organization. The literal translation of 'Boxer' is 'the Righteous and Harmonious Fists'.

British South African Company Formed by Cecil Rhodes from the amalgamation of two companies: the Central Search association and the Exploring Company Ltd.

Buffer state Small state positioned between two much larger ones.

Cadre screening movement A campaign aimed at checking the loyalty of core groups of the CCP

Capital ships The most powerful ships in a navy.

Capitalism An economic system in which the production of goods and their distribution depend on the investment of private capital.

Capitulations Exemption of foreign merchants and their agents from Turkish taxation and law.

Central Bank A national bank, which controls a nation's currency and interests rates.

Central Executive Committee The governing committee of the KMT.

Central Powers The wartime alliance of Germany, Austria, Turkey and Bulgaria.

Charismatic Inspiring great enthusiasm and loyalty.

Civil war in Mexico Conflict in Mexico, 1910–20; initially a revolt against the Diaz regime and then became a multi-sided civil war.

Clan cabinet A cabinet composed of relatives.

Coaling station A base where steamships can be fuelled with coal.

Collective security Security gained through joining an alliance or signing an agreement where the security of each state is guaranteed by the others.

Comintern The Communist international movement set up in 1919 to organize worldwide revolution.

Concentration Camp scandal In the final stages of the Boer War (1899–1902) in order to defeat the guerrilla tactics of the Boers the British relocated the civilian population in concentration camps where a large proportion died of disease.

Condominium Joint control of a territory by two states.

Conference of Ambassadors Standing committee set up to supervise the carrying out of the Treaty of Versailles.

Confucian past The philosophy of Confucius (551–479 BC), which stresses the importance of practical moral matters, was adopted by the Chinese Empire as the basis of its education system and the Imperial exam system for the civil service.

Congress The US parliament.

Conscription Compulsory military service.

Consortium An association of states with a common aim.

Consular courts A court presided over by foreign officials to protect the interests of their countrymen, who were trading or working in a country such as Japan or China. These courts were recognized by treaty.

Continentalist strategy A policy that was primarily concerned with the North American continent.

Counter-revolutionary Person who opposes a revolution and wants to reverse its results.

Coup d'état A sudden action resulting in a change of government.

Covenant Rules and constitution of the League of Nations.

Curzon line Frontier proposed by British foreign secretary, Lord Curzon for Poland's eastern frontier with the Soviet Union.

Dare to Die Units Suicide squads, which volunteers joined to achieve martyrdom in fighting the enemies of China. In Guangzou such a unit was led by a woman, who was compared to Joan of Arc (1412–30), the French heroine of the Hundred Years' War.

Deliberative chamber An assembly appointed to debate or discuss issues.

Demilitarized Having all military defences removed.

Détente A process of lessened tension or growing relaxation between two states.

Devalue Reduce the value of.

Dictated peace A peace treaty that is dictated to the defeated state(s) rather than negotiated.

Dogmatic or empiricist deviations Opinionated or independent thought.

'Dogmeat General' Nickname given to Zhang Zongchang because he liked a gambling game called Pal Gow, which in north eastern China is called 'eating dog meat'.

Dollar diplomacy The furthering of diplomatic aims by using economic pressure and the offer of loans.

Dominions The British Dominions of Australia, Canada, New Zealand and South Africa were self-governing, but part of the British Empire and Commonwealth, of which to this day they are still members.

Downing Street The London residence of the British prime minister.

Dunkirk In May 1940 the British Expeditionary Force in France was forced to retreat to Dunkirk and was only rescued by a risky sea evacuation.

El Dorado Spanish for a fabulously wealthy city or state.

Elite The ruling classes.

Entente A friendly understanding between states, rather than a formal alliance. The Anglo-French *Entente* was sometimes called the *Entente Cordiale* because it led to the restoration of good Anglo-French relations.

Eupen and Melmedy After the League consulted the population about their wishes these territories were integrated into Belgium in 1925.Navy League A German pressure group which agitated for a large German navy.

Executive committee A committee which can take key decisions.

E-yu-wan The name is an abbreviation for the area the base eventually covered on the frontiers of Henan and Anhui.

Fascist Party The Fascist Party was formed in Italy by Mussolini in 1919. Its programme combined social reforms and a tax on war profits with an intensely nationalist foreign policy.

Filipinos The inhabitants of the Philippines.

Five-Year Plans Plans to modernize and expand the economy over a five-year period.

Foot binding Traditional Chinese custom whereby young girls' feet were tightly bound to control their growth. Small feet were considered a mark of beauty.

Formal annexation Taking over full control of a territory by another power.

Free city Self-governing city under the protection of the League of Nations.

Free trade zone An area where countries can trade freely without restrictions.

Free trade Trade between nations unimpeded by tariffs.

Fulfilment A policy aimed by Germany at extracting concessions from Britain and France by attempting to fulfil the Treaty of Versailles.

GDP (gross domestic product) The financial value of all goods and service produced by a country.

General staff A group of officers responsible for planning operations and administering an army.

Genro Term used for a group of Japanese elder statesmen, who were seen as the founding fathers of modern Japan.

German measures to stabilize the mark In November 1924 the devalued German currency was replaced temporarily by the Rentenmark and then in August 1924 by the new Reichsmark, which was put on the gold standard. Theoretically this meant that paper banknotes could be converted into agreed, fixed quantities of gold.

Gold standard A system by which the value of a currency is defined in terms of gold. The value of the pound was linked to gold. On 20 September 1931 the pound was forced off the gold standard and its value fell from $4.86 to $3.49.

Hawks Politicians and generals who wanted Japan to follow an aggressive foreign policy.

Hyperinflation Massive daily increases in the prices of goods and in the amount of money being printed.

Ice-free port A seaport that is free of ice in the winter, so that it can be used throughout the year.

Ideology A system and set of ideas and theories.

Imperial overstretch Term describing the point when an empire has been overextended.

Imperial War Cabinet A cabinet made up of prime ministers of the self-governing Commonwealth countries.

Imperialism The policy of acquiring and controlling dependent territories carried out by a state.

Inter-Allied commissions Allied committees set up to deal with particular tasks.

International civil service A permanent administration made up of officials from all the member states.

International law Law concerning international relations – relations between states.

Isolationist Remaining aloof from international politics.

Jameson raid Armed intervention in the Transvaal led by the British politician in Cape Colony, Leander Starr Jameson, over the New Year weekend of 1895–96.

Jihad A struggle against the enemies of Islam.

Jingoism Extreme patriotism supporting an aggressive foreign policy.

Khedive The title used by the governor and ruler of Egypt and the Sudan.

Kiaochow In 1897 the Germans seized Kiachow in revenge for the murder of two missionaries. They also secured mining rights in the neighbouring province of Shantung.

Kwantung Army Japanese army guarding south Manchurian railway and stationed in Liaodong Peninsula since 1907.

Left Term used to denote parties stretching from the Liberals to the Communists.

Legation Embassy.

Legation quarter The area in Beijing where foreign diplomats, businessmen, etc., and their families lived.

Locarno Spirit The optimistic mood of reconciliation and compromise that swept through Europe after the signing of the Locarno Treaties.

Luftwaffe The German air force.

Maginot line A line of concrete fortifications, which France constructed along its borders with Germany. It was named after André Maginot, the French Minister of Defence.

Magyar Ethnic Hungarians.

Mahdi Arabic word meaning the redeemer of Islam. The Sudanese Sheikh, Muhammad Ahmad (1845–85), claimed to be the Mahdi.

Manchukuo The name given to the Japanese-dominated state of Manchuria under Puyi, the deposed Emperor of China.

Mandated status Ex-German or Turkish territories entrusted to the Allied powers as mandates to govern in accordance with the interests of the local population.

Marco Polo Bridge incident A minor confrontation between Chinese and Japanese troops near Marco Polo Bridge outside Beijing, July 1937, which rapidly escalated into a major war. The Japanese Kwantung Army was conducting manoeuvres just outside Beijing, when Chinese troops fired into the area.

Marxist–Leninist theory Doctrines of Karl Marx's teaching, which were modified by Lenin to suit the situation in Russia.

Maxim gun The first machine gun invented in 1883.

Mein Kampf Literally 'My Struggle': Hitler's major political work in which he outlined his beliefs and political intentions.

Merchant marine A fleet of cargo vessels.

Military mission A small military presence sent to advise on military matters.

Milliard One thousand million; now largely superseded by the term billion.

Minorities Treaty Treaty guaranteeing the rights of the ethnic minorities.

Monopolies Sole control of supplying a commodity exercised by a company or group of companies.

Moratorium Temporary suspension of payments.

'Mutilated victory' A victory which was scarred by the refusal of the Allies to give Italy what had been promised.

Multilateral Agreements or action between or by more than two states.

Nanjing massacres For six weeks in December 1937–January 1938 Japanese troops committed mass murder in Nanjing.

Nationalism A patriotic belief by a people in the virtues and power of their nation.

National Socialism German National Socialism had many similarities with Fascism, but its driving force was race, and in particular anti-Semitism.

Navy League A German pressure group which agitated for a large German navy.

Nazi Party (NSDAP) The National Socialist German Workers Party. In 1921 Hitler became chairman. The party was banned after the Munich putsch in 1923, but refounded in February 1925. On 14 July 1933 it was declared the only legal party in Germany.

'New Imperialism' The period of intensive colonization by the European powers, Japan and the USA roughly in the period 1890–1914.

Non-aggression pact An agreement between two or more countries not to resort to force.

Opportunism Seizing the opportunity when it occurs.

Pandemic An epidemic on a global scale.

Pan-German League A German political society that believed that Germany should extend its frontiers to include all Germans – in Poland, Switzerland and Austria.

Partisans Resistance fighters or guerrillas.

Passive resistance Refusal to co-operate, stopping short of actual violence.

Peace bloc A group of states committed to opposing aggressor powers.

People's Court A special court set up to try 'enemies of the people'.

People's war Popular war fought by the mass of the people.

Permanent Court of International Justice An institution set up at The Hague, the Netherlands, by Article 14 of the Covenant of the League of Nations in 1920.

Philanthropy The desire to help humanity.

Plebiscite A referendum, or vote by the electorate on a single issue.

Politbureau The political Bureau of the Central Committee of the Communist Party.

Power politics International relations that are based on force rather than moral principles.

Power vacuum Territories left undominated by another state after the withdrawal or collapse of the original ruling power.

Pressure groups Associations formed to promote a particular interest by influencing government policy.

Productive pledges The possession of mines and factories as pledges or guarantees of German payment of reparation.

Proletarian nation A nation that lacked an empire and raw materials. Like the proletariat (workers) it was poor.

Protection Stopping foreign goods by levying tariffs or taxes on imports.

Protectorate A territory that is controlled and protected by another state.

Provisional government A government in power until the holding of elections.

Psychic crisis A crisis caused for an individual by outside events, which he or she is unable to come to terms with.

Putsch Takeover of power.

Quinine An anti-malaria drug.

Ratified Having received formal approval from parliament.

Reich Empire.

Reichswehr The German army, 1919–35.

'The Red Spear Society' Formed by peasants and farmers to protect villages primarily from the warlords, but also from tax collectors and later communists and the Japanese.

Reparations Compensation paid by a defeated power to make good the damage it caused in a war.

Republic A state ruled by a president rather than a monarch.

Rhineland separatism A movement favouring separation of the Rhineland from Germany.

Right Term used to denote parties stretching from Conservatives to Nazis or Fascists.

Ruhr The Ruhr in west Germany had the largest concentration of coal mines and steel mills in Europe.

Rump Austria What was left of Austria after its partition.

Russo-Austrian Bulgarian war scare In 1885 the Russians kidnapped the ruler of Bulgaria because he refused to become a Russian puppet. This risked war with Austria, which wished to minimize Russian influence in Bulgaria.

Schlieffen Plan It envisaged a two-front war against France and Russia. France was to be defeated within a month by a flanking movement through Belgium, Holland and Luxembourg and then the mass of the German army would move eastwards to deal with Russia. The plan was later revised to omit Holland.

Scorched earth policy A military strategy aimed at destroying anything of use to the advancing enemy.

Secret annex Secret addition to a treaty.

Security Council One of the most important councils of the United Nations, with powers to authorize peace-keeping operations and sanctions.

Sedan The traumatic defeat of the French by the Prussians in September 1870.

Self-determination A state's right to decide its own future.

Senate The upper house of the US Congress.

Showa restoration Attempts in the early 1930s to restore the power of the emperor. Showa was the title of Emperor Hirohito's reign, 1926–89.

Signatory powers Powers signing a treaty.

Social cohesion The social unity of a country.

Social imperialism A policy aimed at uniting all social classes behind plans for creating and expanding an empire.

South Slavs Formed the main ethnic group in Bosnia and Herzegovina, which Austria occupied in 1878.

Sovereign Self-ruling, fully independent.

Soviet Communist elected council after the model of those initially set up in the USSR.

Staff talks Talks between officers of the planning and administrative departments of national armies.

Standing Committee A permanent committee.

Status quo A Latin term to denote the state of affairs as it exists at the moment.

Straits zone The shores along the Straits of Dardanelles and Bosphorus were occupied by Allied troops.

Strategic aims Aims intended to gain military or economic security for a state.

Stresa Powers The powers who attended the Stresa Conference in 1935.

Successor states The states created from former Austro-Hungarian and Russian territory.

Sudeten Germans Ethnic Germans who had been settled in the Sudetenland since the thirteenth century.

Synthetic materials Objects imitating a natural product but made chemically.

Tariffs Taxes placed on imported goods to protect the home economy.

Teller Amendment An amendment (or qualification) put forward by Senator Henry Teller to a joint resolution by the US Congress limiting the freedom a victorious US would have in Cuba.

Tong-haks A nationalist movement that was strongly opposed to Western culture and domination.

Trade deficit A situation that occurs when a country imports more than it sells.

Treaty of Mutual Assistance A treaty between two or more states whereby each state would assist the other in the event of war.

Treaty Powers Those powers which had signed treaties with China giving them territorial concessions and commercial privileges.

Triple Entente The name often applied to the co-operation of Britain, France and Russia 1907–17.

Triplice An agreement between three powers to work together.

Triumvirate A ruling group of three people.

Two-front war A war in which fighting takes place on two geographically separate fronts.

United front A coalition of parties, usually to oppose a foreign aggressor.

Universal conscription The law by which all young males – and nowadays young females – have to serve for a period in the armed services.

Unrestricted submarine warfare Sinking by German submarines (called U-boats) of all merchant ships, Allied or neutral, engaged in carrying goods to or from Allied states.

USSR The Union of Soviet Socialist Republics. The new Bolshevik name for Russia.

Volte-face An about turn; a sudden and complete change of policy.

Wahabbist Referring to a fundamentalist Islamic reform movement founded by Muhammad Ibn Abd al-Wahhab (1703–92)

War guilt Carrying the blame for starting the war.

Warlords Military leaders in China who were able to take complete control over a Chinese regions thanks to their military strength.

Waterloo In 1815 the British defeated Napoleon in the Battle of Waterloo.

Westernizers Those who believed that the Japanese state should modernize along European lines.

White Russians The name given to members and supporters of the counter-revolutionary 'White' armies, which fought against the Bolshevik Red Army in the Russian Civil War (1918–21).

'White Terror' Terror practised by nationalist or reactionary forces.

'Yellow Press' The new popular press, which published jingoistic and sensational reports.

Yugoslavia Until 1929 Yugoslavia was known as the kingdom of Serbs, Croats and Slovenes.

Zinoviev letter A letter from Zinoviev, the head of Comintern, to the leader of the British Communist Party urging him stage strikes and other subversive activities, which was published in the Daily Mail a few days before the October general election. It may well have been a fake, but it helped the Conservatives win the election.

Zionists Supporters of Zionism, a movement for re-establishing the Jewish state.

Index

E

F

G

H

I

J

K

X

Y

Z

The Publishers would like to thank the following for permission to reproduce copyright material.

Photo credits

p.7 © Deutsches Bundesarchiv via Wikipedia Commons (public domain); **p.14** © LSE Library via https://flickr.com/photos/35128489@N07/22473779343 (public domain); **p.19** © Granger, NYC/TopFoto; **p.26** © Painting by Carl Roechling, 1902 via AKG Images; **p.36** © DEA/ BIBLIOTECA AMBROSIANA via Getty Images; **p.45** Via Wikipedia Commons (https:// creativecommons.org/licenses/by-sa/4.0/deed.en); **p.46** © Granger, NYC/TopFoto; **p.60** © Via Wikipedia Commons (public domain); **p.67** © Bettmann via Getty Images; **p.72** © Via Wikipedia Commons (public domain); **p.84** © U.S. Naval Historical Center. Courtesy of the San Francisco Maritime Museum, San Francisco, California, 1969 (public domain); **p.92** © Davis Jr/Stringer/ Hulton Archive via Getty Images; **p.100** © Harlingue/Roger Viollet via Getty Images; **p.105** © Mary Evans Picture Library; **p.119** Library of Congress, Prints & Photographs division, Washington/LC-DIG-ggbain-37463; **p.121** © Popperfoto/Getty Images; **p.122** Illustrated London News; **p.127** Library of Congress, Prints & Photographs division, Washington/ LC-USW33-019081-C; **p.131** Picasso's Guernica courtesy of The Print Collector/Alamy Stock Photo © Succession Picasso/DACS, London 2019; **p.133** © Fox Photos/Getty Images; **p. 140** © Via Wikipedia Commons (public domain); **p.145** © Mary Evans Picture Library; **p.148** © Hulton-Deutsch Collection/CORBIS/Corbis via Getty Images; **p.162** © Rolls Press/Popperfoto/ Getty Images; **p.174** © Via Wikipedia Commons (public domain); **p.175** © Via Wikipedia Commons (public domain); **p.183** © Via Wikipedia Commons (public domain); **p.191** © Roger Viollet/Getty Images; **p.193** © Via Wikipedia Commons (public domain); **p.195** © China: Muleteers crossing the Luding Bridge over the Dadu River in Luding County, Garze Tibetan Autonomous Prefecture, Sichuan, c.1900/Pictures from History/Bridgeman Images; **p.212** © CORBIS/Corbis via Getty Images; **p.214** © Library of Congress; **p.217** © Punch Cartoon Library/ TopFoto; **p.219** © Punch Cartoon Library/TopFoto.